To the Scholers,
Jeannette and David,
Emily and Abigail

PRAYER
AND THE
NEW TESTAMENT

ROBERT J. KARRIS

A Herder and Herder Book
The Crossroad Publishing Company
New York

The Crossroad Publishing Company
481 Eighth Avenue, New York, NY 10001

Printed in the United States of America

Library of Congress Card Number: 00-104966

ISBN 0-8245-1874-8

1   2   3   4   5   6   7   8   9   10   04   03   02   01   00

Contents

Preface to the Series

THE COMPANIONS TO THE NEW TESTAMENT SERIES aims to unite New Testament study with theological concerns in a clear and concise manner. Each volume:

- engages the New Testament text directly
- focuses on the religious (theological/ethical) content of the New Testament
- is written out of respect for the integrity of the religious tradition being studied. This means that the New Testament is studied in terms of its own time and place. It is allowed to speak in its own terms, out of its own assumptions, espousing its own values.
- involves cutting-edge research, bringing the results of scholarly discussions to the general reader
- provides resources for the reader who wishes to enter more deeply into the scholarly discussion.

The contributors to the series are established scholars who have studied and taught the New Testament for many years and who can now reap a wide-ranging harvest from the fruits of their labors. Multiple theological perspectives and denominational identities are represented. Each author is free to address the issues from his or her own social and religious location, within the parameters set for the series.

It is our hope that these small volumes will make some contribution to the recovery of the vision of the New Testament world for our time.

Charles H. Talbert
Baylor University

Introduction

WHILE I WAS PLANNING this book, I dreaded walking into bookstores and libraries to peruse their titles on prayer and spirituality. Talk about instantaneous discouragement as I saw hundreds of titles and shelves upon shelves of books! What could I add? Could I improve upon the scholarly 1995 book by Oscar Cullmann, *Prayer in the New Testament?* And how could I trump the recently reprinted 1998 book by John Koenig, *Rediscovering New Testament Prayer*, which deals so marvelously with the various themes of prayer in the New Testament? When I asked two colleagues what they would want in a book on prayer and the New Testament, they independently said that they wanted a book that brought in parallel passages and prayers from outside the New Testament. Their idea struck a harmonious chord with me, and my readers will almost immediately note how different this Karris book on prayer is from others. For example, I interpret the Lord's Prayer by means of Jewish texts whose wording I actually provide. A prayer of Moses, supplied by the Jewish historian Josephus, but not found in the Old Testament, will help us understand Luke's theology of God's purpose.

Another feature of this book is that it is largely taken up with some of the major hymns of the New Testament. I treat the Pauline hymn of Philippians 2:6-11, the hymn that forms John's prologue, Mary's *Magnificat*, Zechariah's *Benedictus*, and Simeon's *Nunc Dimittis* from Luke's Gospel, and the hymns of Revelation. So in a real sense this book is a sequel to my 1996 *Symphony of New Testament Hymns*, which focused primarily on hymns in the Pauline tradition.

A further benefit of my book is that I have situated the theme of prayer in the total context of an individual New Testament book. So I do not focus immediately on what, for example, James 5:13-18 has to say about prayer, but I set my discussion in the framework of the entire letter of James. And that is why my chapters are generally so long, for I take great pains and space to situate prayer texts in context. After an opening chapter on prayer and the historical Jesus, I move to chapters on prayer in Luke-Acts and prayer in the Gospel of John and 1 John. Then come chapters on prayer in Paul and the hymns of Revelation. I conclude with a chapter on prayer in James. Each chapter stands on its own and could be used for a course or for independent reading in a course or for conferences in retreats or for private devotions.

In developing each of my six chapters, I did not use a cookie cutter. Each chapter is unique. The chapter on Paul is the shortest, and the chapter on prayer in Luke-Acts is the longest. The length could just as easily have been turned around. To paraphrase what Ralph Vaughan Williams said about his Fourth Symphony: I don't know how it came out the way it did, but this is what I wrote. And I'm proud of it!

A friend has called these chapters "scholarly, readable, and practical." Indeed, I wanted to introduce my readers to the latest scholarship on the subject. I apologize in advance for books and articles I may have omitted and for my failure to treat your favorite passage or favorite New Testament author. In this series "scholarly" is not to be equated with exhaustive bibliography and endless dialogue in footnotes with colleagues in the field. My goal in the writing of this book has been to make scholarly materials understandable and even fun. So I've written with a lightness that should aid communication. And in writing the way I do, I take the risk of not being taken seriously in scholarly circles. As a student said of one of my publications: "This book can't be scholarly! I can understand it!" Finally, I have tried to bring these scholarly materials out of the clouds and down to earth.

I thank Robert Heller of Crossroad for suggesting me as an author and my series editor, Charles H. Talbert, for his professional help and encouragement. This book is better because of the critical suggestions of Peter Williams in Rome, Barbara Bowe in Chicago, and David M. Scholer in Pasadena. They have helped me wring the water out of my writing. All the deficiencies of my study are to be laid at my door. Deep gratitude goes to Mrs. Theresa Shaffer, librarian for interlibrary loans at St. Bonaventure University, for her expert and most willing search for titles, common and rare.

Unless otherwise noted, the translations of biblical texts are based on the New Revised Standard Version.

Titles mentioned under "Suggested Further Readings" are not cited again in the bibliography.

I am grateful to The Franciscan Institute of St. Bonaventure University for permission to quote from my translation of St. Bonaventure's Commentary on St. Luke's Gospel.

I dedicate this book to friends I've known for decades. May the Lord bless and keep the Scholers, Jeannette and David, Emily and Abigail, now and always.

Robert J. Karris
St. Bonaventure University

1

Prayer and the Historical Jesus

Don't Flatten Your Metaphors

WHILE WORKING on this topic, I was reminded of Peter Sellers's movie *The Return of the Pink Panther*. For those who don't know the movie, the "pink panther" was a large, precious diamond that had been fiendishly and inventively stolen and that Inspector Clouseau, the bumbling French detective, was assigned to recover. I leave the rest of the story to your imagination, recollection, and future movie watching. My interest lies in the diamond, the pink panther itself. About the size of an egg, it was so brilliant, so beautiful, and it had no setting. Unlike a fine diamond set in a crown or in a ring, the pink panther could be admired from almost all angles as the light danced around and through it. My contention is that the key words of Jesus' prayer, the Lord's Prayer, are like that pink-panther diamond and are to be appreciated from all angles. It seems to me that there is a tendency in contemporary scholarship to house this magnificent diamond in a single setting.

Let me take the example of N. T. Wright (1997), who is of the opinion that the diamond of *abba*/father should be given the primary setting of the liberation of the exodus. God is father as God rescues the Israelites from Egyptian slavery and forms them into a people by giving them a covenant and land. In a sense what Wright says of God corresponds to the image we Americans have of George Washington, who is the father of our country. He saved us from the oppressive slavery of the British and formed us into a nation. Even though he died some two

1

hundred years ago, we still refer to him as our father, for his influence continues in our lives. Of course, we would have to ask in what sense George Washington continues to be "our" father.

We come to Jesus' prayer, the Lord's Prayer, which is couched in metaphors, and rarely realize that we have been socialized into thinking that these metaphors have one and only one meaning. Thus, "father" means "intimacy." "To hallow" means "reverence for God's name." "Bread," of course, means "physical bread." But here we stumble, for ecclesiastical tradition has socialized us into thinking of the bread of life, the Eucharist. And "debt" means "sin." But what did these metaphors mean at the time of the historical Jesus? How do the words and actions of the historical Jesus help us to interpret the metaphors he used? For after all, the Lord's Prayer is most probably from the historical Jesus.

Let me make my point from yet another angle. Here I quote from Hans Dieter Betz (1995, 413), whose magisterial work on the Sermon on the Mount has valuable information and insight: "Much of the language of prayer is deliberately ambivalent, so as to stimulate the thinking of the orants." Is this the last refuge of exegetes when they cannot explain difficult expressions or words, for example, whether "deliver us from evil" in Matthew 6:13 refers to deliverance from "the evil one" or from "evil"? Betz (1995, 389) concludes: "Since prayer language tends to be general, one need not decide on only one of the possibilities of interpretation." While on the subject of liturgical prayer, I offer one further point. The composer borrows from tradition but creatively adapts that tradition. In what follows we will be able to see how Jesus adapts traditional elements from key Jewish prayers of his time.

So there you have it. The image of the pink-panther diamond encourages us not to flatten metaphors. And the wording of liturgical prayer is ambivalent to keep us supplicants on our spiritual toes.

THE JESUS SEMINAR AND ITS CRITICS

Before I deal with the Lord's Prayer, I have to make a few more introductory remarks, and this time about the frequently contentious contemporary quest for the historical Jesus and the key role of the Jesus Seminar in this quest. Those who want more detailed information should consult the fine book by Mark Allan Powell (1998). In what follows and as I quote from the fellows of the Jesus Seminar and other students of the historical Jesus I will do my best to stay above the sharp repartee they often engage in. I sample this polemic to show my readers that scholars have deep feelings about this issue. N. T. Wright (1996, 30 n. 4) makes this comment about the 1993 book of Robert Funk and Roy Hoover, founder and fellow of the Jesus Seminar respectively : "The introduction . . . makes a great point of how this version is independent of church control, and concludes (xviii) 'the Scholars Version is authorized by scholars.' Were there, I wonder, any wry smiles in the Seminar at this explicit statement of the papacy of the scholars?" And later Wright (1996, 44) gives the most lavish praise to the major work of John Dominic Crossan (1991) and then writes: "It is all the more frustrating, therefore, to have to conclude that the book is almost entirely wrong." And John Dominic Crossan (1999, 358) returns the favor in his evaluation of Wright's book (1996): "I find in your book a Jesus, a Judaism, and a God, all empty at the core and hollow at the heart."

Luke Timothy Johnson's *The Real Jesus* (1996) is an unremitting critique of the Jesus Seminar and had best be read while wearing burnproof gloves. And Robert W. Funk (1996) shows that he, too, can sling mud: "The third questers, like Raymond E. Brown and John P. Meier in the United States, take critical scholarship about as far as it can go without impinging on the fundamentals of creed or challenging the hegemony of the ecclesiastical bureaucracy. In their hands, orthodoxy is safe, but critical scholarship is at risk."

Behind the scenes of this chapter members of the Jesus Seminar and their critics are dueling. And while openly confessing that the findings of the Jesus Seminar have enriched my thinking, I unabashedly lay my cards on the table. I am not a fellow of the Jesus Seminar; I find the general anti-institutional orientation of the Jesus Seminar to be unfounded; I assign a far greater role to faith in my pursuit of history. Indeed, I fear that I'll get every scholar of the historical Jesus angry with me, for the ultimate argument of this chapter is that both the fellows of the Jesus Seminar and their critics are in error if they champion their viewpoint as the only way of looking at things. And in fairness to all sides I cite the scholars' own words as far as possible.

I will conclude these introductory matters by taking a brief look at Jesus' religious background. Behind the general agreement in the opinions of the three scholars I mention below, my readers will notice the various emphases given by different students of the historical Jesus.

The Religious Upbringing of Jesus, Peasant and Genius

I am convinced that we must look into the Jewish roots of Jesus' prayer life, and in particular we should look into what E. P. Sanders (1992) has called "common Judaism." We don't have time to consider in any detail the *Shema*, which Jews said twice a day. Nor the Eighteen Benedictions, which came to be said thrice a day by Jews. And again we don't have time to consider the three annual pilgrimage festivals of Israel: Passover, Pentecost, and Booths. Nor do we have time to look at the nonpilgrimage feast of the Day of Atonement. And finally, we don't have time to consider the Jewish sacrificial system and the role of Sabbath celebrations. But all of these played a significant role in Jesus' socialization into Jewish religion and heritage. In an appendix to this chapter, I have reproduced five prayers, which James H. Charlesworth (1986) has argued date to the time of Jesus. Interested readers can consult them at their leisure and gather an even deeper understanding of the Jewish roots of Jesus' prayer. In the course of my discussion of the various words of the Lord's Prayer I will cite salient portions of these prayers. In outlining my viewpoint, I am not far removed from that of a member of the Jesus Seminar, Marcus J. Borg. Borg (1987, 40) writes: "As a faithful Jew, he [Jesus] would have recited the *Shema* upon rising and retiring each day. . . . Presumably, he participated in the Jewish festivals and went on pilgrimage to Jerusalem. From the gospels, it is clear that he was very familiar with his Scriptures, the Hebrew Bible. He may have known it from memory, a feat not uncommon among the learned. The Psalms were probably his 'prayer book.'"

John P. Meier, who has already written two very large books about the historical Jesus, generally agrees with the above assessment. He writes (1991, 278; see also 1994, 299): "One therefore has to allow for a high degree of natural talent—perhaps even genius—that more than compensated for the low level of Jesus' formal education. . . . Jesus comes out of a peasant background, but he is not an ordinary peasant." Notice that Meier concedes Jesus' peasant background but insists on his extraordinary nature.

John Dominic Crossan (1994, 25–26) emphasizes that Jesus was an illiterate peasant: "Furthermore, since between 95 and 97 percent of the Jewish state was illiterate at the time of Jesus, it must be presumed that Jesus also was illiterate, that he knew, like the vast majority of his contemporaries in an oral culture, the foundational narratives, basic stories, and general expectations of his tradition but not the exact texts, precise citations, or intricate arguments of its scribal elites." Crossan notes that Jesus knew his Jewish tradition, but his emphasis lies elsewhere.

From my quotations of the writings of Borg, Meier, and Crossan the astute reader will already notice how the scholars are arguing. Even when saying the same thing, for example, that Jesus was a peasant, scholars give a different twist to that fact. But I emphasize that behind these differences there is common agreement that Jewish religious tradition nourished Jesus' spiritual and prayer life.

THE WORDING OF THE LORD'S PRAYER

Authors as diverse as Joachim Jeremias (1978, 94–95), John P. Meier (1994, 292), and Stephen J. Patterson (1998, 103) generally agree on the original wording of the Lord's Prayer, which occurs in a context of teaching about prayer, almsgiving, and fasting in Matthew 6:9-13, in the context of Jesus' instructions on prayer in Luke 11:2-4, and in a context of instruction in a writing that stems from the end of the first Christian century, *Didache* 8:2. The note after Matthew 6:13 in the NRSV rightly indicates that the conclusion, "For the kingdom, and the power, and the glory are yours forever," is ancient, but not part of the original Greek text. While acknowledging the views of Hans Dieter Betz (1995, 370) and James Barr (1988, 44–45) that call into question the existence of an original text, I contend that the form of the Lord's Prayer upon which I will comment contains the core of Jesus' prayer. I follow the wording given by John P. Meier (1994, 292):

Address:	Father,
You Petitions:	hallowed be your name.
	Your kingdom come.
We Petitions:	Our daily bread give us today.
	And forgive us our debts, as we forgive our debtors.
	And do not lead us to the test.

Before I examine the individual components of the Lord's Prayer, I mention that the Jesus Seminar is of the opinion that Jesus did not teach his disciples this prayer. John Dominic Crossan (1991, 294) declares: "Still, despite the fact that the Lord's Prayer must be a very early summary of themes and emphases from Jesus' own lifetime, I do not think that such a coordinated prayer was ever taught by him to his followers." Like Crossan, the general membership of the Jesus Seminar does not think that Jesus *composed* the Lord's Prayer. I follow the majority scholarly opinion that Jesus did compose this prayer. And even if the fellows of the Jesus Seminar are correct that Jesus never composed the Lord's Prayer, my commentary on the key single prayer texts they attribute to Jesus will prove helpful to my readers. After the address to God as father, these single prayer texts are: your name be revered; let your domain come; give us the bread; forgive our debts (see Hal Taussig, 1999). I now proceed to examine these and other components of Jesus' prayer.

Father

The significant contributions of Joachim Jeremias (1978) have dominated the discussion of the meaning of the Greek word *pater*. Jeremias, it seems to me, made a number of steps in setting up his hypothesis. First, Jesus' prayer was first uttered in Aramaic. Literally, *abba* is Aramaic for "the father." Put another way, it is the determinative form of *ab* (father). Further, it is used as a vocative. Second, we know from Galatians 4:6 and Romans 8:15 that the early Christians used the Aramaic word *abba* in addressing God as "father." Where did they get this Aramaic word except from the Lord's Prayer? Third, *abba* is a word of intimacy, used by children and adults in referring to their fathers. Fourth, Jesus' prayer is that of an individual, not of the nation. Fifth, there is no evidence in Palestinian Jewish liturgical sources that an individual addressed God as *abba*. Sixth, Jesus' usage of *abba* is unique and reveals his self-consciousness. Jeremias's own words (1978, 97) seem to meld Jesus' address to God with the Spirit-prayer of Galatians 4:6 and Romans 8:15: "The final point, and the most astonishing of all, however, has yet to be mentioned: in the Lord's Prayer Jesus authorizes his disciples to repeat the word *abba* after him. He gives them a share in his sonship and empowers them, as his disciples, to speak with their heavenly father in just such a familiar, trusting way as a child would with his father."

Jeremias's view of *abba* has been subjected to great scrutiny. The most comprehensive critical article is by Joseph A. Fitzmyer (1992). The briefest and most accessible is by John Ashton (1992). The very title of James Barr's article, "'Abba' Isn't 'Daddy'" (1988), indicates the direction of his criticism. Of course, as Barr knows so well (1988, 38–39), Jeremias never said that to address God as *abba* was to engage in baby talk. As a matter of fact, Jeremias (1978, 62) explicitly said the opposite: "One often reads (and I myself believed it at one time) that when Jesus spoke to his heavenly Father he took up the chatter of a small child. To assume this would be a piece of inadmissible naivety." But Jeremias's interpretation clearly left the door open for people to take *abba* as Daddy. A second attack on Jeremias has come from his apparent concern to make Jesus' prayer unique. If you remove Jeremias's artificial restrictions of private as opposed to national prayer and Palestinian Judaism as opposed to Diaspora Judaism, one can see that "father" occurs quite frequently as a name for God. I will return to this point momentarily. Moreover, in the Dead Sea Scrolls in the heart, as it were, of Palestinian Judaism around the time of Jesus has come to light a private prayer that addresses God as "my father" (*abbi*). I refer to 4QApocryphon of Joseph (4Q372): "[16]. . . And he (Joseph) said: 'My father and my God, do not abandon me in the hands of gentiles, [17]do me justice, so that the poor and afflicted do not die.'" Joseph A. Fitzmyer (1992, 53), however, downplays the significance of this text: "Yet it is still not the same as the Aramaic *abba*." Finally, Hans Dieter Betz (1995, 374) writes concisely: "None of the recensions of the Lord's Prayer has the Aramaic *abba*, not even in Greek transliteration, whereas the references to the *abba* (Gal 4:6; Rom 8:15; Mark 14:36) show no evidence of knowing the Lord's prayer." Yet the fellows of the Jesus Seminar, who gave this address a rare red or almost certain vote, do not engage in this debate. As Funk and Hoover (1993, 327) simply state: "He [Jesus], of course, frequently used 'Abba' to address God."

What sense are we to make of all this scholarly discussion about *abba* as Jesus' address to God? As a general comment, I observe that once an opinion is established it is very difficult to change it. In the case at hand, despite repeated scholarly statements, even by Joachim Jeremias himself, that Jesus of Nazareth did not call God "Daddy," this opinion has captured the popular and scholarly mind. On the popular front, see Herman C. Waetjen (1999, 54): "*Abba* is children's speech. . . . It is an expression of intimacy and may be translated into English as 'Papa' or 'Daddy.'" For a systematician's rendition, see Edward Schillebeeckx (1979, 256–71), whose influential Christology contains this chapter: "Jesus' Original *Abba* Experience, Source and Secret of His Being, Message and Manner of Life." We educators have done a superb job over the last thirty years teaching people this hypothesis. How can we expect them to change their minds in a few months? But change, although difficult, is a fact of contemporary life as the experts make new discoveries and reevaluate old tenets and procedures. Why, we may even have had our minds boggled as we experienced such contemporary wonders as one-day hospital stays for procedures that only as recently as ten years ago required a stay of seven days.

Relative to specific comments, I make a batch. First and to belabor the obvious, it is certain that Jesus did not call God his Daddy. Second, it is certain that the Lord's Prayer, in any version that is available to us (Matthew 6:9, Luke 11:2, or *Didache* 8:2), does not contain the Aramaic word *abba*. Third, it is probable that Jesus did call God his father. The arguments of Mary Rose D'Angelo (1992a; 1992b) to the contrary fail to convince. The evidence from the Lord's Prayer and from Luke 10:21-22/Matthew 11:25-27 is very significant in this matter. Fourth, it is possible to argue from the existence of the Aramaic word *abba* in Mark 14:36, Galatians 4:6, and Romans 8:15 to the fact that the historical Jesus used *abba* in addressing God. Note how cautiously John Ashton (1992, 7; *emphasis mine*) words his argument in this regard: "But even the single attribution of the term to Jesus (in the prayer in Gethsemane) *lends plausibility* to the suggestion that Christian usage was prompted by an authentic tradition of Jesus' own prayer." The argument of John P. Meier (1991, 266) does not raise this possibility to a probability.

As we begin our investigation of how various writings applied the metaphor "father" to God, I state in advance that the Old Testament and other Jewish writings frequently refer to God as father of the Jewish people and that even individual petitioners refer to God as father. All too often, efforts to prove that Jesus' use of *abba* for God was unique have obscured these facts.

Intimacy

Intimacy is one of the obvious meanings of "father." What was said above under *abba* is sufficient on this topic, and I say no more about it here.

Power and Authority

Power and authority constitute another meaning of "father." John P. Meier (1994, 300) graphically writes:

> While a 1st-century father might be a symbol of love for his children he was most certainly a symbol of sovereign power over their lives and fates . . . and so he was the object of obedience and reverence, even fear, as well as love. Conversely, at various times ancient kings, however ghastly and bloody their political record, boasted of being the fathers of their people insofar as they protected and cared for them, especially the poor and the weak (or so said the state propaganda). Father and king were therefore not contradictory symbols in religious discourse.

Mary Rose D'Angelo (1992a, 623–26) highlights another dimension by indicating the role of "father" in Roman Imperial Theology. Among the texts she quotes there is a late text from the first of four discourses on kingship or empire delivered by Dio Chrysostom (died after A.D. 112). She writes (1992a, 624): "It is Zeus, as the common provider and father of gods and human beings, who nurtures the good ruler and ousts the bad. Thus in Dio's theology, the reign of God the father is the protection and warrant of the empire." Part of the third conclusion that D'Angelo (1992a, 630) gives to her article is: "If indeed 'father' was used by Jesus, the context is less likely to be familial intimacy than resistance to the Roman imperial order."

Liberator

Since this view is largely associated with the name of N. T. Wright and since his intricate thought prohibits summary, I quote Wright at length. I warn my readers that it is he who spells God as "god." His argument (1996, 262–63) goes as follows:

> The "religious" meaning [of faith], stressed at various points in the gospels, focused on the insistence that Israel's god was to be seen as the "father" of his people. This, it must be emphasized, was not a new thought. . . . Nor is it simply a matter of "father" being one miscellaneous appellation among many for YHWH. Nor, yet, is it to be explained solely in terms of Jesus' "religious experience." It is particularly associated, as the passages in the note indicate, with his great acts of deliver-

ance, namely the exodus and the return from exile. To invoke this god as "father" is to stir up associations of the great coming deliverance.

In a long footnote (1996, 262 n.73) Wright assembles his evidence. I leave aside his references to later Rabbinic literature and note in advance that the address "father" as "liberator" occurs in the widest spread of Jewish literature: the Law, the prophets, wisdom literature, Josephus, Philo, and the pseudepigrapha. I give one quotation from each.

Deuteronomy 32:6: "Do you thus repay the LORD, O foolish and senseless people? Is not he your father, who created you, who made you and established you?"

Isaiah 63:16: "For you are our father, though Abraham does not know us and Israel does not acknowledge us. You, O LORD, are our father; our Redeemer from of old is your name."

Wisdom 14:3: "But it is your providence, O Father, that steers its course, for you have given it a path in the sea and a safe way through the waves."

Josephus, *Jewish Antiquities* 5.93: This is what Joshua says as he addresses the people: "Seeing that God, the Father and Lord of the Hebrew race, has given us to win this land and, being won, has promised to preserve it to us for ever. . . ." Joshua 22 does not contain this statement.

Philo, *On Abraham* 12.58: "But he to whose lot it falls, not only by means of his knowledge, to comprehend all the other things that exist in nature, but also to behold the Father and creator of the universe, has advanced to the very summit of happiness."

Jubilees 1:25: The Lord said to Moses in a move of restoration: "And I shall be a father to them, and they will be sons to me."

Having examined all the evidence Wright assembles, I judge that with the exception of two passages it supports the point he is making that God is seen in Jewish tradition as liberator/father.

Father Supplies Refuge and Forgiveness

If one examined very carefully the passages assembled by Wright, one would notice that there is no reference to Qumran. If one emphasizes what Qumran has, one arrives at a different picture. As Mary Rose D'Angelo (1992a, 621) maintains, three functions of "father" seemed to have been particularly important in antique Judaism and in Qumran in particular. "First, 'father' functions to designate God as the refuge of the afflicted and persecuted, especially those persecuted by the unbelieving. Second, 'father' frequently accompanies a petition for or an assurance of forgiveness. These two functions are grounded by a third: 'father' evokes the power and providence that govern the world."

I quote two pieces from the vast literature of Qumran in support of D'Angelo's contention. In the *Hymns* from Qumran we find a powerfully beautiful hymn of lament which moves into thanksgiving. I quote the key portions of 1QH 9:

> [6]As for me, from ruin to annihilation, from sickness to disease, from pains to tortures, [7]my soul reflects on your wonders. . . . [23]For in the mystery of your wisdom you have rebuked me, [24]you have hidden the truth a while, [your favor, until] the ordained time. Your rebuke has been changed into happiness and joy for me, [25]my disease into everlasting healing and unending [bliss,] the scoffing of my rival into a crown of glory for me, and my weakness into everlasting strength . . . [33]with my steps there is bountiful forgiveness [34]and great compassion when you judge me, until old age you support me. [35]For my mother did not know me, and my father abandoned me to you. Because you are a father to all the sons of your truth. [36]In them you rejoice, like one full of gentleness for her child, and like a wet-nurse, you clutch to your chest all your creatures.

Here the prayer virtually breaks off.

Earlier in treating *abba*/father I quoted from the retelling of the Joseph story in the 4QApocryphon of Joseph (4Q372). Here Joseph is praying as he finds himself in dire straits among foreigners:

> [14]And in all this, Joseph [was delivered] [15]into the hand of foreigners, consuming his strength and breaking all his bones up until the time of his end. And he shouted [and his call] [16]summoned the powerful God to save him from their hands. And he said: "My father and my God, do not abandon me in the hands of gentiles, [17]do me justice, so that the poor and afflicted do not die."

Here we have references to God as a father who rescues and forgives in texts from a community in Israel at the time of Jesus of Nazareth.

Gifts of Torah, Forgiveness, Deliverance, and Sustenance in Jewish Prayers from Jesus' Time

Many scholars were reluctant to quote Jewish prayers as evidence for the Lord's Prayer, for they argued that these prayers were later and thus provided no evidence for Jesus' prayer. However, as I briefly indicated above, in recent times James Charlesworth (1986) has gathered together the results of the investigations of various Christian and Jewish scholars on these prayers and has concluded that five of them may well date from Jesus' time. I quote the salient portions. The full texts of these prayers may be found as an appendix to this chapter.

Gift of Torah: In Blessing 4 of the Eighteen Benedictions from the Cairo Genizah we read: "Favor us with your knowledge, our Father, and with your Torah's understanding and wisdom. Blessed are you, Adonai, who favors people with knowledge."

In the *Ahabah Rabbah* we read: "Our Father, our King, for the sake of our forebears who trusted in you, whom you did teach laws of life, be gracious to us and teach us likewise. Our Father, merciful Father, who are ever compassionate, have pity on us and inspire us to understand and discern, to perceive, learn and teach, to observe, do, and fulfill gladly all the teachings of your Torah."

In the *Qaddish* we find: "(We pray) for Israel, for our teachers and their disciples and the disciples of their disciples, and for all who study Torah, here and everywhere. May they have abundant peace, lovingkindness, ample sustenance and salvation from their Father who is in heaven. And say: Amen."

Forgiveness: In Blessing 6 of the Eighteen Benedictions from the Cairo Genizah we find: "Forgive us, our Father, for we have sinned before you. Wipe out and remove our transgressions from before your eyes, for great is your mercy. Blessed are you, Adonai, who is quick to forgive." Blessing 6 of the Eighteen Benedictions in the traditional liturgy links together "father" and "king": "Forgive us, our Father, for we have sinned. Pardon us, our king, for we have transgressed, for you forgive and pardon. Blessed are you, Adonai, who is gracious and quick to forgive."

Deliverance and Sustenance: Both deliverance and sustenance occur in the third section of the Grace after festive meals: "O God, our Father, tend and nourish us, sustain and maintain us, grant us deliverance. Speedily, Lord our God, grant us relief from all our troubles."

The prayers from which I have just quoted are prayers that Jesus may well have said on a regular basis.

Summary and Conclusion on Father

So there you have it—massive materials on just one word, but a very important word indeed. I would venture that many in our Western tradition have taken Joachim Jeremias's understanding of Jesus' use of "father" as normative and have thereby flattened this potent metaphor into one narrow meaning. In a slightly different context Walter Brueggemann (1997, 81) makes a comment on Jewish discourse that is apropos of my argument: "I intend only to contrast this particularistic, polyvalent mode of discourse with the pervasive Western, Christian propensity to flatten, to refuse ambiguity, to lose density, and to give universalizing closure." It is wonderful that Jesus revealed that God is as intimate to us as a father is. But as we have seen above in great detail, intimacy is just one of the dimensions of the rich metaphor "father" and may arguably be the least conspicuous at Jesus' time. Jesus' use of the metaphor "father" seems to accentuate its political dimension, for the father God that Jesus proclaimed is opposed to all other exclusive claims to dominance, be these those of imperial Rome or of even our own earthly father. But I stop here, lest I be accused of flattening the metaphor of father.

Hallowed Be Your Name.

The first of the "you" petitions seems very simple, that is, until we examine it. Don't our children give us the first clue as to the complexity of this petition when they pray: "Hello-ed be your name," as if they were saying a big Hi! to God.

This petition is filled with the biblical code words "to make holy" and "name," which we need to crack open in order to appreciate what it is being said to God and especially what we are asking for. I use a very prosaic example. When we were children growing up in the Karris household, Mom, whose parents came from Austria, used to employ the word *Schwabbelhanus* when we would make a mess. Later on when as adults we would talk among ourselves and use that code word, nonfamily members would look at us with blank stares, as if to ask: What are you talking about? They didn't know the code.

While talking about code, I ask the seemingly naïve, but important, hermeneutical question: Did Jesus know the entire biblical code that scholars say is behind "to hallow" and "name"? Did he expect his disciples to know this code? In his valuable treatment of the Lord's Prayer, John P. Meier (1994, 299) articulates his presupposition that Jesus was nourished on the Scriptures of Israel. He then almost makes Jesus as skilled as a contemporary exegete who can plot thematic trajectories through Old Testament prophet, wisdom teacher, Qumran, and Jewish synagogue. I remind my readers of what I said earlier in this chapter about the positions scholars have on Jesus' religious upbringing. Here is what Meier says (1994, 297): "Granted the trajectory we have seen from Ezekiel through Ben Sira and Qumran to the *Qaddish*, Jesus' petition most probably carries the same theological concentration: God alone can rightly and fully manifest himself in all his power and glory, that is to say, God alone can sanctify his name, which, it is hoped, he will do so soon."

With that as introductory background, I return to the code words "name" and "to hallow." I take "name" first, for its code can be rather easily cracked. "Name" stands for the person as we would say to someone who is disparaging our integrity: "You're ruining my name!" If someone is ruining our name, they are attacking our person. And how do we defend our good name? We can sue in the courts for defamation of character. We can defend ourselves by telling others the truth and by doing the truth in the hope of dispelling the lies being spread about us.

Continuing some of the imagery from "father" in the address of the Lord's Prayer, I note that children can bring disgrace on the family name. If the children turn out bad, people start to talk about "bad parents." If children turn out well, they bring honor on the family name. I recall hearing a proud parent boast: "My daughter graduated from Harvard Law School and is now a partner in a prestigious New York law firm." The daughter's honors reflect brilliantly back on her parents.

And these somewhat homey examples lead me back to the Bible. I ask: Did not Israel, God's children, often disgrace God's name by what they did? Did God not hear the Gentiles mocking God's name as they conquered the land God had given to Israel and led God's people away in chains? I quote a rather long passage from Ezekiel 36:16-23 and ask my readers to note how God's "name" and God's "holiness" are intertwined:

> The word of the LORD came to me: Mortal, when the house of Israel lived on their own soil, they defiled it with their ways and their deeds. . . . I scattered them among the nations, and they were dispersed through the countries. In accordance with their conduct and their deeds I judged them. But when they came to the nations, wherever they came, they profaned my holy name, in that it was said of them, "These are the people of the Lord, and yet they had to go out of his land." But I had concern for my holy name, which the house of Israel has profaned among the nations to which they came. Therefore, say to the house of Israel, Thus says the Lord God: It is not for your sake, O house of Israel, that I am about to act, but for the sake of my holy name, which you have profaned among the

nations to which you came. I will sanctify my great name, which has been profaned among the nations, and which you have profaned among them. And the nations shall know that I am the Lord, says the Lord God, when through you I display my holiness before their eyes.

In this long quotation from Ezekiel we see that the author depicts God's dealings with Israel with the two code words "holiness" and "name." Israel does not defile God's name and gift of land when they act righteously. When they act unrighteously, they defile the land and God's name and are sent away captives. Instead of bringing glory to God's name, they have brought disrepute. Surely, "name" indicates who God is. And so, too, does "holiness." Holiness points to who God is as wholly other. For all others are unholy. And unholy actions defile the person, the nation, and the land and also profane the name of the God who selected the person and the nation and gave the gift of the land. This view of holiness may seem to be outside our ken until we reflect a little. In those instances when someone has broken into our homes or cars we instinctively say: "I feel defiled." Someone has defiled us by breaking into what is the sanctuary of our home. Or if you've ever been in the presence of evil, you feel that you have to cleanse yourself from the polluting force.

It seems likely to me that behind Jesus' prayer "Hallowed be your name" lies not only Ezekiel 36 but also and especially the *Qaddish*, which is a Jewish prayer dated to Jesus' time. I quote the first and fourth sections, refer my readers to the appendix for the entire prayer, and advise them to note how concise Jesus' petition is and at the same time how traditional it is. I use the translation of Philip Birnbaum (1995, 46, 48):

> Glorified and sanctified be God's great name throughout the world which he has created according to his will. May he establish his kingdom in your lifetime and during your days, and within the life of the entire house of Israel, speedily and soon. And say: Amen.

> (We pray) for Israel, for our teachers and their disciples and the disciples of their disciples, and for all who study the Torah, here and everywhere. May they have abundant peace, loving-kindness, ample sustenance and salvation from their Father who is in heaven. And say: Amen.

From the first section of the *Qaddish* we see how closely "name," "hallowing," and "kingdom" are related. God's name is to be hallowed. God's kingdom is coming. And if your eye goes back over the fourth section, you will note that mention is made of "Father who is in heaven."

I think that my consideration of the first "you" petition of the Our Father has brought us to the brink of another major issue facing interpreters of this prayer. Is its meaning ethical or eschatological? The ethical interpretation means that we should not take God's name in vain or use it lightly in taking oaths. This ethical sense is fostered by the Jesus Seminar, whose translation of this petition is: "Your name be revered" (Funk and Hoover 1993, 148). Towards the end of his treatment on "sacred names" Robert Funk (1996, 208) writes: "The term [*Abba* or Father] suggests that Jesus understood himself to have a particularly intimate relationship to God. Moreover, he taught his disciples to address God in a similar fashion. He also taught his disciples to hold the name of God in reverence." As his footnote indicates, Funk is referring to the first petition of the Lord's Prayer (Luke 11:2 and Matthew 6:9).

Or is "hallowed be" what biblical scholars call a theological passive, that is, that God will make God's name holy? In this eschatological interpretation, fostered as we saw above by John P. Meier, God is doing through the ministry of Jesus what God will finally do when he destroys Gog, Magog, and other evil powers (Ezekiel 38–39). If this is the meaning of "hallowing God's name," then N. T. Wright (1997, 15) is correct. We have not just intimacy, but revolution. Not just familiarity, but hope. But if Funk and the fellows of the Jesus Seminar are correct, then Jesus' petition fits into those concerns of his day, witnessed especially at Qumran, that Jews revere God's name and not pronounce the sacred name. And since there is no other gospel material that has the same wording, that is, "hallowed be your name," we cannot turn to that source as a way of adjudicating the case at hand.

But if "name" and "hallowing" are indeed symbols, then we shouldn't expect them to be one-dimensional. That is, Meier, Wright, and Funk are all right.

Your Kingdom Come

There is little doubt among scholars that Jesus' entire life revolved around preaching and enacting God's kingdom. But scholars diverge when it comes to interpreting whether God's kingdom is future or present. I let John P. Meier speak for those who accentuate its futurity and John Dominic Crossan for those who champion a present meaning. I advise my readers to page back to what I said about Jesus' religious upbringing. John Dominic Crossan argues that Jesus' land was thoroughly Hellenized and that therefore one can legitimately use Greek writings from Diaspora Judaism to interpret Jesus' teaching.

John P. Meier (1994, 298) focuses on the rare expression in the Lord's Prayer that the kingdom "comes" and states the problem clearly: "In OT prophecies, all sorts of eschatological realities (God, the hoped-for king, days, etc.) were said to come—but, pointedly, not the kingdom of God or some equivalent phrase." And then Meier (1994, 299) adroitly goes on to solve this problem by stating: "Rather according to the OT, it is God as king who is the one who comes, and that is the meaning of Jesus' petition." I quote two of the Old Testament passages Meier uses in support of his position. Isaiah 35:4 reads: "Say to those who are of a fearful heart, 'Be strong, do not fear! Here is your God. He will come with vengeance, with terrible recompense. He will come and save you.'" Zechariah 14:9 occurs in a context of God conquering the nations who stand against Jerusalem: "And the Lord will become king over all the earth. On that day the Lord will be one and his name one." As Meier (1994, 299) concludes: "In short, when Jesus prays that God's kingdom come, he is simply expressing in a more abstract phrase the eschatological hope of the latter part of the OT and the pseudepigrapha that God would come on the last day to save and restore his people Israel."

In his treatment of "your kingdom come" Meier has also given an answer to the vexing question: Is God's kingdom present or future? In his opinion it is future. As a matter of fact, Meier (1994, 235) goes so far as to say: "Future transcendent salvation was an essential part of Jesus' proclamation of the kingdom. Any reconstruction of the historical Jesus that does not do full justice to this eschatological future must be dismissed as hopelessly inadequate" (1994, 235). If Meier is correct, then the reconstruction of the historical Jesus undertaken by Crossan and other fellows of the Jesus Seminar is "hopelessly inadequate."

As I read the fellows of the Jesus Seminar, they maintain that God's kingdom is present. That is, Jesus did not preach that God's kingdom would come in the future, especially with earthquakes and other apocalyptic events. As John Dominic Crossan (1991, 294) says: "I repeat, however, that there is nothing apocalyptic about the Lord's Prayer, and its serves, unless rendered too exclusively spiritual, as a beautiful summary of the themes and emphases in Jesus' vision of the kingdom of

God." One way of putting the matter is to say that the fellows of the Jesus Seminar interpret the Lord's Prayer in an ethical rather than an eschatological way. Crossan (1994, 56) depicts his alternative to the future kingdom as present or sapiential vision. "The term *sapiential* underlines the necessity of wisdom—*sapientia* in Latin—for discerning how, here and now in this world, one can so live that God's power, rule, and dominion are evidently present to all observers. One enters that kingdom by wisdom or goodness, by virtue, justice, or freedom. It is a style of life for now rather than a hope of life for the future." From the vast Jewish tradition Crossan selects non-Palestinian "wisdom" references to the kingdom of God from Philo of Alexandria (*Special Laws* 4.135-136) and Wisdom of Solomon 10:10 as his evidence. Wisdom 10:10 says: "When a righteous man fled from his brother's wrath, Wisdom guided him on straight paths. She showed him the kingdom of God and gave him knowledge of holy things." Jesus, an illiterate peasant, but with an oral brilliance, championed this here-and-now kingdom of God. And an important aspect of the present kingdom of God was Jesus' "open commensality," which we will touch upon in the first "we petition" of the Lord's Prayer.

Summary on the Petition "Your Kingdom Come"

John Dominic Crossan and John P. Meier have made it clear that "the kingdom of God" has different meanings. Indeed, it is a polyvalent symbol. John P. Meier and others have taken it to mean primarily the eschatological restoration and salvation of God's covenant people. John Dominic Crossan and the fellows of the Jesus Seminar take it sapientially. One enters God's reign now by following God's wisdom as enunciated by Jesus. Indeed, it is both. And this is the point argued by Gerd Theissen and Annette Merz (1998, 252), who quote from Jewish liturgical texts at the time of Jesus to provide their answer that God's kingdom is both present and future. One prayer is the eleventh petition from the Eighteen Benedictions. In their translation this petition reads: "Restore our judges as before . . . and be king over us, you alone." Another prayer is from the first section of the *Qaddish*, which I referred to just a few pages ago: "Magnified and sanctified be his great name in the world . . . may his kingdom be established during your life and during your days, and during the life of all the whole house of Israel, even speedily and at a near time." They (1998, 252) conclude: "It can be inferred from the examples given that in a liturgical context

Jews in the time of Jesus could equally praise the present rule of God and ask for its coming without seeing an irresolvable contradiction here." Yes, God's kingdom is God's business and our business. And yes, please, do not flatten the metaphor "kingdom of God" into one meaning and one time reference.

Our Daily Bread Give Us Today

It's almost impossible to discuss this petition without immediately sensing its symbolism. As Hans Dieter Betz (1995, 399) writes: "The term 'bread' (*artos*) also has multiple meanings. There is hardly any doubt that it refers to real, not merely 'spiritual,' bread, but in antiquity generally bread was never taken as something merely material."

But before I get into possible biblical referents for the symbol of bread, I share a story from the time of St. Francis of Assisi. Massimo Montanari (1994, 51) writes:

> With a few possible exceptions, white bread made from wheat remained a delicacy available only to a few. . . . In a sermon to the lay Cistercian brothers, Humbert of Romans recounted . . . a significant episode: "Brothers often come to us from poverty, attracted by the hope of a better life. It happened once upon a time that a man, from a family which only ate black bread, wanted to become a brother in order to eat white bread. On the day of his admission, prostrate before the bishop, he was asked: 'What do you desire?' He answered: 'White bread, and often!'"

Yes, instead of saying "I desire to serve the Lord in penance," the peasant wanted white bread. For white bread not only provided nutriment, it also indicated the good life and social class. And in one of those quirks of history, contemporary health-conscious Americans proscribe white bread and prescribe black bread, and the poor eat white bread and the rich black bread.

But let us return to our Jewish and biblical context. From a Jewish context three possible referents for a deeper meaning of "bread" come to mind right away. Recall God's gift of manna, of which Moses says in Exodus 16:15: "It is the bread that the Lord has given you to eat." Then there was the gift of the bread of wisdom. Recall how Wisdom invites people to eat of her food and drink of her potions in Proverbs 9:5: "Come, eat of my bread and drink of the wine I have mixed." And in an eschatological context Isaiah 25:6-7 promises rich fare and the best wines in the end time: "On this mountain the LORD of hosts will make for all peoples a feast of rich food, a feast of well-aged wines, of rich food filled with marrow, of well-aged wines strained clear. And he will destroy on this mountain the shroud that is cast over all peoples, the sheet that is spread over all nations; he will swallow up death forever." Are any of these referents or all three of them in mind in this first "we petition"?

Perhaps, we can come to an answer and also deepen our search if we ask about the meaning of one of the most controversial words in the entire New Testament. In talking about the Greek word *epiousios* Hans Dieter Betz (1995, 397): contends: "for which a fully convincing explanation and translation cannot be given even today." In the title of this section I used the translation of John Meier (1994, 292): "Our daily bread give us today." While Meier's translation seems straightforward, he has made a decision to translate the rarest of Greek words, *epiousios*, as "daily," that is, to take the word as coming from *epi*, an empty prefix here, and *ousa*, the present participle of the verb *eimi*, "to be." Thus, the prayer deals with "bread for today." Other scholars derive the meaning of *epiousios* from *epi*, again an empty prefix here, and *ousa*, the present participle of the verb *eimi*, "to come." In this derivation *epiousios* means "bread for the coming (day)." Finally, *epiousios* can come from the preposition *epi*, which conveys goal or purpose, and the noun *ousia*, which means "essence, being, substance." In this derivation *epiousios* means "bread for subsistence, necessary for existence" (see Joseph A. Fitzmyer 1985, 905; see also Hans Dieter Betz 1995, 397–99).

The Jesus Seminar has: "Provide us with the bread we need for the day" (Funk and Hoover 1993, 327) and definitely has taken *epiousios artos* to mean "bread we need," that is, the bread necessary for existence. And that is the meaning also taken by Fitzmyer (1985, 905) and Betz (1995, 399).

But not all scholars would agree with this translation that accentuates the present need for bread. Joachim Jeremias favors a future meaning and translates this "we petition": "Our bread for tomorrow/give us today" (1978, 95). But Jeremias does not mean that this future dimension means that the present need for bread is neglected. He writes (1978, 102):

> the petition about "bread for tomorrow" . . . does not sever everyday life and the kingdom of God from one another, but it encompasses the totality of life. . . . In a world enslaved under Satan, in a world where God is remote, in a world of hunger and thirst, the disciples of Jesus dare to utter

this word "today"—even now, even here, already on this day, give us the bread of life.

N. T. Wright also combines future with present dimensions of "give us our daily bread." In his popular exposition of the Lord's Prayer he (1997, 41) expounds on this meaning: "Matthew, in line with Jesus' whole agenda, means 'give us, *here and now*, the bread of life which is promised for the great Tomorrow.'" And what that "bread of life" means is shown in Jesus' table fellowship with outcasts and sinners. Wright (1997, 39–40) continues: "Jesus was re-inventing the Kingdom of God around his own work; and at the heart of it was the great sign of welcome to all-comers, welcome to the party, to the Messianic Banquet, to the renewed people of God. Jesus was offering all and sundry the daily bread that spoke of the Kingdom of God."

Can we legitimately collapse these three possibilities into two: present and necessary bread; future bread? We need God's gifts of bread and of wisdom today. We hope for the future bread of the Messianic banquet. And we do so in dependence on our God, to whom we pray. Or is such collapsing of possibilities a frontal attack on the nature of the symbol "bread"?

Another dimension to the symbolism of this petition is found in its redundancy. I wonder whether we say this petition of the Lord's Prayer so often that we fail to note its double redundancy. Twice it mentions "we": It is *our* daily bread that we pray that God give *us* today. Twice, too, this petition refers to "today": Give us our *daily* bread *today*. What is going on? Jesus' petition, although spoken by a member of the chosen people, is universal in scope and includes all people. To make this point as clear as possible, "our/we" are repeated. Not just you disciples and I, not just all the Jewish people, but everyone is included in the "we" who stand under the universal sustainer of life. And it is indeed we, who must work together to provide bread. For it is not just the product of one person, but of many working together: farmer, miller, baker, deliverer, and seller. And bread, which stands for the necessities of life by a literary device technically called synechdoche, is required not once a week, but daily. Could one express the frailty of human life and human dependence on God and human interdependence more powerfully that this? We humans need food today, for our hunger will not be assuaged by recollections of past feasts or by the hope of tomorrow's table of delights. I give Betz (1995, 379) the final word, and it is an ethical word: "Finally, therefore, the petition 'give us' involves an obligation on the part of the petitioners. . . . Only if the petitioners act in the same manner they expect of God and of other human beings are they justified in presenting this petition. In other words, the imperative 'give us,' while being addressed to God, implies a self-addressed demand to the petitioners themselves."

This level of the symbolism of "our bread" is well and good in as far as it goes. But if we believe, along with the fellows of the Jesus Seminar, that Jesus put his prayer into action, then we have to look for yet another level of the meaning of "our food." I ask: With whom did Jesus share his food, so that it became "our food"? Was it just with his kin, acquaintances, disciples, and religiously good people?

John Dominic Crossan (1991), E. P. Sanders (1985; 1993), and N. T. Wright (1997) have taught us well that the historical Jesus freely associated with sinners and other outcasts at table and made his food "our food." I summarize Crossan's views first, for his is the more dominant voice in the United States.

Crossan calls Jesus' table fellowship with sinners and outcasts his "open commensality." For Crossan (1994, 69) the social category of commensality "means the rules of tabling and eating as miniature models for the rules of association and socialization. It means table fellowship as a map of economic discrimination, social hierarchy, and political differentiation." If you recall my opening story about the peasant who wanted to join the monastery so that he could eat the white bread of the wealthy, you have an instance of commensality. By eating white bread, the poor chap was moving across social and economic boundaries. Crossan (1994, 69) goes on to apply this social category to what he knows of the historical Jesus and his eating with tax collectors and sinners. This activity earned Jesus the epithet of being a glutton, a drunkard, and a friend of tax collectors and sinners (see Matthew 11:19/Luke 7:34). Righteous Jewish men didn't engage in such indiscriminate table fellowship. Crossan (1994, 69) concludes: "He (Jesus) makes, in other words, no appropriate distinctions and discriminations. . . . All of those terms—tax collectors, sinners, whores— are in this case derogatory terms for those with whom, in the opinion of the name callers, open and free association should be avoided."

From his analysis of Jewish law E. P. Sanders makes a strong point about what "sinners" means in the almost certainly true charge against Jesus that "he eats with tax collectors and sinners" (Q: Matthew 11:19/Luke 7:34). He writes (1993, 227): "'Sinners' in the Hebrew Bible, when used generically to refer to a class of people, refers not to those who occasionally transgress, but to those who are outside the law in some fundamental way. . . . The significance of the fact that Jesus was a friend of the wicked was this: he counted within his fellowship people who were generally regarded as living outside the law in a blatant manner."

It is impossible here to treat the Last Supper. Suffice it to say that in the view of John Dominic Crossan (1998, 423–44) the later church put restrictions on Jesus' "open commensality" as it established rules for what type of sinner was allowed to participate in the Lord's Supper. In an excellent, but little-known, book Francis J. Moloney (1997) visits much of this same territory and challenges the churches to open their doors wide to both saints and sinners who want to come together to pray and break bread.

Conclusion on "Our Daily Bread"

Perhaps, our heads are spinning as we come to the end of this look at the rich metaphor of "our bread" in the first "we petition" of the Lord's Prayer. On one level this petition is very similar to the universal thrust of the Jewish "Grace after Meals," which can be seen in the appendix to this chapter. On yet another level this universal dimension shines forth in Jesus' table fellowship as he shares "our bread" not in the abstract, but in his ministry with "outcasts and sinners." And finally, there is a future dimension, I would contend, as Jesus' table fellowship anticipates God's future dining with all and sundry. What a rich metaphor we have in "bread"! And it is one that the evangelists, each in his own way, will develop in their stories of Jesus.

Allow me to return to the story with which I opened this section. Did the young man from the peasant family who ate only black bread truly know what he was asking for? Sure, he wanted white bread and wanted it often. But did he really know who his confreres in the monastery would be? The movie *The Name of the Rose* is accurate in showing that medieval monasteries could have distinguished and less than distinguished members. Did the righteous who came to Jesus' table know that they might be breaking bread with rogues and roués? Crossan, Sanders, and Moloney have done us a great service as they have displayed this shocking dimension of Jesus' ministry before our

very eyes. Do the churches need to recover this dimension of the symbol of "our bread"?

And Forgive Us Our Debts,
As We Forgive Our Debtors

I have used the translation of John Meier (1994, 292). A quick compar-
ison with a Jewish prayer from the time of Jesus will show the uniqueness of Jesus' prayer. I quote the sixth benediction of the Eighteen
Benedictions. I use the translation of Lawrence A. Hoffman (1998, 39):
"Forgive us, our father, for we have sinned before you. Wipe out and
remove our transgressions from before your eyes, for great is your
mercy. Blessed are you, Adonai, who is quick to forgive." Two things
are immediately obvious as one compares this prayer to the second
"we petition" of the Lord's Prayer. First, the sixth benediction uses different words for human weakness, that is, it talks about "sin" and
"transgressions" whereas the Lord's Prayer speaks of "debts" and
"debtors." And second, this "we petition" is reciprocal: "And forgive
us our debts, *as* we forgive our debtors."

Does this petition refer to "real" debts or does it use "debts"
metaphorically? Hans Dieter Betz maintains that real debts are not in
view and argues against scholars who maintain this position. The terminology of debt and debtors comes from law and commerce. Betz
(1995, 402) goes on to maintain: "two facts are presupposed: (1) the
social concept that all human affairs are fundamentally those of
mutual obligations and that this also includes our relationship with
God; (2) the realization that these obligations, at least to a significant
degree, remain unfulfilled." He concludes (1995, 404) his consideration of this petition: "The peculiar situation exists therefore that the
petitioners, even though they find themselves in the condition of
injustice (vs. 12a), still need a basis of justice to make a justifiable
appeal for mercy (vs. 12 b)."

It seems to me that Betz may have too quickly dispensed with a consideration that the word "debts" may point to real monetary debts and
has soared into fine and more abstract considerations of justice and
injustice. In this regard scholars of the historical Jesus offer a necessary
corrective. In considering the versions of this petition found in
Matthew and Luke, Funk and Hoover (1993, 149) write: "Again,
Matthew seems to have preserved the more original petition regarding
debts: Luke has begun the transition to 'sins,' but does not quite com-

plete it. Eventually, 'sins' or 'trespasses' was to take the place of real, monetary debts. Yet for Jesus this petition undoubtedly had to do with the plight of the oppressed poor, whose debts were probably overwhelming."

John Dominic Crossan (1991, 294) is clearer: "God forgives us our debts, that is, the offerings or punishments due for our sins, and we forgive our neighbors their debts, that is, the returns or penalties due for their loans." But it is N. T. Wright (1997, 55–56) who is clearest of all:

> Among the many meanings which this [petition] had for Jesus' followers was that they were to practice the great old biblical command of Jubilee. Not only were they to forgive one another their sins and offences; they would have no debts from each other. . . . The problem of debt was very serious in Jesus' time. When the revolutionaries took over the Temple at the start of the Jewish war against the Romans, thirty years after Jesus' day, the first thing they did was to burn the records of debt. The early church certainly believed that Jesus was talking about actual debts. The Lord's Prayer makes sense, not just in terms of individual human beings quieting their own troubled consciences, vital though that is, but also in terms of the new day when justice and peace will embrace, economically and socially as well as personally and existentially. So this clause in the prayer is anchored, like all the others, in the career and announcement of Jesus.

With this petition, it seems to me, we are again caught up with our notion of metaphor. Should we interpret "debts" literally as financial obligations owed someone else or should we interpret "debts" as a metaphor for our indebtedness to God for our unjust lives of failing to meet our moral obligations? Or it may be that in this instance we can have our cake and eat it at the same time. The first part of the verse uses "debts" metaphorically whereas the second part of the verse uses "debts" literally. In the first part we pray that God will forgive us our debts, taking "debts" here as a metaphor for our sins and transgressions. In the second part we are dealing with the literal meaning of "debt" and pray "as we forgive those who owe us money and land."

Before I conclude this brief section, allow me to make two quick points. The first deals with the biblical ideal of Jubilee. See the description of the Jubilee in Leviticus 25, where on the fiftieth year people who have sold their property get it back (vs. 13) and those who enslaved themselves because of poverty get freedom for themselves and their children (vs. 54). John Howard Yoder (1994) may have gone too far in arguing that Jesus' inaugural sermon in Nazareth in Luke

4:16-30 proclaims the Jubilee year, but the second "we petition" of the Lord's Prayer would resonate with the Jewish law of Jubilee.

My second quick point is that the reciprocity in this petition is found in other places in the genuine Jesus tradition. See the parable in Matthew 18:21-35. Also consult the teachings of "forgiveness for forgiveness" in Luke 11:4a/Matthew 6:12, Mark 11:25/Matthew 6:14-15, and Luke 6:37c; "measure for measure" in Luke 6:38c/Matthew 7:2b and Mark 4:24b; and "judgment for judgment" in Luke 6:37a/Matthew 7:1-2a. As Crossan (1991, 294) notes: "The point, however, is not sequentiality or causality, 'we do in order that God does,' but rather simultaneity and mutuality, 'we do and God does.'" In these teachings we are at the heart of the teaching of the historical Jesus.

And Do Not Lead Us to the Test

On one level this petition doesn't make too much sense. For if we Americans pray to be freed from testing, we are praying to die. None of us is going to get out of this life without testing and its attendant pain and anxiety. From cradle to nursing home we are tested. There are medical tests, as described in the sentence: "They want me to get a stress test and then some more tests after that." There are educational tests. I would dread to have to prepare for and take my three days of written doctoral comprehensive tests again. Many states require us to take our cars in for an annual test. The car of a friend of mine recently flunked its test. And then there are the tests to our virtue. Why, the other day in Wal-Mart I heard an exasperated mother say to her daughter: "Melissa, you're testing my patience!" And then there are the daily chores that test our physical strength. Perhaps, you are among many others who complain: "I just can't do what I used to!"

Perhaps, we can eliminate most of the contemporary "testings" we have to endure in the United States. The final "we petition" doesn't ask that God not lead us to medical, educational, or mechanical tests, for these largely didn't exist for Jesus and his listeners. It seems that this petition has to do with moral testing, but what kind? Garden variety testing or the big test in the sky?

I look to the Bible for an answer and tell you in advance that I think that a large portion of its meaning is eschatological, that is, we pray that God not lead us to commit apostasy—fail in the ultimate test and abandon belief in God. May it be that in our ordinary experiences of testing we find the grounds for using them as a metaphor for our moral and faith relationship with God?

It may also be helpful at the very beginning to note that the Jesus Seminar gave this petition a "gray" vote. The fellows of the Jesus Seminar are saying: "Jesus did not say this, but the ideas contained in it are close to his own" (Funk and Hoover 1993, 36). Their translation is: "And please don't subject us to test after test" (1993, 148). It is Stephen Patterson (1998, 103 n. 34), a fellow of the Jesus Seminar, who gives us an inkling of why the Jesus Seminar voted as it did: "The final petition was designated 'gray,' on the suggestion that the appeal for deliverance might be more at home in the early church's experience of persecution."

One problem is the meaning of the Greek *peirasmos*. In translating it as "test," I have followed John Meier's translation. This translation seems to have fine biblical warrant in God's testing of God's people in their formative years in the desert. See, for example, Exodus 16:4, where "testing" is linked with God's gift of bread: "Then the Lord said to Moses, 'I am going to rain bread from heaven for you, and each day the people shall go out and gather enough for that day. In that way I will test them, whether they will follow my instructions or not.'" See also Exodus 20:20 and Deuteronomy 8:2, 16. And there are the wisdom tales of God's testing of righteous Tobit and Job. And in all these instances the testing is to see whether God's people and righteous ones will remain steadfast and not deny God and thereby commit apostasy. That is, "testing" is not to be equated with "temptation" to ordinary, quotidian sin. And a particular time for such "testing" would occur during the last days. Raymond E. Brown (1965, 315–16) writes:

> The word for "trial, temptation" here is *peirasmos*. While this word can refer to ordinary temptation, it also has a specialized reference to the final onslaught of Satan. Ap [Revelation] 3:10 contains a promise of Christ: "Because you have kept my command and stood fast, I will keep you from the hour of trial (*peirasmos*) which is coming on the whole world, to try those who dwell on earth."

A second problem emerges from the entire notion of "testing" and can be formulated in this manner: Does God determine that people sin and thereby turn their backs on their God? Commentator after commentator addresses this problem. I let John Meier (1994, 302) speak for them all:

> In keeping with their strong monotheism, usually expressed by mythic stories rather than by philosophical theology, they [the biblical writers]

frequently attributed all events directly to God, with no great concern
about whether these events were good or bad. The important point was
to exclude any second power, good or evil, that might seem equal to God.
. . . Worrying about whether God directly causes or merely permits evil
may lie beyond the horizon of this utterly simple prayer.

Having said all this, I still am attracted to a late Jewish prayer which
both Joachim Jeremias and Hans Dieter Betz adduce to interpret this
petition. Notice how Jeremias (1978, 104) brings this fifth-century A.D.
prayer into Jesus' backyard: "How the verb [in James 1:13] is really to
be construed is shown by a very ancient Jewish evening prayer, which
Jesus could have known and with which he perhaps makes a direct
point of contact." Betz (1995, 410) is equally clever at bringing this
later prayer into Jesus' ken: "Jewish prayers preserved from a later time
may allow one to suppose that either they or their antecedents were in
use at the time of Jesus." The prayer both Jeremias and Betz cite is
found in Babylonian Talmud Tractate *Berakoth* 60b:

> Blessed is He who causes the bands of sleep to fall upon my eyes and
> slumber on my eyelids, and gives light to the apple of the eye. . . . [A]ccus-
> tom me to the performance of religious duties, but do not accustom me
> to transgression, and bring me not into the power of sin, or into the
> power of iniquity, or into the power of temptation, or into the power of
> contempt. And may the good inclination have sway over me. . . . Blessed
> are Thou, O Lord, who gives light to the whole world in your glory.

This prayer has some similarities to a psalm prayer from Qumran,
to which John Meier (1994, 365 n. 49) makes reference. I quote 11Q5
19:12-16: "I too have loved your Name and I have looked for sanctuary
in your shade. The memory of your power strengthens my heart. I relax
in your goodness. Pardon my sins, YHWH, and cleanse me from my
iniquity. Bestow on me a faithful and knowing spirit; may I not be dis-
graced in the calamity. May Satan not rule over me or an unclean
spirit; may neither pain nor evil purpose take possession of my bones."
    These two prayers suggest the context for the final petition of the
Lord's Prayer. It acknowledges that the power of sin and iniquity exist
and buffet believers. In the terms of the Lord's Prayer the power of sin
and iniquity will be negated when God's name is hallowed and God's
kingdom comes. As Betz (1995, 411) says: "By granting these [first
three] petitions, God would in effect eliminate the source of evil forever, so that by not granting them God allows this evil to persist and
thus to exert its lure of temptation."
    As I come to the conclusion of this final "we petition," I realize that

I have come close to falling over the precipice of flattening the metaphor, "test." But surely, "test" has both an eschatological and an ethical dimension, for this metaphor, too, is polyvalent.

CONCLUSION ON PRAYER AND THE HISTORICAL JESUS

I make these summary points. First, I have set the ball of interpretation in motion for the Lord's Prayer and have put it into your court. I would suggest that each of its metaphors has at least two meanings: father, name, making holy, kingdom, bread, debts, test. Don't let this insight out of your sight. Don't do it lip service as you might say: "I'd love a flat stomach." If there's no pain, there's no gain in the battle against flattening biblical metaphors. It's so easy to say "father" certainly means "this" and "our daily bread" certainly means "that" and not take the effort to walk around the "pink-panther" diamond and to see and appreciate some new angles. If I might paraphrase the theme song from the rejuvenated musical *Cabaret*: What good is sitting around in your room looking at the four walls of the same old meanings?

Second, the Jesus Seminar's interpretation of the various clauses of the Lord's Prayer is what is technically called a present or ethical interpretation in contrast to a future interpretation, such as that of John Meier. Theissen and Merz (1998, 262–63) provide a helpful summary of the contrast between ethical and future/eschatological interpretations of the five commonly accepted petitions. But as we saw earlier, they themselves take the petition "your kingdom come" in both a future and a present sense. Put another way, why cannot both meanings be present in all five petitions? Why do scholars fight over an either-or? Let's look at both sides of the same coin. Recall what Hans Dieter Betz said earlier about the blessedly ambiguous nature of liturgical prayer.

Third and with gratitude to Hans Dieter Betz (1995, 411) I would suggest that the entire prayer is a sort of frank discussion between two good friends. That is, Jesus is saying to God: "If you'd be doing a better job of hallowing your name and bringing about your kingly rule, then we won't be in such a mess of evil. And we won't have to pray that you not lead us into temptation." But God could well reply: "Are you and your companions sharing your food with others and forgiving their debts, so that there is more justice in the earthly realm? You know, this justice business is a two-way street."

Fourth, as Anton Vögtle (1978), James Charlesworth (1986), Hans Dieter Betz (1995, 378), and many other scholars have taught us, the Lord's Prayer is a largely traditional Jewish prayer. Study of the Jewish prayers in the appendix to this chapter will provide some of the evidence that has led scholars to this conclusion. What is unique in this prayer is not so much Jesus' address of God as "father," as Joachim Jeremias would have it. Rather the fellows of the Jesus Seminar are on the right path in teaching us that Jesus' uniqueness is to be found in the fact that he put his life on the line for the petitions of his prayer. He embodied the petition for "our bread" by his table fellowship with sinners. He taught the forgiveness of real debt, just as his followers today appeal for the forgiveness of third- and two-thirds-world debt. His teaching on love of enemies, turning the other cheek, and not serving Mammon were the ethical components of the coming of God's kingdom in the present. And as a traditional Jew, versed in the examples of the great pray-ers of his tradition, namely, Abraham, Moses, and Elijah, he entered into frank exchange with the Father about the state of the world. In our subsequent chapters on prayer in Luke-Acts and prayer in John and 1 John we will see how the evangelists probed the depths of Jesus' life with God in prayer and how Luke put special emphasis on Jesus' prayer in public and in private.

Fifth, metaphors are interpreted by one's culture. In 1979 Morton W. Bloomfield and his colleagues published a work with the exhaustively exact title of *Incipits of Latin Works on the Virtues and Vices, 1100–1500 A.D., Including a Section of Incipits of Works on the Pater Noster*. They listed 1260 incipits or beginnings of works on the Our Father (#8001 to #9261). Number 8654 contains the beginning words of St. Francis of Assisi's "Exposition of the Our Father." In his work and in most of the other 1,259 commentaries on the Lord's Prayer you will see how medieval people interpreted it. They largely interpreted one Scripture passage by means of others, and they also borrowed heavily and without citation from previous interpreters. One will look in vain for any consideration of what we today call "the historical Jesus." In 1983 the English translation of Leonardo Boff's book on the Lord's Prayer was published. In the very title of the book this liberation theologian indicates the interpretive matrix he will use in reading the metaphors of the Lord's Prayer: *The Lord's Prayer: The Prayer of Integral Liberation*. Since ours is an age of historical inquiry, I have tried to interpret the Lord's Prayer in the context of the search for the historical Jesus undertaken by fellows of the Jesus Seminar and by others.

While some would call such a venture a trip to the core of "subjectivism," I stand undaunted and repeat the old adage that my investigations with contemporary methodologies nurture my faith. Or if I might put my quest in a medieval and monastic context, I use contemporary methodologies so that I might experience the object of my faith: God and Jesus the Lord. And my prayer is that my study will nurture and enliven the faith life of my readers, too.

The final point about contextualization concerns the issue of patriarchy, because feminists ask probing questions about the role of patriarchy in our Bible and in our churches. Mary Rose D'Angelo (1992a; 1992b) has dealt with these issues in twin articles and laid an excellent foundation toward a solution on the use of "father" in the Lord's Prayer. In a more accessible format Elizabeth A. Johnson (1992, 80–82) has wonderfully and briefly addressed the issue of patriarchy and Jesus' use of "father" under the rubrics of frequency and exclusivity. The earliest Gospel, that of Mark, uses "father" to refer to God four times while the latest Gospel, that of John, uses "father" in reference to God 109 times. And if we ask what the earliest strands of the gospel tradition say about the frequency with which Jesus refers to God as "father," we arrive at the following results. Jesus refers to God as "father" once in Mark, once in the special source that Matthew and Luke share (Q), twice in the material that Luke alone has, once in the material that Matthew alone has, and seventy-three times in John. So the earliest traditions show us that when Jesus talked about God, "father" was not always on his lips. And if one asks whether the historical Jesus used "father" exclusively to refer to God, the answer is a resoundingly No. Take the parables of Jesus, for example, which talk of God's kingdom as a woman baking bread (Luke 13:20-21) or of God's search for men and women under the imagery of a woman in search of lost money (Luke 15:8-10). In this regard, the studies of the Jesus Seminar have marvelously shown us the diverse imagery Jesus used to refer to God and how all-inclusive and nondomineering he was. Marcus Borg (1999, 241–42) paints a captivating portrait of Jesus, compassionate and non-dominating: "As a lens through which we see God, Jesus enables us to see much. What we see is deeply Jewish. . . . God is passionate about justice. . . . God's passion for justice led Jesus to side with the poor and marginalized and to indict the religious and political elites, including Jerusalem and the temple as the center of the native domination system. Indeed, Jesus' passion for justice in the name of God was the cause of his death: he challenged and suffered the wrath of the powers." Is this the portrait of a Jesus who would bless those who use his prayer to justify their domination over others? And finally, lest my readers get the wrong impression, I emphasize that Jesus' frequent use of "father" in addressing God in the Fourth Gospel is not a function of patriarchy but of the author's high Christology.

Elizabeth Johnson (1992, 82) concludes her observations on Jesus and patriarchy with these correct and sharp words: "The difficulty with the appeal to Jesus' use of father to restrict other options in naming toward God thus becomes apparent. It presses speech that was pluriform, subtle, and subversive into an exclusive, literal, and patriarchal mold, and simply does not do justice to the evidence at hand." Yes, indeed. Don't flatten the metaphor of "father."

As I come to the last paragraph of this chapter, my readers may be disappointed that I did not conclude with irenic words. But as I indicated at the beginning of this chapter, emotions run high when scholars talk about the historical Jesus. So much is at stake. There are so many presuppositions, spoken and unspoken. And thanks be to God that such study is a matter of life and death for many of us, scholars and nonscholars alike. And if we return to the Pink Panther story with which I opened this chapter, we may learn a lesson from Inspector Clouseau and not take our efforts too seriously. There are laughs aplenty as we see ourselves and others stumble toward the door of truth.

FOR FURTHER READING

Ashton, John. 1992. "Abba." *Anchor Bible Dictionary*, 1: 7–8. New York: Doubleday.

Betz, Hans Dieter. 1995. *The Sermon on the Mount: A Commentary on the Sermon on the Mount, including the Sermon on the Plain (Matthew 5:3–7:27 and Luke 6:20-49)*, 370–413. Hermeneia. Minneapolis: Fortress.

Birnbaum, Philip. 1995. *Daily Prayer Book: HA-SIDDUR HA-SHALEM.* New York: Hebrew Publishing Company.

Borg, Marcus J. 1987. *Jesus a New Vision: Spirit, Culture, and the Life of Discipleship.* New York: HarperSanFrancisco.

Cullmann, Oscar. 1995. *Prayer in the New Testament*, 37–69. Overtures to Biblical Theology. Minneapolis: Fortress.

Fitzmyer, Joseph A. 1993. "Abba *and Jesus' Relation to God.*" In

According to Paul: Studies in the Theology of the Apostle, 47–63, 132–42. New York: Paulist Press.

Houlden, J. L. 1992. "Lord's Prayer." *Anchor Bible Dictionary*, 4: 356–62. New York: Doubleday.

Jeremias, Joachim. 1978. *The Prayers of Jesus*. Philadelphia: Fortress.

Taussig, Hal. 1999. *Jesus Before God: The Prayer Life of the Historical Jesus*. Santa Rosa, Calif.: Polebridge Press. This book arrived too late for me to enter into serious dialogue with its contents.

Wright, N. T. 1997. *The Lord and His Prayer*. Grand Rapids: Eerdmans; Cincinnati: Forward Movement Publications.

APPENDIX ON JEWISH PRAYERS FROM JESUS' TIME

I give some scholarly arguments for dating the following prayers to the time of Jesus and including them here as "evidence" for Jesus' prayer life. I have followed the considered opinions of experts in these fields. My chief consultant has been James H. Charlesworth (1986, 411–436). Charlesworth (1986, 419) argues that besides the *Shema*, which is not a prayer in the strict sense, there are at least five prayers that "are very early, certainly proto-rabbinic: the Grace after Meals, the *'Ahabah Rabbah* (With Abounding Love), the *'Alenu lesabbeah* Prayer (It is our duty to praise), the *Qaddish* (Magnified and sanctified . . .), and the *Tefillah* (*Shemoneh 'Esreh* or Eighteen Benedictions)." I quote these prayers from modern translations and introduce each with brief commentary.

The Shema

I quote the *Shema*, based on Deuteronomy 6:4-9, from the text provided by Lawrence A. Hoffman (1997, 83):

"Hear O Israel: Adonai is our God; Adonai is One. Blessed is the One the glory of whose kingdom is renowned forever. You shall love Adonai your God with all your mind and body and strength. Keep these words, which I command you today, in mind. Instruct your children about them. Use them when you sit at home and when you walk about, when you lie down and when you stand up. Bind them to your hand as a sign and set them between your eyes as a symbol. Write them on the door posts of your house and on your gates."

Hoffman (1997, 93) comments: "The Jews were saying the *Sh'ma* twice daily as early as the first century. . . ." Hoffman (1997, 93) also states: "Originally, the invitation, 'Hear O Israel,' evoked a psalm-like doxology without the word 'kingdom': 'Blessed be his glorious name forever and ever.'. . . The accent on God's ultimate reign on earth is usually viewed as a response to Roman rule. Jesus too preached 'the coming of the kingdom' which must have been an important doctrine as early as the first century, and became more so, as the wars against Rome were fought."

Following the opinion of Hoffman, an expert in Jewish liturgical history, I omit from consideration the remaining two paragraphs of the *Shema*, which come from Deuteronomy 11:13-21 and Numbers 15:37-41. What is also clear is that the *Shema* is the conclusion of the covenant-making ceremony of Deuteronomy 5, which included the Ten Commandments. These are the words that the Israelites/Jews are to take to heart at least twice each day. As E. P. Sanders (1992, 236) rightly maintains, the recitation of the *Shema* was one of the five building blocks of "Common Judaism."

The Eighteen Benedictions or Tefillah

Scholars give a number of answers to the questions of who said these prayers, when they were composed, and in what form. Joachim Jeremias (1978, 72) gives the maximalist interpretation: "In the morning and in the evening, they (the men) would recite the *Shema*, framed by benedictions and followed by the *Tephilla*; in the afternoon the latter was prayed alone."

E. P. Sanders (1992, 204) and Lawrence A. Hoffman (1998, 31) are much more minimalist. Although Rabban Gamaliel II is credited with instituting the Eighteen Benedictions at Yavneh in Israel near the end of the first century C.E., these benedictions had a long prior history. Hoffman (1998, 31) writes: "Gamaliel inherited no single collection of blessings that everyone used. He inherited a practice of saying a proto-*Amidah* that varied from place to place, as well as examples of what these proto-*Amidot* contained: their typical topics, the kind of things people prayed for here and there, in as many different ways as there were people." For a similar view see Joseph Heinemann (1975, 31–32).

I follow the procedure of Sanders (1992, 204–5) and quote some of the Eighteen Benedictions in full and then list the topics covered by the others. The benedictions I quote give a sampling of the wordings for a particular topic, give two examples of addressing God as "our Father" (#4 and #6), and four examples of prayers for liberation and restoration (#7, #10, #11, and #14). I use the translation of the shorter version of the Eighteen Benedictions found in Hoffman (1998, 38–42).

Blessing 1—"Ancestors"
Blessed are you, Adonai, our God and our ancestors' God, Abraham's God, Isaac's God, and Jacob's God, great, mighty, and revered God, supreme God,

master of heaven and earth, our protector and our ancestors' protector, our security in each and every generation. Blessed are you, Adonai, Abraham's protector.

Blessing 2—"God's Power"

You are mighty, you humble the proud, you are strong, you judge the wicked, and you live forever. You support the dead, cause the wind to blow and bring down the dew, and sustain life, giving life to the dead. In the blink of an eye you bring salvation. Blessed are you, Adonai, who gives life to the dead.

Blessing 3—"Sanctification of God's Name"

Holy are you, and your name is revered; there is no god other than you. Blessed are you, Adonai, the holy God.

Blessing 4—"Knowledge"

Favor us with your knowledge, our Father, and with your Torah's understanding and wisdom. Blessed are you, Adonai, who favors people with knowledge.

Blessing 6—"Forgiveness"

Forgive us, our Father, for we have sinned before you. Wipe out and remove our transgressions from before your eyes, for great is your mercy. Blessed are you, Adonai, who is quick to forgive.

Blessing 7—"Deliverance"

See our affliction and fight our fight. Redeem us for the sake of your name. Blessed are you, Adonai, who redeems Israel.

Blessing 10—"Gathering the Exiles"

Sound a great shofar for our freedom, and lift up a banner for the gathering of our exiles. Blessed are you, Adonai, who gathers the dispersed among his people Israel.

Blessing 11—"Justice"

Restore our judges as in days of old, and our counselors as in former times, and reign over us, you alone. Blessed are you, Adonai, who loves justice.

Blessing 14—"Jerusalem and David"

Have mercy, Adonai our God, in your great mercy on Israel your people and on Jerusalem, your city, and on Zion where your presence dwells, and on your palace and on your habitation and on your righteous servant David's kingdom. Blessed are you, Adonai, David's God, who builds Jerusalem.

Blessing 5 treats the topic "repentance."
Blessing 8 treats the topic "healing."
Blessing 9 treats the topic "years" or "good crops."
Blessing 12 treats the topic "heretics."
Blessing 13 treats the topic "the righteous."
Blessing 15 treats the topic "prayer."
Blessing 16 treats the topic "sacrificial service."
Blessing 17 treats the topic "grateful acknowledgment."
Blessing 18 treats the topic "the priestly blessing."

Grace after Meals

Joseph Heinemann (1975, 90) writes: "There can be little doubt that Grace itself as well as the 'Invitation to Grace' goes back to earliest times. Very likely its origin must be sought in the large community meals which were customary in the Second Temple period; such meals are known to us also from the Dead Sea Scrolls." I quote the first three benedictions in a modified translation from Heinemann (1975, 91–92). I remind my readers of Jesus' many meals with all and sundry, in the course of which he probably said this prayer. I call your attention to the mention of liberation from slavery in Benediction 2 and the plea for deliverance and the use of "our Father" in Benediction 3.

"1. Blessed are you, Lord our God, King of the universe, who sustain the whole world with goodness, kindness, and mercy. God gives food to all creatures, for God's mercy endures forever. Through God's abundant goodness we have never yet been in want. May we never be in want of sustenance for God's great name's sake. For ours is a God who sustains all, does good to all, and provides food for all the creatures he has created. Blessed are you, O Lord, who sustains all."

"2. We thank you, Lord our God, for having given a lovely, good, and spacious land to our ancestors as a heritage; for having brought us forth from the land of Egypt and freed us from the house of slavery; for your covenant which you have sealed in our flesh; for your Torah which you have taught us; for your laws which you have made known to us; for the life, grace, and kindness you have bestowed on us; and for the sustenance you grant us daily, at every season, at every hour. For everything, Lord our God, we thank you and bless you. Be your name forever blessed by all as it is written: 'And you shall eat and be satisfied, and bless the Lord your God for the good land God has given you' (Deuteronomy 8:10). Blessed are you, O Lord, for the land and the sustenance."

"3. Have compassion, Lord our God, on Israel your people, on Jerusalem your city, on Zion the abode of your glory, on the royal house of David your anointed one, and on the great and holy Temple that bears your name. O God, our Father, tend and nourish us, sustain and maintain us, grant us deliverance. Speedily, Lord our God, grant us relief from all our troubles. Lord our God, O make us not dependent on the gifts and loans of human beings, but on your full, open, and generous hand, that we may never be put to shame and disgrace. Rebuild Jerusalem the holy city speedily in our days. Blessed are you, O Lord, who in your mercy rebuild Jerusalem. Amen."

'Ahabah Rabbah (Great Love)

James Charlesworth (1986, 420) writes: "Heinemann (1977, 129, 174) traces the original form of this benediction to the period before the destruction of Jerusalem; it was recited by the priests (see *m. Tamid* 5:1)." Philip Birnbaum (1995, 73) says simply that this blessing "is very old and was probably instituted by the men of the Great Assembly in the early period of the second Temple." In contemporary Jewish prayer books such as Birnbaum's it is the second blessing before the recitation of the *Shema*. I use and modify the translation of Birnbaum (1995, 74–76):

"With a great love have you loved us, Lord our God. Great and abundant mercy have you bestowed upon us. Our Father, our King, for the sake of our forebears who trusted in you, whom you did teach laws of life, be gracious to us and teach us likewise. Our Father, merciful Father, you who are ever compassionate, have pity on us and inspire us to understand and discern, to perceive, learn and teach, to observe, do, and fulfill gladly all the teachings of your Torah. Enlighten our eyes in your Torah. Attach our heart to your commandments. Unite our heart to love and reverence your name, so that we may never be put to shame. In your holy, great and revered name we trust—may we thrill with joy over your salvation. O bring us home in peace from the four corners of the earth, and make us walk upright to our land, for you are the God who performs triumphs. You have chosen us from all peoples and nations and have forever brought us near to your truly great name, that we may eagerly praise you and acclaim your Oneness. Blessed are you, O Lord, who has graciously chosen your people Israel."

'Alenu (Our Duty)

James Charlesworth (1986, 420) writes: "This prayer clearly predates 70 C.E. since it 'was composed against the background of the Temple service' (Heinemann, 1977:273; so also *EncJud* 2: col. 557)." I modify the translation of Philip Birnbaum (1995, 136, 138).

"It is our duty to praise the Master of all, to exalt the Creator of the universe, who has not made us like the nations of the world and has not placed us like the families of the earth; who has not designed our destiny to be like theirs, not our lot like that of all their multitude. We bend the knee and bow and acknowledge before the supreme King of kings, the Holy One, blessed be he, that it is he who stretched forth the heavens and founded the earth. His seat of glory is in the heavens above. His abode of majesty is in the lofty heights. He is our God. There is none else. Truly, he is our King. There is none besides him, as it is written in his Torah: 'You shall know this day, and reflect in your heart, that it is the Lord who is God in the heavens above and on the earth beneath. There is none else' (Deuteronomy 4:39).

"We hope therefore, Lord our God, soon to behold your majestic glory, when the abominations shall be removed from the earth and the false gods extermi-nated; when the world shall be perfected under the reign of the Almighty, and all humanity will call upon your name, and all the wicked of the earth will be turned to you. May all the inhabitants of the world realize and know that to you every knee must bend, every tongue must vow allegiance. May they bend the knee and prostrate themselves before you, Lord our God, and give honor to your glorious name. May they all accept the yoke of your kingdom, and do you reign over them speedily forever and ever. For the kingdom is yours, and to all eternity you will reign in glory, as it is written in your Torah: 'The Lord shall be King forever and ever.' (Exodus 15:18). And it is said: 'The Lord shall be King over all the earth. On that day the Lord shall be One, and his name One' (Zechariah 14:9)."

Qaddish (Hallowed)

I follow the early dating of the Qaddish given by James Charlesworth (1986, 420): "The simple form of the eschatological hopes for the establishment of the kingdom of God and the absence of any allusion to the destruction of the Temple may indicate that this prayer predates 70 c.e. (*EncJud* 10: col. 661)." I use the translation of the *Kaddish D'Rabban* by Philip Birnbaum (1995, 46, 48):

"Glorified and sanctified be God's great name throughout the world which he has created according to his will. May he establish his kingdom in your life-time and during your days, and within the life of the entire house of Israel, speedily and soon. And say: Amen.

"May his great name be blessed forever and to all eternity.

"Blessed and praised, glorified and exalted, extolled and honored, adored and lauded be the name of the Holy One, blessed be he, beyond all the bless-ings and hymns, praises and consolation that are ever spoken in the world. And say: Amen.

"(We pray) for Israel, for our teachers and their disciples and the disciples of their disciples, and for all who study the Torah, here and everywhere. May they have abundant peace, loving-kindness, ample sustenance and salvation from their Father who is in heaven. And say: Amen.

"May there be abundant peace from heaven, and life, for us and for all Israel. And say: Amen.

"He who creates peace in his celestial heights, may he in his mercy create peace for us and for all Israel. And say: Amen."

2

Prayer in Luke-Acts

ROM THE STOREROOM of contemporary studies on prayer in Luke-Acts I want to bring forth both the old and the new. David M. Crump (1992, 1–11) has given a helpful overview of previous studies on prayer in Luke-Acts. The studies by Wilhelm Ott (1965) and Louis Monloubou (1976) have underscored Luke's presentation of Jesus as the paradigm of prayer and the teacher who gave instructions to his disciples about persistence in prayer during time of trial. Oscar G. Harris's 1966 Vanderbilt doctoral dissertation made the important contribution that it was probable that Luke's primary thought about prayer was that through it God guided the course of salvation history (pp. 244–45). Ludger Feldkämper (1978) advanced the discussion to a much higher level as he investigated the implicit Christology behind the figure of Jesus at prayer. And David M. Crump (1992) himself has argued that Luke's presentation of Jesus at prayer is a function of Luke's theology and Christology. Finally, Steven F. Plymale (1990; 1991) has intimated that Luke followed the practice of historians of his day by adding prayers to his work as a means of conveying his understanding of salvific history. Unfortunately, these studies are largely inaccessible. The monographs of Ott and Feldkämper are in German. Monloubou wrote in French. Harris's dissertation was never published. And the works of Crump and Plymale are in scholarly serials.

I will pursue the following outline. First, I will stress Luke as a historian and biographer who wants to show how the events he will describe in his two-part history happened according to God's will and plan. Second, I will study the canticles in Luke's Infancy Narrative, which have largely been omitted in most of the aforementioned monographs on prayer in Luke-Acts because these studies equate prayer with intercession. Third, I will give brief consideration to those Gospel passages that depict Jesus at prayer but give no content to his prayer. Fourth, I will deal with those passages that spell out the content of Jesus' prayer. Fifth, I will look at the role of prayer in Acts. Sixth, I will address the problem created, especially in Acts, by Luke's frequent use of angels to direct human affairs. What does this "supernaturalism" have to do with prayer and especially our prayer today? Throughout each section I will feel free to introduce "practical suggestions on prayer." And I trust that at the end of this chapter you will agree with me that Luke-Acts conveys "a sense of God," radiates joy and happiness in the presence of that God, and calls us to prayer with justice.

LUKE'S PURPOSE IS
TO MANIFEST GOD'S PURPOSE

It seems probable to most of us Lukan interpreters that the preface in Luke 1:1-4 applies to both the Gospel and Acts. Further, Luke's purpose, as stated in that preface, is at least twofold. He wants to write history as a means of bolstering faith and as means of edification. Thus, it is clear that what Luke says about Mary, Jesus, the early church, and Paul at prayer will have exhortatory intent. It is also clear that Luke does not recount fact after fact after fact, but interprets the events he narrates and does so primarily by showing how they accord with God's plan.

Charles H. Cosgrove (1984) and John T. Squires (1993) have helped me greatly to see how dominant the thematic of "God's plan and purpose" is in Luke-Acts. In brief, Luke describes the salvific event of Jesus and the spread of the Gospel from Jerusalem to the ends of the earth as the fulfillment of God's plan, a plan manifested in the Scriptures and through angels. Although men and women retain their freedom, this plan will be obeyed and will win out. Let me single out some significant passages as evidence of this pervasive theme. The very first words of Jesus recorded in Luke's Gospel are: "Did you not know that I *must be* about my Father's business?" (Luke 2:49). As Jesus journeys to Jerusalem, he pronounces his firm resolve: "Yet today, tomorrow, and the next day I *must be* on my way, because it is impossible for a prophet to be killed outside of Jerusalem" (Luke 13:33). The risen Jesus tells his male and female disciples: "These are my words that I spoke to you while I was still with you – that everything written about me in the law of Moses, the prophets, and the psalms *must be* fulfilled." In his Pentecost sermon Peter preaches: "This man, handed over to you *according to the definite plan and foreknowledge of God*, you crucified and killed by the hands of those outside the law" (Acts 2:23). Finally, Paul gives voice to God's insistence that the Gentiles are included in God's plan of salvation: "To this day I have had help from God, and so I stand here, testifying to both small and great, saying nothing but what the prophets and Moses said *would take place*: that the Messiah *must* suffer, and that, by being the first to rise from the dead, he *would proclaim* light both to our people and to the Gentiles" (Acts 26:22-23).

To get a better fix on Luke's use of the "divine plan" and how it might relate to what he says about prayer, I present a parallel from Josephus, the Jewish historian and contemporary of Luke. This parallel from *Jewish Antiquities* 4.40-51 consists of a prayer of Moses not found in the story presented in Numbers 16 of the rebellion of Abiram and Datham and shows how a historian could fashion prayers to convey his theology. Josephus insists that Moses acted in accordance with God's will and "divine providence." And Josephus's reworking of Numbers 16 ends with an earthquake. I put the salient passages in italics and modify the translation of H. St. J. Thackeray (1957, 494–501):

> Moses said: "Lord of all that is in heaven and earth and sea, since you are the witness most worthy of belief for my actions, how that all things have been done *in accordance with your will* and how for their performance you did devise a way, taking pity on the Hebrews in all adversities, come and lend your ear to my words. . . . I, who had secured for myself a life of ease, through my prowess and *at your will*, thanks too to what Raguel, my father-in-law, left me, abandoning the employment of those good things, devoted myself to tribulation on behalf of this people. At first for their liberty and now for their salvation, great are the toils that I have undergone, opposing to every peril all the ardor of my soul. Now therefore, when I am suspected of knavery by men who owe it to my exertions that they are yet alive, well may you yourself
>   who showed me that fire on Sinai
>   and did cause me then to listen to your voice and to behold all those prodigies which I was permitted by that place to see;
>   who bade me make speed to Egypt and reveal *your will* to this people,
> who did tumultuously upset the well being of the Egyptians,
>   and granted us escape from the yoke of their bondage,

and made the power of Pharaoh less than my own;

who, when we knew not whither to go, did change the deep into dry land,

and when the sea had been beaten back, brought up its surging billows to the Egyptians' destruction,

who into our empty hands granted arms for our protection,

who did cause sweet water to flow for us from polluted springs and

in the depth of our distress did find means to bring us drink from the rocks;

who when the fruits of the earth failed us preserved us with sustenance from the sea,

and who from heaven did send down food unheard of before,

who did put into our minds a scheme of laws and an ordered constitution

O come, Lord of the universe, to judge my cause and to attest, as witness incorruptible, that neither have I accepted a present from a single Hebrew to pervert justice, nor in the interest of wealth condemned a poor person who was in the right, nor, acting to the detriment of the public weal, have allowed thoughts so wholly alien to my conduct to enter my mind, as to give the priesthood to Aaron not by your command but through my favoritism. Prove now once again that *all is directed by your providence, that nothing befalls fortuitously, but that it is your will that overrules and brings everything to its goal.* Prove that you care for those who would benefit the Hebrews, by pursuing with vengeance Abiram and Datham, who accuse you of such insensibility as to have been defeated by artifice of mine. . . ." So he spoke, weeping throughout , when suddenly the earth shook. . . .

Before moving on to Luke-Acts, let me make some further observations about the significance of this important parallel from Josephus. First, historians interpreted the traditions that they uncovered in their research not only by speeches (as in Acts), but also by prayers that they composed or modified from traditional materials. Second, the middle section of this prayer consists of traditional materials and is formed by "who" clauses and fifteen participles. It is similar to the hymns in the Pauline epistles, for example, Philippians 2:6-11 and Colossians 1:15-20, which also have "who" clauses and/or participles and which contain traditional materials. Third, Josephus's theological and political agenda is manifest in this passage. Josephus, soldier in the rebellion against Rome turned Roman ally, seems to be sitting for the ethical portrait he paints of Moses. Josephus seems to be treating the rebellious Abiram and Datham as predecessors of the Jews who rebelled against the legitimate authority of the Romans. As the Lord did to Abiram and Datham in the past, so the earth will quake and swallow up today's rebels. Fourth, in Josephus's theology all of Moses' activities had been ordained by God's will and providence and did not happen fortuitously. See the number of times Josephus underscores God's will: "in accordance with your will"; "and at your will"; "prove now once again that all is directed by your providence, that nothing befalls fortuitously, but that it is your will that overrules and brings everything to its goal." Fifth, Josephus is building upon the commonly accepted view that Moses was a man of prayer. Finally, this section from Josephus has a number of parallels with Acts 4:23-31, which will be the final prayer passage we will examine. Can I help it if Luke's style of using literary *inclusions* has rubbed off on me, so that I begin and conclude my look at prayer in Luke-Acts with the same passage?

In summary, it will be my thesis that Luke, like Josephus, adapts traditional hymns and prayers in his Gospel and Acts to foster his theology and Christology. Luke's three hymns are found in his Infancy Narrative and are in response to God's fulfillment of promise. To them I now turn.

THE CANTICLES IN LUKE'S INFANCY NARRATIVE

Before I engage in explorations of each one of these three canticles, I remind my readers that they have largely been neglected by the major monographs on prayer in Luke-Acts. Also, I will agree with Raymond E. Brown (1993) that Mary's *Magnificat*, Zechariah's *Benedictus*, and Simeon's *Nunc Dimittis* are traditional hymns that Luke has adapted.

Mary's Magnificat (Luke 1:46-55)

St. Bonaventure of Bagnoregio (1217–1274), a Parisian doctor, administrator par excellence as general minister of the Order of Friars Minor and cardinal of the Holy Roman Church, and mystic, dedicated a six-hundred-folio volume of his *opera omnia* of nine volumes to a commentary on St. Luke's Gospel. In translating and annotating his commentary on Mary's *Magnificat*, I have found that his insights can enrich contemporary scholarly discussions of Mary's prayer. I will interweave some of his outstanding commentary into my presentation to show how far contemporary exegesis has come in the last seven hundred years. And since Raymond E. Brown (1993) has summarized so well what contemporary scholarship is saying about the *Magnificat*, I will follow his outline, will rely heavily upon his summaries, and refer interested readers to his virtually exhaustive bibliographies.

Role of Scripture Passages in Mary's Magnificat

St. Bonaventure was a master of interpreting Scripture by Scripture. Raymond E. Brown (1993, 358–60) lists twenty-four biblical or Jewish allusions to Mary's *Magnificat* and uses this evidence to support his contention that the lowly Mary of Nazareth did not compose the *Magnificat*. Bonaventure, who held the medieval opinion that Mary authored her prayer, would only have been aware of twenty of these allusions. Four of them were beyond his ken, for example, the writings of Qumran. In his exegesis of Mary's *Magnificat*, Bonaventure has forty-five percent (nine out of twenty) of the Scripture allusions that Brown discovers and finds many more. Having meditated on how Mary's prayer accords with passages from the Law, the prophets, and the psalms, Bonaventure concludes his explanation of Mary's *Magnificat* with these telling words. The cardinal writes:

> Thus, the Blessed Virgin begins her canticle from the greatness of the highest beginning and finishes it in eternity's end, for she praises him who is "the Alpha and the Omega, the beginning and the end," as Revelation 1:8 says. And indeed she does so quite fittingly because her canticle shows that the fulfillment of all promised blessings has come about, and therefore brings about the fulfillment of all praise and canticles and even of the scriptures.

In brief, it is fitting that when all promised blessings were fulfilled in the conception of Jesus, Mary would give expression to her joy at this salvific event by drawing upon choice prayers from all the Scriptures.

The Structure of Mary's Magnificat

Raymond Brown (1993, 358–59) and other scholars find this structure: Introduction (1:46-47); First Strophe (1:48-50); Second Strophe (1:51-53); Conclusion (1:54-55). Bonaventure's analysis of the structure of what he calls Mary's "Song of Joy" accords with that of Stephen Farris

(1985, 114–16). In Luke 1:46-47 Luke describes "the disposition of the one singing praise," a disposition consisting of gratitude (1:46) and rejoicing (1:47). The second section of Mary's Song of Joy conveys the twofold "motif clause" of her prayer. In 1:48 she expresses gratitude for and rejoices over God's bestowal of grace, "which made her lovable in God's sight and praiseworthy in human sight." And as Bonaventure notes: "And humility was the disposition for the reception of grace, as Isaiah 66:2 has: 'To whom shall I have regard except to the poor, and contrite of spirit, and the one who trembles at my words?'" Verse 49 gives the second reason for Mary's gratitude and joy: the miracle of God's power, which is great and holy, in the incarnation. And, like Raymond Brown, Bonaventure finds a scriptural allusion for this in Psalm 111:9: "He has sent redemption to his people. . . . Holy and terrifying is his name." Bonaventure calls the last six verses "the extension of divine praise." Here are Bonaventure's own words:

> And this [final section] consists of the praise of divine mercy in its work of human redemption, already begun in the conception of the Virgin. For the work of our redemption is declarative of God's *mercy* and *power,* and makes manifest God's *largess* and *veracity. Mercy* in the revelation of fallen humanity; *power* in the prostration of the devil; *largess* in the bestowal of the Holy Spirit; and *veracity* in the fulfillment of promise.

Bonaventure develops the meaning of "mercy" in his commentary on Luke 1:50, of "power" in his commentary on Luke 1:51-52, of "largess" in his commentary on Luke 1:53, and of "veracity" in his commentary on Luke 1:54-55.

Contemporary Appropriation of Mary's Magnificat

As Raymond Brown's summary of the discussion on the *Magnificat* from 1976–1992 indicates so well (1993, 650–53), there has been great discussion these last two decades concerning the relationship between liberation theology and Mary's *Magnificat.* One cannot expect thirteenth-century Bonaventure to be aware of late twentieth-century concerns, but it is informative to see that he was cognizant of the problems involved in interpreting Luke 1:51-53 and to learn how he handled those troublesome verses. He writes that verse 51 praises God for "casting down the proud demons and the riches of the unjust." While Bonaventure does not give any explanation of what he means by "the riches of the unjust," he does acknowledge that riches can be unjustly obtained and that it is characteristic of God to right the wrong of unjustly obtained wealth. In his exegesis of verse 52, Bonaventure interprets "God has deposed the mighty from their thrones" to refer to "the proud demons and also tyrannical potentates." And he quotes four Scripture passages in support of this position: Daniel 5:19-20 and its message about God's overthrow of Nebuchadnezzar, Sirach 10:18, Luke 18:14, and 1 Samuel 2:7-8. Raymond Brown also cites 1 Samuel 2:7-8 as the biblical allusion behind this verse. Bonaventure knew of good rulers such as saintly King Louis IX of France (d. 1270), whom God would not cast down, but God did not favor "tyrannical potentates." In dealing with verse 53, Bonaventure's main comment is brief and to his point: "For true largess is to give to the poor, and not to the rich, as Proverbs 13:25 has: 'The just eats and fills his soul, but the belly of the wicked is never to be filled.'"

Perhaps, no single group has contributed to liberation theology and the shift from a more spiritualized interpretation of Mary's *Magnificat* to a more social interpretation than Latin American Roman Catholics. And their exegesis, often lived out in their own experience, has trickled up to their bishops and from them has gone across the ocean to Rome. In his 1987 encyclical, *The Mother of the Redeemer*, Pope John Paul II exegetes Mary's *Magnificat* in this way:

> Mary truly proclaims the coming of "the Messiah of the poor" (cf. Isaiah 11:4; 61:1). Drawing from Mary's heart and from the depth of her faith expressed in the words of the *Magnificat*, the Church renews ever more effectively in herself the awareness that the truth about God who saves and the truth about God who is the source of every gift cannot be separated from the manifestation of his love of preference for the poor and humble. That love, which is celebrated in the *Magnificat*, is later expressed in the words and works of Jesus. (#37)

While it would be interesting to track how the official churches have received liberation theology's interpretations of Mary's *Magnificat*, that project is beyond the scope of this book. Suffice it to say that there have been some uneven sections of road and even unexpected turns in the road of its reception. Also, interpreters today are not worthy of their hire if they neglect the insights that liberation theology has provided into the meanings of Mary's Song of Joy.

I now ask, along with many other contemporary Lukan scholars, how the context of Luke-Acts may help us in appropriating Mary's prayer. These scholars are persuasively reminding us that individual passages in Luke-Acts must be interpreted primarily via other texts in that same body of writing. So while it may be helpful to investigate the original setting of the prayer that Luke has incorporated into his Gospel as Mary's *Magnificat*, it is more important to ascertain its function in the entirety of Luke-Acts. I can only hint at the highlights here and refer my readers to my earlier works (1983;1990) for more detail.

First, Luke has inserted the canticles of Mary, Zechariah, and Simeon into his Gospel to accentuate who God is, how God has been faithful to promises made of old, and to carry forward the story of God's fulfillment of those promises in the advent of John and especially of Jesus, Son of God and Savior.

Second, from the Lukan text a number of things are clear about Mary. She is young and of marriageable age, considers herself lowly, and is obedient to the angel Gabriel's revelation of God's plan that she will conceive and give birth to the Son of God. At the beginning of Acts she is described among the 120 praying and awaiting the coming of the promised Holy Spirit. If we ask the question of whom Mary represents, the answers are rightly multiple: Israel, the lowly, and faithful who depend on and trust in God for salvation.

Finally, I single out two of the multiple themes, first sounded in Mary's *Magnificat* that will find further refinement and development in the rest of Luke-Acts. The theme of the lifting up of the poor and lowly (1:52) echoes throughout Luke-Acts and is given primary expression in Jesus' inaugural sermon in Nazareth (4:16-30). Jesus preaches the good news to the poor (4:18; 7:22), cures lepers and other marginalized men and women, and teaches that one must invite the poor, the crippled, the lame, and the blind to one's banquet (14:13). The parable of poor Lazarus and Dives (16:19-31) gives fine expression to this reversal theme. Indeed, the stone rejected by the builders has become the cornerstone (20:17) as Jesus, rejected by the rulers, has been raised up by God to be the cornerstone of reconstituted Israel. And one wonders whether the fate of King Herod Agrippa, graphically depicted in Acts 12:23, is not that of a proud ruler being struck down from his throne: "And immediately, because he had not given the glory to God, an angel of the Lord struck him down, and he was eaten by worms and died."

And as Bonaventure recognized so well, the beginnings of salvation are in fulfillment of God's promises. Throughout Luke-Acts the theme sounds of the fulfillment of promise and of the universal dimensions behind the phrase "the children of Abraham" (1:55). As John the Baptist declares, "God can raise up children to Abraham from these stones" (3:8). A woman, bound by Satan for eighteen years, is "a daughter of Abraham" (13:16) and will be liberated by Jesus. And people will arrive from the east and west, north and south, and recline at table with Abraham, Isaac, and Jacob in God's kingdom while the self-right-eous are cast out (13:28-29). After his death Lazarus finds himself in the bosom of Abraham while Dives is far, far away (16:19-31). Jesus defends the just actions of the chief tax collector Zacchaeus and declares that he is "a descendant of Abraham" (19:9).

Surely, the Lukan co-text helps us to appropriate the multiple mean-ings of Mary's *Magnificat*. But my readers may raise the serious prac-tical question: What can Luke 1:46-55 possibly have to say to me during Vespers when I am supposed to pray it as a new entity, now cast off from its original context in Luke-Acts? I make four comments.

My first comment, although in story form, warns us again not to spiritualize the meaning of the *Magnificat*. In Part First of his *Tales of a Wayside Inn*, Henry Wadsworth Longfellow (1902) tells "The Sicil-ian's Tale: King Robert of Sicily" and shows that listening to the *Mag-nificat* chanted at Vespers in Latin can be very dangerous:

> Robert of Sicily, brother of Pope Urbane . . . Apparelled in magnificent attire, With retinue of many a knight and squire, On St. John's eve, at ves-pers, proudly sat, And heard the priests chant the *Magnificat*. And as he listened, o'er and o'er again Repeated, like a burden or refrain, he caught the words, *"Deposuit potentes De sede, et exaltavit humiles."* And slowly lifting up his kingly head He to a learned clerk beside him said, "What mean these words?" The clerk made answer meet, "He has put down the mighty from their seat, And has exalted them of low degree." Threat King Robert muttered scornfully, "Tis well that such seditious words are sung Only by priests and in the Latin tongue; For unto priests and people be it known There is no power can push me from my throne." And leaning back, he yawned and fell asleep.

As the tale goes on, an angel, successfully masquerading as King of Sicily, does have Robert put down from his throne and has him reduced to court jester. After about three years of deep humiliation the real king does indeed repent, is exalted back to his throne, and is found by his courtiers kneeling upon the floor, absorbed in silent prayer. Although Longfellow's tale seems to make the point that King Robert had to become more pious, not more just, to get his throne back, it, nevertheless, clearly shows how difficult it is to take the sting out of the political bee of Luke 1:51-53.

Second, it seems to me that in interpreting Mary's *Magnificat* we are caught in a hermeneutical web. In his investigation of seven Old Tes-tament prayers such as Hannah's in 1 Samuel 2:1-10, which have been inserted into narrative contexts, Samuel E. Balentine (1993, 213–24) has shown how the biblical authors have taken a general text and particularized it by applying it to a specific individual. In our efforts to assimilate Mary's prayer, we may first try to enter into her dispositions of gratitude, joy, and praise for the gift of Jesus, the Messiah, the Son of God. Next I would suggest we pray-ers have to universalize what Luke has particularized before we can universalize it again and then particularize it in our own contexts.

Lest the interpretive web involved in interpreting Mary's *Magnificat* trap us in a web of incomprehension, I give a simple sample reformulation of Mary's prayer for a contemporary American context.

"I confess and praise you, God, as the God who has worked wonders in my life. Make me like Mary, archetype of us believers, as I struggle to believe that with you nothing is impossible, especially in the face of the enormous ills in our world. Raise that mighty arm of yours and once again free us from the slavery of Egypt and bring all of us into the land of milk and honey. Help us to cast out from our families the tyrants of abuse, from our schools the warriors of violence, and from our streets the barons of drugs. Open the minds and hearts of more billionaires and millionaires to share their wealth with the millions of deprived throughout the world. Open my eyes to see how I can bring the poor and the disadvantaged of my neighborhood and city to my table of plenty. I praise you for your faithfulness in remembering graciously our patriarchs and matriarchs in the faith and ask you to deepen my faith and trust in your love for all your children whether they're like us or not. Help me to recognize the need for a just peace with my prickly neighbor next door and our do-nothing alderman downtown. I suppose, dearest God, that I'm really asking for it, for I'm asking that you dispel the coziness of my faith, so that it may embrace more generously your plan of fullness of life for all of your children, for all of creation. So be it. Amen."

My third consideration also comes from Balentine (1993, 276) and builds upon the image of a God who accomplishes what is humanly impossible (Luke 1:37) and ties in with my first point from Longfellow's tale. What did the nuns, monks, and priests hope to accomplish by singing and reciting the *Magnificat* day after day at Vespers? In the simplest of terms they were engaged in the church's happy obligation of giving praise to God. But as Balentine reminds us, they were keeping alive a revolutionary memory. For to participate in the ministry of praise "is to remember and to give thanks with Hannah (and Mary) that the lowly can be lifted up, the powerful can be brought down. Without doxology both the lowly and the powerful will be tempted to conclude that the *status* is *quo*, that possibilities unseen are inauthentic and unlikely, that the world's power to define reality is ultimate and unchallenged." So even the canons and bishops who shuffle to Vespers on a Sunday at St. Peter's in Rome are unwitting participants in God's revolutionary cause of reversal.

Finally, Samuel Terrien (1995) has analyzed forty-six composers' renditions of the *Magnificat*. These musical gems might help one appreciate various dimensions of Mary's Song of Joy. One of my favorites is the liberation-sounding artistic interpretation by the contemporary Polish composer, Krzysztov Penderecki. And when I want a joyous interpretation of Mary's Song, I turn to J. S. Bach.

My computer counting tool has informed that I have hammered over sixteen thousand keystrokes in my commentary on Mary's Song of Joy. That effort was worthwhile, for Lukan treatises on prayer have generally neglected Luke's canticles. I hope that my treatment of Mary's *Magnificat* has offered an introduction to many of the important issues for the interpretation and appropriation of first-century prayers and might help us to pray Luke 1:46-55 more meaningfully.

Zechariah's Benedictus (Luke 1:68-79)

In this section I will also draw upon the rich commentary of St. Bonaventure as a spur to some fresh reflections on the prophetic prayer of the just and old priest Zechariah, which is used in churches at Morning Prayer and is called the *Benedictus*. And since the *Benedictus* has engendered less contemporary commentary than the *Magnificat*, my observations will be briefer.

Allusions to Scripture in Zechariah's Benedictus

Raymond Brown (1993, 386–89) discovered forty-four allusions to Scripture and to Jewish writings in Luke 1:68-74, 78-79. Eleven of these allusions would have been unknown to Bonaventure, who, for example, knew nothing of Qumran or of the *Testaments of the Twelve Patriarchs*, each of which provides Brown with four allusions. In his interpretation of Zechariah's *Benedictus* Bonaventure invokes the Old Testament (including Wisdom and Sirach) sixty-six times and the New Testament twenty-nine times. Brown and Bonaventure have the same biblical allusions about twenty-five percent of the time (eight of thirty-three), but this does not mean that Bonaventure viewed the *Benedictus* as less dependent on Scripture than the *Magnificat*. Sometimes it's merely a question of what biblical passages Brown decided to select as allusions. For example, for Luke 1:68a "Blessed is the Lord, the God of Israel," Brown found four biblical allusions, and Bonaventure found three. But neither one cites the same biblical allusions the other does. In any case, the Hebrew Scriptures are the "source book" for the *Benedictus*, and Bonaventure opened up many of the pages of this source book seven hundred years ago.

The Structure of the Benedictus

Raymond Brown (1993, 656–61) has shown how much of recent scholarship on Zechariah's *Benedictus* has focused on its structure. While many of these structural analyses may be overly refined, they do point to the thematic development and repetition that pulsates through the *Benedictus*. I offer Bonaventure's analysis of the structure of the *Benedictus* as a way of seeing more clearly its thematic unity. By singling out "redemption" as the key concept of the *Benedictus*, Bonaventure is able to draw into its thematic orbit two other important themes: God's fidelity to promises; liberation from various and sundry enemies. Bonaventure writes: "The first part (1:68-69) deals with thanksgiving and praise for the gift of our redemption, according to which God's remediative dispensation *has been accomplished through Christ*. The second part (1:70-71) concerns redemption *already promised by the Prophets*. . . . The third part (72-75) focuses on redemption *promised to the patriarchs*. . . . The fourth part (76-79) treats of redemption as already *begun in the precursor*." In the next section I will explore the three themes of salvation, God's fulfillment of promises, and liberation from enemies.

Contemporary Appropriation of Zechariah's Benedictus

I now ask, as I did in my treatment of Mary's *Magnificat*, how the context of Luke-Acts may help us in appropriating Zechariah's prayer.

Neither the *Benedictus* nor Luke-Acts in general will let us forget that redemption has come about because of God's fidelity to promise. Yes, all peoples will be blessed through Abraham. What the prophets longed for is coming to pass. And it is coming to pass in David's house. As the angel tells the shepherds: "To you is born this day in the city of David a Savior, who is the Messiah, the Lord" (2:11). The blind beggar at Jericho will shout twice: "Jesus, Son of David, have mercy on me!" (18:38-39). The risen Lord Jesus gives a succinct formulation of this thematic: "'These are my words that I spoke to you while I was still with you— that everything written about me in the law of Moses, the prophets, and the psalms must be fulfilled" (24:44). And Paul in his sermon at Pisidian Antioch lends an eloquent and developed voice to this thematic (Acts 13:16-47). One of Paul's most telling truths in this context is this: "Of this man's [David's] posterity God has brought to Israel a Savior, Jesus, as he promised" (Acts 13:23).

Truly, salvation and redemption are God's long-awaited gift, but from what are those who pray the *Benedictus* saved? Here the redundancy of the *Benedictus* will not let us forget that all is not well in the world, in ourselves, and among ourselves: "saved from our enemies" (1:71); "from the hand of all who hate us" (1:71); "rescued from the hands of our enemies" (1:73); "the forgiveness of their sins" (1:77); "to give light to those who sit in darkness and in the shadow of death" (1:79). Who are these enemies? Who are the people who hate us? From what sins are we to be forgiven? What constitutes the darkness and death's shadow in which we sit? Bonaventure's commentary and the co-text of Luke-Acts supply some hints at answers.

Cardinal Bonaventure's comments on "the enemies" indicate that he did not think that Zechariah was referring primarily to ethnic or national enemies. Rather, in Bonaventure's eyes the enemies are broader, spiritual, even cosmic in dimension. On Luke 1:71 he writes:

And this salvation consists in *the liberation from enemies*, that is, from the demons, as the psalm reads: "Rescue me from my enemies" (59:2) and as Colossians 1:13 has: "He has delivered us from the power of darkness.". . . *From the hand of all who hate us*, that is, from the hand or power of all persecutors, whether demons or human.

And on Luke 1:77 Bonaventure notes:

To give, it says, *knowledge*, but not any kind of knowledge, but *of salvation*. Because without knowledge there is no salvation. . . . *Of salvation*, it says, but not of any kind whatsoever, but *spiritual*. And therefore, the text adds: *through forgiveness of their sins*. Bede writes: "Lest you think that temporal salvation is promised, the text adds 'through forgiveness of their sins.'"

Finally, Bonaventure uses the same two passages from Isaiah that Brown detected and indicates in his commentary on Luke 1:79 that the salvation begun by "the Lord God of Israel" extends to the Gentiles: *"To enlighten those who sit in darkness and the shadow of death.* This must be construed: He visited to enlighten, that is, to enlighten those who sit in darkness, that is, the Gentiles who are erring. Isaiah 9:2 has: 'The people, who walk in darkness, have seen a great light. A light has arisen for those who dwell in the region of the shadow of death.' And again in Isaiah 42:6-7 we read: 'I have given you as a light to the Gentiles, so that you may open the eyes of the blind and bring forth the prisoner from prison, and those that sit in darkness out of the prison house.'"

The title of Susan R. Garrett's excellent book *The Demise of the Devil* (1989) points to a dominant theme in Luke-Acts. The victory over the forces of evil, sung by Zechariah, will be Jesus' work in the remainder of the Gospel. In his summary of Jesus' ministry Peter preaches: "That message spread throughout Judea, beginning in Galilee after the baptism that John announced: how God anointed Jesus of Nazareth with the Holy Spirit and with power; how he went about doing good and healing all who *were oppressed by the devil"* (Acts 10:38). At the beginning of his ministry Jesus wrestles with the devil in the wilderness (Luke 4:1-13). During his ministry he does battle with the likes of "the legion" of demons who drives the Gerasene demoniac to the margins of society (Luke 8:26-39). And Jesus' passion begins when Satan enters into Judas Iscariot (Luke 22:3).

And the universal dimension of salvation is not only rooted in Abraham, who was promised that in him all peoples would be blessed, but also in Simeon's canticle: "a light of revelation to the Gentiles" (Luke 2:32). And the risen Jesus instructs his male and female disciples "that repentance and forgiveness of sins is to be proclaimed in his name to all nations, beginning from Jerusalem" (Luke 24:47). And it is Paul who is the capital preacher of this universal salvation. In his third description of his "conversion" Paul quotes the Lord Jesus, who says to him: "I will rescue you from your people and from the Gentiles—to whom I am sending you to open their eyes so that they may turn from darkness to light and from the power of Satan to God" (Acts 26:17-18).

It is high literary and theological finesse that fashions Isaiah 42:7 as the link between Luke 1:79 and Acts 26:18.

Finally, John the Baptizer, of whom Zechariah sings in Luke 1:76-77, will be a preacher of repentance and the forerunner of Jesus. Luke tells John's story with a few brush strokes in Luke 3:1-20, but they are enough to show how dearly John's fidelity to his prophetic vocation cost him.

On the more practical side I suggest here, as I did above in my discussion of Mary's *Magnificat*, that we need to take the universal truths or themes of Zechariah's *Benedictus* and struggle in prayer to particularize them. Again I give a simple sample particularization. "Today I praise and thank you, my faithful God and Lord. Deepen my faith in you and your saving power as I struggle with the news that my best friend has cancer. I acknowledge and confess my need for your saving touch from my enemies, whose names today are blindness to the needs of others and proud self-reliance. Help me to keep my head screwed on straight with your values, as I contemplate the fiery prophet John the Baptizer. If I'm going to lose my head as John lost his, let it to be over something that truly counts. Amen."

Nunc Dimittis (Luke 2:29-32)

In my treatment of this, the briefest of the three canticles in Luke's Infancy Narrative, I will again call upon the assistance of St. Bonaventure. His comments reveal two other sides of his multifaceted personality and may challenge contemporary Bible readers to let the Spirit blow them along the paths of mysticism and into the ranks of extraordinarily fine preachers.

Structure and Old Testament Allusions

I again compare twentieth-century Raymond Brown and thirteenth-century St. Bonaventure. Bonaventure's initial structural analysis of Simeon's *Nunc Dimittis* is straightforward: "There are two parts to this canticle. First is the spiritual consolation of the old (2:29). Second is the exalted commendation of the infant (2:30-32)." Brown's analysis (1993, 457) corresponds to the scholarly language of our time and is more complex: "Basically it consists of three distychs or bicola (29ab,

30-31, 32ab), with the last of the three exemplifying synonymous parallelism."

Brown (1993, 458) writes that there seem to be five biblical echoes in the *Nunc Dimittis,* and all five are from Second Isaiah. Bonaventure had already detected three of those echoes: Isaiah 40:5; 49:6; 52:10. And we may note that in their commentaries on the figure of aged Simeon, both Brown (1993, 457) and Bonaventure refer to the consolation expressed by truly ancient Jacob upon seeing Joseph who he had hoped against hope was still alive. Bonaventure writes: "Already in genuine consolation he could say what Jacob said to Joseph in Genesis 46:30: 'Now I may die happy, because I have seen your face and leave you alive.'"

Appropriation of the Messages of Simeon's Nunc Dimittis

We can appropriate some facets of the *Nunc Dimittis* if we take its theme of universal salvation and see how this becomes a leitmotif in Acts. I have given much space to this theme in what I said above about appropriation of Zechariah's *Benedictus* and refer my readers to that section. As Brown says (1993, 615) in his characteristic conciseness: The *Nunc Dimittis* "lays out the program for the spread of the Christian message described in Acts."

Bonaventure, who had a mystical bent, uses the Song of Songs to reflect upon the old priest Simeon. Perhaps, we can learn from Bonaventure's commentary on Luke 2:28 to take into our arms "the consolation of Israel" and hold on for dear life to what we value deeply:

> *And he took him in his arms.* Behold the devotion of this old man to comprehend and hold onto this little child. And by his devotion he exposes himself totally to Christ, so that he could say what the Song of Songs 1:12 has: "My lover is a sachet of myrrh that will lie between my breasts." For he wanted to fulfill what the Song of Songs 8:6 says: "Place me as a seal upon your heart, as a seal upon your arm." Indeed, upon both your arms. Yes, both to show how strongly he is to be comprehended and held. The Song of Songs 3:4 reads: "I have found him whom my soul loves. I took hold of him and would not let him go."

During my months of translating Bonaventure's commentary on Luke, I was sometimes reminded of those times I have been privileged to hear rhetorically and theologically arresting preachers in the

African-American community. And Bonaventure can shine with the best of them. Hear what preacher Bonaventure has to say about the meaning and future of the child in Simeon's arms. I quote from the conclusion to his commentary on Simeon's *Nunc Dimittis* where he summarizes much of the Christology to be narrated in the remainder of Luke-Acts:

> Therefore, Christ is glorified because of *the salvation of all people, the light for the Gentiles*, and *the glory for the Jews* . . . and because of *the peace* he brings to console an old man. So in this canticle Christ is praised as *peace, salvation, light,* and *glory*. He is *peace*, because he is *the mediator*. He is *salvation*, because he is *the redeemer*. He is *light*, because he is *the teacher*. He is *glory*, because he is *the rewarder*. And in these four consist the perfect commendation and magnification of Christ, indeed the most brief capsulation of the entire evangelical story: *incarnation* in peace; *preaching* in light; *redemption* in salvation; *resurrection* in glory.

And after a pause for us to catch our breath, Bonaventure concludes: "And because this canticle contains in itself the fullness of the praise of Christ and the consolation of a dying old man, it is, therefore, sung in the evening at Compline." Yes, how fitting it is for members of the church to sing this canticle as they say goodbye to their day (or days). Yes, how fitting it is for members of the church to sing Simeon's song as they rejoice in the gift they hold in their hands, Jesus, their Savior. Yes, how appropriate it is for members of the church to put the words of Simeon's chant into their mouths as they rejoice in their God whose name is "the one who fulfills promises."

As I have done with Mary's *Magnificat* and Zechariah's *Benedictus*, allow me to contemporize Simeon's *Nunc Dimittis*. I pray: "Lord, I've come to the end of yet another day. Thanks for it. I don't know how many more nights you've in store for me. I thank you for the ones you've given me. Forgive me for the times I've squandered them on things unworthy. Help me to be grateful for Jesus, your Son, and the life I've enjoyed in his service. Lord, continually broaden my horizons, so that my days, few or many as they may be, may be spent in extending my love beyond the narrow confines of my heart and the circle of love it has formed. Amen. And Good Night."

Conclusion to the Canticles
of Luke's Infancy Narrative

Luke begins his work of fifty-two chapters by creating the atmosphere of prayer and worship of God. Whether in private home or in public temple the three canticles are sung, and sung by a teenage lay woman and two old priests. None of them use the philosophical language of the book of Wisdom or of Philo of Alexandria. As Bonaventure and Brown have shown so well and in such great detail, their prayers are a cento of Old Testament passages. For them theology is a reworking of the language of sacred history and prayer. They invite us to make their hymns our theology, to praise the God who has wrought great wonders in Israel's past and now in the gift of Jesus, the Messiah and Son of God, and to be saved from all our enemies. Truly, these canticles, inserted by Luke into his history, convey his theology in doxological form.

It is small wonder that the church has taken the prayers of Mary, Zechariah, and Simeon into the daily round of its liturgy of the hours. They are magnificent prayers. And they are also marvelous introductions to the story of God's designed fulfillment of promises that Luke will narrate in the remaining fifty chapters of his Gospel and Acts. In this context of "conclusion" I quote in modified form from the conclusion of Stephen Farris's monograph on these hymns (1985, 160): "But in using these hymns the Church takes up and declares anew its Jewish heritage. Just as Luke suggested, we in the Gentile Church are built upon the foundation of pious Israelites who received the gospel with joy. Not only are we built upon 'the foundation of the apostles and prophets' whose activities are recounted in Acts, but also upon the foundation of the humble sons and daughters of Abraham, whose worship still echoes in the hymns of Luke 1–2."

PASSAGES IN LUKE (-ACTS) THAT MENTION
PRAYER, BUT GIVE NO CONTENT
TO THE PRAYER

This may seem like a strange category, but any careful reading of Luke-Acts will show that while there may be frequent mention of Jesus or members of the early church praying, infrequently is any content given to their prayers. For the sake of simplicity I will not give much consideration to the passages contained in Acts, but will concentrate on those passages that deal with Jesus' prayer. For readers interested in investigating the significance of content-less prayer passages in Acts, I list them here with the assurance that in a subsequent section I will be making general remarks about them and will give specific attention to the content-full prayer in Acts 4:23-31. See Acts 1:14; 2:42; 3:1, 8-9; 4:21; 6:4, 6; 8:15, 24; 9:11, 40; 10:2, 4, 9, 30, 31; 11:5, 18; 12:5, 12; 13:2, 3; 14:23; 16:13, 16, 25; 20:36; 21:5, 20; 22:17; 24:11, 14; 26:7; 27:23, 29, 35; 28:8.

The Gospel passages that simply mention Jesus at prayer are: 3:21 (Jesus' baptism), 5:16 (withdrawal to pray), 6:12 (choice of the Twelve), 9:18 (Peter's confession), 9:28-29 (Jesus' transfiguration), 11:1 (before teaching Lord's Prayer). Let me make a number of observations about these six passages. First, these passages are often drawn upon as support that the historical Jesus was a man of prayer. See my earlier chapter, "Prayer and the Historical Jesus," and the conclusion of James D. G. Dunn (1975, 20–21): "It is therefore more than probable that *prayer was Jesus' regular response to situations of crisis and decision*" (emphasis in original). Second, while we may surmise from Luke's Gospel that Jesus prayed the psalms (see 23:46), was a mystic (see 10:18), and frequently attended synagogue and was accustomed to the prayers recited there (see 4:15-16), these reflections do not give us the specific content of his prayer in the aforementioned six instances.

Third, scholars such as Oscar Harris (1966, 219–20) are right on target when they view these six passages as clear examples of Luke's intention to present Jesus as a model of good conduct. This view is at least seven hundred years old and was given wonderful articulation by St. Bonaventure (d. 1274) in his commentary on Luke 3:21:

> In all circumstances the Lord is found *praying* . . . in order to demonstrate what is said in Luke 18:1 below: "They must always pray and not lose heart." For he prayed at *the reception of baptism* . . . so that he might provide a model of praying to those approaching baptism.—In *the solitude of the desert*, as Luke 5:16 below has . . . so that he might give an example to contemplatives.—During his *preaching*, as Luke 6:12 below says . . . so that he might give an example to preachers.—In *performing miracles*, as John 11:41 says . . . so that he might supply an example to those engaged in such work.—In *suffering*, as Matthew 26:39 has . . . so that he might give a model to those enduring suffering.—In *the administration of the Body of the Lord*, as Luke 22:17 has . . . so that he might provide a model for priests.—In a *spirit of commendation*, as Luke 23:46 below says . . . so that he might supply a model for those who are dying. And thus in all circumstances is one to pray.

My fourth point brings Ludger Feldkämper and David Crump into the discussion. The titles of their monographs encapsulate their correct and major insights that Luke is presenting Jesus as more than a model of faithful prayer. For Feldkämper Jesus at prayer is the mediator of salvation (*Der betende Jesus als Heilsmittler nach Lukas*). For Crump Jesus is the intercessor for his disciples, not only in heaven, but also on earth. Their primary way of arriving at their conclusions is close literary analysis of text in context. I give one example from each.

Here is a digest of how Feldkämper (1978, 103–4) approaches the notation of Jesus at prayer in Luke 6:12 before he chooses the Twelve. Jesus' prayer begins his Sermon on the Plain. And it is a sign that in his teaching Jesus instructs entirely through the power of God. Luke depicts Jesus at prayer right after he had given voice to the Jewish religious leaders' rejection of Jesus in 6:11. Through prayer Jesus renews his resolve to be obedient to God's will, even though it may mean rejection and suffering. But rejection of Jesus does not spell defeat, for Jesus has chosen the Twelve to continue God's work and to be the nucleus of reconstituted Israel. All of Jesus' work for salvation and that of the church, the reconstituted Israel, is work in the power of God. Jesus' prayer is a sign of that. For Feldkämper's analysis to make sense, one must sit with it and must change one's definition of prayer. In the six examples at hand, prayer does not necessarily mean intercessory prayer but communication with God. Jesus is open to receive God's revelation and communicate it in turn to others. And Jesus does this in word and deed. And since what the Father communicates to Jesus in prayer is salvific, Jesus at prayer is to be seen as the mediator of salvation.

Let me give an example of a similar type of exegesis from what David Crump (1992, 42–48) says about Jesus' prayer and his transfiguration (Luke 9:28-36). At the end of his presentation of Jesus' Galilean ministry Luke prepares for Jesus' determined journey to Jerusalem (9:51–19:28) through Jesus' twofold prediction of his passion. It is no coincidence that one of these predictions occurs before Jesus' transfiguration (9:21-22) and one after (9:44). Also it is with full intent and purpose that Luke has Jesus, Moses, and Elijah—all three great men of prayer—discussing Jesus' "exodus, which he was about to accomplish in Jerusalem" (9:31). And it is fine Lukan theology that the voice from the cloud says: "This is my Son, my Chosen. Listen to him" (9:35). Yes, listen to what Jesus has to say about his rejection, passion, and resurrection (see 9:22). Given this setting, I summarize Crump's conclusions (1992, 48). Through his prayer (see 9:28) Jesus is in communion with his Father and receives confirmation of and encouragement for the new phase in his journey through the gift of his transfiguration. But Jesus' transfiguration is not just a private gift, but is also revelation for Peter, John, and James. In a very concise statement Crump concludes (1992, 48): "As in Peter's confession, Jesus prays and those who are with him receive new insight into who he really is."

In summary, the minicourse I have given on the approaches of Feldkämper and Crump can be applied to the remaining four content-less prayers of Jesus. I am grateful to these two scholars for inviting me to look with new eyes at these six passages. We have been accustomed by studies of New Testament Christology to focus on the titles of Jesus, for example, Son of God, Messiah, and have neglected to see what the story line of the Gospel may be telling us about Jesus. Luke's repeated narrative emphasis on Jesus at prayer tells us much about Jesus as Son of God in communion with his Father and as eschatological prophet along the lines of Moses, leader out of slavery, founder of a new people, and man of prayer par excellence.

I conclude this section with my fifth point, which introduces the connection between Jesus' content-less prayer and Jesus' interpretation of and compliance with God's will and purpose. With the possible exceptions of Luke 5:16 and 11:1, the other four content-less references to Jesus at prayer deal with major turning points in Jesus' life: the inauguration of his public ministry at his baptism (3:21); the selection of the Twelve, who represent reconstituted Israel (6:12); Peter's profession of faith and Jesus' first prediction of his passion and resurrection (9:18-22); Jesus' transfiguration and resolve to embark on his "exodus" in Jerusalem (9:28-36). If we take these passages and connect them with the Lukan theme of the Gospel story as the fulfillment of God's will and plan, then we will begin to glimpse the validity of some of the conclusions of Harris and Crump. Jesus' prayer and God's will are closely connected. Harris may have misstated the connection when he maintained that God guides the course of salvation history through prayer. Rather Jesus and others come to know God's will and plan through prayer. In any case, there may be lessons aplenty in this aspect of Luke's presentation of Jesus at prayer. Jesus, even though he was mediator of salvation, had no blueprint of salvation imprinted on his brain. He learned to grasp his Father's will through prayer. Nor was he a puppet in his Father's hands, as we will learn from the next batch of prayer passages in Luke's Gospel.

Jesus' Prayers and His Teaching on Prayer

It is perhaps not coincidental that five of the six references to Jesus' content-less prayer occurred in Luke's Galilean phase of Jesus' ministry where he preached God's kingdom, healed the sick, and gathered reconstituted Israel around him in the persons of his male and female disciples and the Twelve. The next selection of passages we put under our investigative lens all occur during the Lukan literary and theological masterpiece called his "Travel Narrative." In Luke 9:51–19:28 Jesus is obedient to God's plan that he go to Jerusalem. And as the acute observer will readily notice, he makes little headway, but teaches his disciples much. For Luke Jesus' "journey" becomes the Christian Way, and what Jesus has to say in prayer and about prayer is vitally important for his disciples, past and present. I will look at Luke 10:21-24, 11:1-13, 18:1-14.

Luke 10:21-24: Jesus' Prayer of Thanks and the Sight-Filled Disciples

One of the first things to notice in the thanksgiving prayer of Luke 10:21-22 is how closely it is tied to its context. From the immediate context I note that Jesus' "rejoicing" (10:21) echoes the "joy" of the returning seventy missionaries who have been victorious over the powers of evil as they preached the arrival of God's eschatological kingdom (see 10:17, 20). Further, Jesus' prayer repeats the theme of 10:16: "whoever rejects me rejects *the one who sent me*," and that one is no one else but Jesus' Father. And in 11:2 Jesus will teach his disciples to address God as "Father." From the total context of Luke's Gospel I point to five instances that give indication of Jesus' relationship to God as Son to Father. At his baptism Jesus hears: "You are my Son, the Beloved. With you I am well pleased" (3:22). At Jesus' transfiguration Peter, John, and James hear this message: "This is my Son, my Chosen. Listen to him" (9:35). On the Mount of Olives Jesus prays: "Father, if you are willing, remove this cup from me. Yet, not my will but yours be done" (22:42). From the cross Jesus addresses his Father twice: "Father, forgive them, for they do not know what they are doing" (23:34) and "Father, into your hands I commend my spirit" (23:46). Finally, I ask my readers to note and take to heart the close relationship between the reversal theme in the person of humble Mary and her *Magnificat* and the reversal theme in Jesus' prayer.

Wisdom motifs pulsate through Luke 10:21. Just like Lady Wisdom, Jesus and his Father search for adherents. From the many distractions that might claim the attention of human beings and lead them away from the pursuit of wisdom, Jesus singles out one: arrogant self-sufficiency. "The things" of Jesus' ministry of God's kingdom only become revelatory for those who are "infants," that is, totally dependent upon God for life, nourishment, shelter, protection, and well-being. Luke 10:22 plumbs this sagacious message to its theological and christological depths. Those who come to Jesus as infants will see the Father in what Jesus says and does, for Jesus in his words, deeds, journey, cross, resurrection, ascension, and sending of the promised Spirit reveals the life plan of his Father.

Luke 10:23-24, for its part, taps into another significant Lukan thematic, that of seeing. The disciples are able to see the fulfillment of what God had promised and what more noteworthy people such as kings and prophets only saw in their dreams. Note how thrice Luke describes that the shepherds saw what the angels had promised them and glorified and praised God for all they had seen (2:15-20). The blind beggar with insistent and persistent faith in Jesus, Son of David, will receive his sight and follow Jesus to Jerusalem (18:35-43). And it is theological irony of the first order that Luke narrates that the people were able to see through total darkness the significance of Jesus' death on the cross: "And when all the crowds who had gathered there for this *spectacle saw* what had taken place, they returned home, beating their breasts in repentance" (23:48). Through his ironic preaching of the Christian kerygma to the two disciples on the road to Emmaus the risen Jesus opens their eyes to see that it was God's will that the Messiah should suffer these things and then enter into his glory (24:31).

In brief, Jesus' thanksgiving prayer in Luke 10:21-22 presents the Lukan Gospel *in nuce.* The Father is no hidden God but has revealed himself in all that Jesus is and does. And only those truly dependent can open themselves to receive such a gracious gift. The self-sufficient find their wisdom in the boredom of living for themselves.

Luke 11:1-13: Jesus' Short Course on Prayer

Luke 11:1-13 is in many ways a short course on prayer for disciples on
the Way. The Lord's Prayer (11:1-4) is followed by the parable of 11:5-
8, which in turn is followed by Jesus' words about asking, searching,
and knocking (11:9-13). There is the nice touch of a literary *inclusion*,
as "Father" is at the beginning of this section (11:2) and at its ending
(11:13).

Luke 11:1-4: The Lord's Prayer

Since I have spent an entire chapter, "Prayer and the Historical Jesus,"
on the Lord's Prayer, I do not intend to repeat all that material, outstanding as it may have been, in this context. I refer my readers to that
chapter for a brief refresher. Once my interested readers have freshened
up their learning, I invite them to peruse what I have to say about the
Lukan context of the Lord's Prayer and its five petitions.

It is the Lukan context of God's fulfillment of promises in Messiah
Jesus that makes these five Jewish petitions a messianic or Christian
prayer. The followers of Jesus who call God "Father" now know more
about God than non-Christian believers. God is not just Father as creator, not just Father as liberator from Egyptian slavery, but also and
especially Father as revealed in the life, death, and resurrection of his
Son, Jesus. He is the Father of Israel, reconstituted by his Son, Jesus.
And as St. Bonaventure observed so powerfully, God is Father as creator, redeemer, and glorifier. For the children will follow the Son into
the Father's glory.

The hallowing of the Father's name is seen especially in Luke-Acts
as Jesus and his disciples engage in the eschatological battle with the
powers of evil that cause God's name to be discredited or unhallowed.
In the immediate context of the Lord's Prayer my eyes are drawn back
to the arresting images of Luke 10:17-19. In the kingdom-preaching
work of Jesus' missionaries Satan does fall like lightning from heaven.
And not even such health-destroying beasts as cobras and scorpions
will stand in the way of Jesus' disciples. Not even the worst enemy of
them all, death, can stand in Jesus' way as he promises paradise to the
repentant thief (23:43) and commits himself totally and confidently
into the hands of his gracious Father (23:46).

Jesus has given his life for God's kingdom, which is given a narrative definition in Luke 4:16-43. The good news of the kingdom of God, for which Jesus was sent (4:43), consists in being empowered by the Spirit, preaching God's love to the poor, proclaiming release to captives, giving sight to the blind, liberating the oppressed, proclaiming God's favor to the outcast and nonreligious, healing the sick, and casting out demons. And this is the kingdom that Jesus' disciples pray for and preach about, as they give witness in Jerusalem, Samaria, and to the ends of the earth. And in Lukan parlance God's kingdom has come to be identified with what Jesus did and taught. It is high missionary theology and Christology that Luke ends his two-volume work with this description of Paul under house arrest, awaiting trial in Rome: "proclaiming the kingdom of God and teaching about the Lord Jesus Christ with all boldness and without hindrance" (Acts 28:31).

The first of the three "we" petitions picks up a dominant theme in Luke-Acts: Who provides food for life and with whom should one share one's food? As we saw in our earlier chapter, one of the emphases in this petition is on "us" and "our." And Luke has gone out of his way to underscore this emphasis as he depicts the religious leaders as harshly criticizing Jesus because of his table fellowship with toll collectors and sinners (see 7:34; 15:1-2). Yet despite their opposition Jesus eats with his critics, too (see 7:36-50; 11:37-55; 14:1-24). And Jesus commands that one share one's table with "the poor, the crippled, the lame, and the blind" (14:13). And even Jesus' male and female disciples don't get the message of being open to the needs of others, for they squabble over places of honor during Jesus' last earthly meal (22:24-27). And it is of capital importance that the two disciples on the road to Emmaus recognize the risen Jesus in the breaking of the bread after they have offered him hospitality (24:13-35) and that the risen Jesus eats with his female and male disciples (24:36-43). Finally, we should not miss this note in the Lukan summary of what was essential in the first Jerusalem community: "They broke bread at home and ate their food with glad and generous hearts" (Acts 2:46).

And surely, the meaning of "bread for today" is not exhausted in the physical sharing of food with those less fortunate. For Luke, "breaking bread" with those in need shades over into sharing Eucharist, as Luke 9:16, 22:19, and 24:13-35 indicate. And of course, one cannot omit the many references to "the breaking of bread" in Acts. I mention just one instance, Acts 20:7-12, where Paul breaks bread with the disciples at Troas and homilizes for ten times twenty minutes, much to the distress of a young man named Eutychus. Finally, Luke uses food and eating together to image life with God in heaven (Luke 13:29).

In sum, the first "we" petition is not just about me and my physical needs but is global in scope and challenging in communal fulfillment.

The second "we" petition reminds us of the sins we have generously contributed to the world's poor moral health. In Luke's Gospel the cardinal vice is greed, as the example parable of the greedy fool in the immediate context teaches (12:13-21) and as Jesus proclaims: "You cannot serve God and mammon" (16:13). And the forgiveness Jesus demands in the Lord's Prayer is echoed earlier and later in his teaching. In Luke's Sermon on the Plain Jesus teaches: "Forgive, and you will be forgiven" (6:37). And in the final section of the Lukan Travel Narrative Jesus tells his disciples: "And if the same person sins against you seven times a day, and turns back to you seven times and says, 'I repent,' you must forgive" (17:4). But lest Jesus the Messiah's demands demoralize us, we can take courage from Luke 15, in which Luke joyfully proclaims God's forgiveness to sinners in three marvelous parables. Perhaps, in all this teaching about forgiveness the challenge remains that given by the father to his older son: You've got to rejoice because your sinful brother has come back to us safe and sound. Forgive, forget, and let's celebrate!

As we saw in the earlier chapter, the final "we" petition is troublesome. The Lukan Jesus himself has sat for the portrait of a person under trial. Tempted thrice at the beginning of his ministry (4:1-13), Jesus is tempted thrice while he hangs on the cross (23:35-39). At his final earthly meal with his disciples the Lukan Jesus refers back to the ministry, conflicted by demons and the sharp criticisms of religious leaders, in this way: "You are those who have stood by me in my trials" (22:28). But as his temptation on the Mount of Olives reveals and as we will see in greater detail momentarily, Jesus' trials and temptations and those in store for his disciples have an eschatological dimension. For they are temptations to abandon faith in God and to say No to God's will (22:39-46). May God, our gracious Father, prevent us from going over the precipice of apostasy.

In conclusion, Peter Edmonds (1980, 140–43) is correct in calling the Lukan Our Father a summary of Luke's teaching on prayer. But we must never forget that Luke 11:2-4, which comes closest to what the historical Jesus said, has many characteristics of a lament. In it the disciple of Jesus wrestles with faith in a gracious God and Father and with the harsh realities of a world where God's kingdom has not come fully, where God's creation is defiled, where tiny children starve by the tens of thousands, and where centuries-old hatreds slam shut the doors of peace and forgiveness. Into this world disciples utter this prayer of ultimate trust in God's graciousness in imitation of Jesus, their Lord, lament that God has not yet brought about his kingly rule, and once again take upon their shoulders the task of being bread and forgiveness to their portion of the world.

Luke 11:5-13: Don't Hesitate to Ask Your Graciously Generous Father

If you've ever tried to do a public reading in liturgy or to preach about the parable of Luke 11:5-8, you know that you have met the challenge of all of your skills. While Luke may well be an artist and a theologian in many sections of his Gospel, he seems to have lost the handle here. Verses 5-7 are one long sentence in Greek and almost defy proper phrasing and pausing. And in all honesty verse 8 is not much better in its clarity of expression. What does the rarest of Greek words, *anaideia*, mean? It seems to me that the RSV, NRSV, and NAB translate this work inaccurately as "persistence" in the phrase "because of his persistence." Recently scholars have been coming to our interpretive rescue with regard to verse 8. You see, behind this parable, and much else in Luke-Acts, lies the Mediterranean culture of honor and shame. But we Americans don't have to go to the Mediterranean basin to appreciate what honor and shame means. How often do we hear parents say to their children: You should be ashamed of yourself! Or we hear ourselves say: "I'm ashamed of myself. I should know better." Upon a moment's reflection we realize that we experience shame when we have gone against some standard of conduct. Or we want our children to develop good standards of conduct, be these of ethics or etiquette.

Seen from the perspective of honor and shame, the Greek word *anaideia* of 11:8 should probably be translated by "shame" or "because of his shamelessness." This translation, however, does not alleviate all our interpretive problems, for we must ask whose "shame" is at stake: that of the importunate friend or that of the friend who's enjoying his cozy domestic rest? Klyne Snodgrass (1997) has made a good case that the "shame" belongs to the importunate friend. That is, the Greek word *anaideia* is negative and means that the "friend" does not know or care about shame. He is shameless and does not abide by society's norms in the case at hand. In plain and simple language, he is rude. So what does this parable mean, especially in the context of 11:3 "give us each day our daily bread," and 11:9 "knock and the door shall be opened to you," and 11:11-13 that tell of the Father's good pleasure toward his children? In what direction(s) are we to take the Jewish "how much more" argument involved in this parable? If we interpret the parable of "The Friend at Midnight" in the light of Luke 11:9-10 (asking, seeking, knocking), then the lesson in prayer is: If human beings respond to a request made by a rude person, how much more will God, gracious Father that he is, grant your request! If, however, the parable of 11:5-8 is seen with reference to 11:11-13, it means: If a person will get up in the middle of the night to assist a rude friend, how much more will a gracious God answer our petitions! And as Snodgrass (1997, 513) concludes his article: "the parable teaches the certainty of a God who hears prayer and responds." And that is a powerful lesson for all of us who pray and may even form the explicit or implicit reason why we persist in prayer.

The final verses of this short catechism on prayer are the ones that deal with persistence in prayer, but not mindless persistence. It is persistence motivated by knowledge of and faith in the goodness of the heavenly Father. The distinctively Lukan reference to the Father's gift of the Holy Spirit (11:13) does not mean that God is only interested in giving "spiritual" gifts to believers. For that would negate the first "we" petition of the Lord's Prayer, which asks for all that we need daily for physical survival. Rather Luke emphasizes how broad our prayer should be and how wondrously manifold are God's gifts. Luke's Big and Little Pentecosts (Acts 2–4) graphically describe how God is true to promise in sending the Holy Spirit upon reconstituted Israel in Jerusalem.

Jesus' Teaching on Prayer in the Parables of Luke 18:1-8, 9-14

Although it is only in the parable of Luke 18:1-8 that Luke teaches about prayer, prayer does function in the parable of 18:9-14 and will offer us the opportunity to explore for a brief moment some inner dispositions that are necessary in the pray-er. Important for both these parables is context. It is Luke's wont to introduce notations of travel in his Travel Narrative of 9:51–19:28. One of these notations occurs in 17:11 "on the way to Jerusalem" and shows that Luke is entering upon the final stages of his presentation of Jesus' way and deals with such themes as the present and future dimensions of God's kingdom. In Luke 17:21 Jesus makes a striking christological claim when he states that "the kingdom of God is among you," that is, it is present in my ministry of teaching and healing. In what follows in Luke 17:22–18:8 Jesus addresses the future dimension of God's kingdom. The first parable for our consideration occurs in and concludes Jesus' teaching about this future dimension. Contrary to Wilhelm Ott's view (1965) Jesus' teaching here does not deal so much with Luke's response to a putative "delay of the parousia," but rather with everyday issues of faith in the midst of opposition.

There seem to be at least three perspectives to the parable of Luke 18:1-8. The first concerns the need "to pray always and not to lose heart" (18:1). From this perspective the widow who comes perseveringly, day after day, in pursuit of justice is a model for the praying community of believers. The second perspective focuses on the beleaguered judge. The implicit argument is from lesser to greater: If this unjust judge cracks under the pugilistic tactics of the widow who blackens his eye (18:5), how much more will God, who really cares for his persecuted children, come quickly to their aid. The third perspective invites us to revisit the figure of the widow. Commentators such as Barbara E. Reid (1996, 190–94) have shown that the widow of this parable occupies a special place in Luke's Gospel, which portrays so many women. Along with orphans the widow is seated on the pedestal of the powerless. Without a male agent to pursue her rights she, like the widows Tamar and Ruth, must do so on her own. She must disobey the laws, written and unwritten of her society, leave the walls of her domestic confinement, appear in public, and walk the street to the judge's bailiwick. Day after long day she badgers the unjust judge for her rights and eventually wins out. She is a model not only for persistent prayer, but is also a heroine for relentless pursuit of justice. In Reid's words: "She embodies godly power in the midst of apparent powerlessness. This is a message that achieves its full flowering in the passion, death, and resurrection of Jesus" (1996, 192).

I make three quick points about the parable of Luke 18:9-14. First, this parable reminds us that the Temple was a place of public and private prayer. It's a fact we know of from Luke's Infancy Narrative, from Jesus' last days in Jerusalem (19:29–22:53), and from Acts. The second point deals with Luke's presentation of the Pharisees, who seem to embody all that is negative in an approach to God. In this instance it is blowing the horn of one's own self-righteousness. In Luke 11:42 they tithe mint, rue, and herbs of all kinds, but neglect justice to their fellow human beings and love of God. In Luke 16:14 it is greed: "The Pharisees, who were lovers of money, heard all this, and they ridiculed him." These may be the faults of the historical Pharisees in so far as they shared our common sinful lot, but the historical Pharisees were not nefarious practitioners of these vices. In the Pharisees Luke offers a countermodel to what he wants the disciples of Jesus to follow. Jesus' disciples must be self-effacing, lovers of God and not of money, and people who walk along the narrow paths of justice. With these dispositions in their minds and hearts the prayers of the disciples will be pleasing to God, whose characteristic, as we remember from Mary's *Magnificat,* is to exalt the humble and to humble the exalted. My third point is closely related to what I have just said and focuses on the dispositions of the tax collector. Note how Luke describes him in 18:13. His posture is one of self-effacement as he stands at a distance and does not even raise his eyes to God in heaven. He beats his breast as a sign of remorse and repentance. His prayer echoes many a penitential psalm, for example, Psalm 50: "God, be merciful to me, a sinner." His confession is that his God is full of mercy. His confession is that he is not holy, and as an acknowledged sinner is in need of God's merciful forgiveness. And God, who shows no partiality, reaches out to this pariah in Jewish society and justifies him. And it is with finest literary intent that Luke's story of repentant Zacchaeus, a chief tax collector, is just around in the corner in 19:1-10.

In conclusion to the prayers and parables on prayer that Luke has included in his narrative of Jesus' Way, I can only say that there are lessons aplenty here for disciples. God's plan is for the shalom of all creatures and God has revealed that plan in Jesus, God's Son. As disciples pray the prayer Jesus taught them, they are called upon to adopt a dependent attitude, on the one hand, and receive good gifts from a gracious God. On the other hand, a courageous widow and a shameless friend offer role models on how to strive for food and reconciliation for all.

Prayers and Prayer Notices in Luke 22–24

When scholars search for prayers in the last section of Luke's Gospel, they normally zoom in on Jesus' prayer on the Mount of Olives and his two prayers from the cross. But if we ask about "prayer notices," we will find some additional important passages. I move through these three chapters one by one.

Luke 22:14-38 has been rightfully called the earthly Jesus' farewell discourse as he eats and drinks with his male and female disciples for the last time, gives them instructions in word and deed about self-sacrificing service to others, warns them about the changed situation of missionary evangelization, and prays with them. Yes, Jesus prays with them. For what is a Passover meal if not praise of God and thanksgiving for the gift of present and future liberation from the forces of slavery? Now this liberation takes place in a body, "given for you," and through blood, "poured out for you as a new covenant" (22:19-20). Of course, Luke doesn't show us the ritual with its various prayers and psalms that lies behind a Passover celebration. Nor does he present us with the ritual for what has come to be called the Last Supper or in Acts, the breaking of bread. Yet those who are obedient to Jesus' command, "Do this in remembrance of me!" (22:19), are engaged in solemn prayer. I refer my readers to the work of Eugene LaVerdiere (1994) for more detail on this much-neglected aspect of prayer in Luke-Acts.

David Crump (1992, 154–57) has done all of us a wonderful service by highlighting the role that the prayer notice of 22:31-32 plays in Luke's theology of prayer. Again in this passage we see that Jesus' kingdom ministry and reconstitution of Israel on the foundation of his disciples and the Twelve involves an eschatological battle with the forces of evil. Jesus says: "Simon, Simon, listen! Satan has demanded to sift all of you like wheat, but I have prayed for you that your own faith may not fail. And you, when once you have turned back, strengthen your brothers." Here in many ways is a preview of the first half of Acts where Peter, repentant and wiser because of his denial of Jesus, leads the Jerusalem community after Pentecost and unto mission to non-Jews, such as Cornelius. But more important than Peter's future role is the role that Jesus assumes in this passage as intercessor. Here is bedrock for Crump's thesis that Luke presents Jesus as his disciples' powerful intercessor during his earthly life. And it is just a short trek across the pages of Luke-Acts to the story of the first Christian martyr,

Stephen, in Acts 7. Luke says this of Stephen, who is on the verge of being stoned to death: "But filled with the Holy Spirit, he gazed into heaven and saw the glory of God and Jesus standing at the right hand of God" (7:55). The heavenly Jesus is at God's right hand making intercession for Stephen and those who believe in him. So what Luke describes Jesus as doing in his heavenly service has its earthly counterpart in Jesus' intercessory work for his disciples and for Peter in Luke 22:31-32. Furthermore, Luke conveys the power of Jesus' intercession in 22:61-62 and 24:34. In 22:61-62 it is the Lord who looks at Peter, who has just denied him. There is no word of condemnation, and Peter goes out and weeps bitterly. In the resurrection tradition of 24:34 the message is short, but mighty: "The Lord has truly been raised and has appeared to Simon." Peter is now fully restored and reconciled to his Lord, who had interceded for him that his faith not fail.

With Luke 22:39-46 we come to the first explicit prayer of Jesus in this section, and it is an important one. Unlike the parallel accounts in Matthew 26:36-46 and Mark 14:32-42, which describe Jesus praying thrice, Luke's Jesus prays just once and does so with a powerful faith and obedience. Yet his faith and obedience, however strong, do not eliminate his struggle to accept God's plan and will: "Father, if you are willing, remove this cup from me. Yet, not my will, but yours be done" (22:42). Jesus' first statement in Luke's Gospel was "Did you not know that I must be about my Father's business?" (2:49). Now after a ministry of teaching, healing, and preaching the good news to the poor, Jesus meets with betrayal by one of his own Twelve and prays to accept that the Scriptures must be fulfilled in this way. Crump (1992, 167) rightly gauges scholarly opinion on this passage: "The consensus among interpreters today views Luke as deliberately presenting Jesus as the paradigmatic prayer-er, who survives the moment of *his* greatest temptation through the intense prayer he offers to his Father." However, Luke's spotlight in this passage is not singular, for he also spotlights the disciples. In contrast to Jesus' robust resolve to align his will with that of his Father, the disciples are asleep. As Luke's literary technique of *inclusion* at the beginning and end of this passage clearly indicates, they are on the brink of "coming into the time of trial." Those readers who recall the final "we" petition of the Lord's Prayer (11:4) are very perceptive indeed. And because of the power of Jesus' intercessory prayer, the Lukan disciples do not fall over the precipice into apostasy. For the points I am making here to have persuasive force, it is not important that Luke 22:43-44 be original, although I think they are. These verses accentuate the sheer intensity of Jesus' prayer.

Before addressing Jesus' two prayers in Luke 23:34, 46, I want to make some general remarks about Luke's soteriology. Luke's Gospel has accurately been called the "Gospel of God's Mercy." And Luke 23:39-43 has rightly been tagged the "Gospel within the Gospel," for it shows how the crucified Jesus, who had come to save outcasts, promises paradise to a criminal, whose shady past we lighten by calling him "the good thief." Further, since Luke is not Paul, he does not use the theological terminology that Jesus died to save us from our sins. Rather Luke is very similar to that other prominent New Testament theologian, John, and uses the terminology that it is God's revelation that saves. Further, in Luke 22–23 Luke uses colors from different religious traditions to paint the portrait of Jesus, faithful Son of God. Jesus is an innocent martyr like the righteous Jewish men and women during the unjust persecution of Antiochus Epiphanes IV. He is the innocent suffering righteous one of Wisdom 2–5, who remains faithful to his Father in the face of dreadful persecution. Although his discussion is technical and refers to the Greek word *dikaios* (righteous) that the centurion uses to refer to Jesus in 23:47, I would like to summarize my points about Luke's soteriology by quoting from Peter Doble (1996, 234–35), who has written a monograph on the subject. Doble writes: "Luke distanced himself from sacrificial or vicarial strands of thought, concentrating on Jesus' *dikaios*-like suffering and death as God's bringing about his plan of salvation through the fulfilling of Scripture. Luke's *theologia crucis* is that the *dikaios* has died and been raised, so Jesus' followers can be sure that God's plan of salvation is nearing fulfillment." And Luke shows so much of this soteriology through the figure of Jesus at prayer.

With the above brief overall background to Luke's passion narrative in mind, I approach Jesus' first prayer: "Father, forgive them, for they know not what they are doing" (23:34). I refer interested readers to David Crump (1992, 79–85) for arguments why this verse is authentic and original. This verse points backward in the Gospel to Jesus' Sermon on the Mount: "Forgive, and you will be forgiven" (6:37). Obedient to his Father, Jesus also practices by his very life what he teaches. But we are also directed further backwards to a prayer that is becoming more familiar to us with each passing paragraph—Mary's *Magnificat*. It seems to me that in Jesus' prayer for forgiveness for those who are unrighteously crucifying him he is reversing the reversal theme of Luke 1:51-53. You would think that Jesus would be praying that God cast down his enemies from their arrogant thrones. Truly, God does not vindicate Jesus by destroying his oppressors but by destroying the power of death over Jesus. The Father will hear his Son's petition and extend bounteous forgiveness and mercy through the preaching of the early Jerusalem church to Jesus' unjust persecutors. Finally, the figure of Jesus, obedient to his Father's will and petitioner of God's forgiveness for his enemies, stands as a model for that first Christian martyr, Stephen. With his last breath Stephen prays: "Lord, do not hold this sin against them" (Acts 7:60). This cross reference between Luke 23:34 and Acts 7:60 clearly reveals Luke's intent of exhorting any innocently suffering members of his churches to perseverance and merciful largess of spirit.

In Luke's Gospel Jesus dies with words that express his utmost confidence in his Father and his Father's will and plan: "Father, into your hands I commend my spirit" (23:46). These words, taken from Psalm 31:5, show us that the Lukan Jesus was familiar with the psalms, Israel's prayer book. I, for one, am of the opinion that we should read all of Psalm 31 as the co-text of Jesus' last words. I particularly refer to these verses: "I am the scorn of my adversaries" (verse 11); "Blessed be the Lord, for he has wondrously shown his steadfast love to me" (verse 21); "Love the Lord, all you his saints. The Lord preserves the faithful" (verse 23). And it is not surprising to me that a Gospel that has prayers or prayer references in almost every chapter describes its main character, Jesus, God's Son, dying with a prayer to his Father on his lips. In Jesus' life and death Luke has shown how God's plan has been realized and offered many an example for Theophilus's imitation. But the Gospel story is not over yet, because we still have to examine, albeit briefly, a few more prayer references in Luke 24, which details God's vindication of Jesus, his Son, the innocent martyr and innocently suffering righteous one.

The first of three references to prayer in Luke 24 is found in Luke's most beautiful story of the two disciples on their way to Emmaus. For our purposes Luke 24:30 and 35 are central: Jesus blessed bread; the disciples proclaim that they recognized the risen Jesus in the breaking of the bread. David Crump (1992, 104–7) is one of the few commentators to draw our attention to the fact that Jesus' blessing over bread is a prayer of thanksgiving. Interested readers might want to check the appendix at the end of my chapter "Prayer and the Historical Jesus" for a text of a Jewish blessing over a meal. I agree with Crump (1992, 105–6): "In other words, for these disciples to say that they were caused to recognize Jesus 'in the breaking of the bread' is tantamount to saying that he was made known to them *while he was at prayer"* (emphasis in original).

The second reference to prayer occurs so quickly in the same Emmaus story that we may miss its significance. Luke 24:34 proclaims: "The Lord has risen indeed, and he has appeared to Simon." The risen Jesus shows the power of the intercessory prayer that he said for Peter in Luke 22:31-32 as he offers reconciliation to the wayward Simon Peter.

Finally, this Gospel of God's mercy ends on the joyful note with which it began in the Temple. God's promises have been fulfilled in Jesus. As Jesus completes the liturgy of his life of revealing God and God's plan of salvation, he blesses his disciples for the first and last time. What Zechariah could not do after he had completed his liturgical service, Jesus does at the completion of his. Jesus' disciples worship him as Son of God, raised by his Father as a sign of his vindication and the authentication of his Son's message and life. And in Luke's wonderful style of parataxis or joining sentences one to another without any apparent logical connection, Luke adds that the disciples experience great joy and are continually in the Temple blessing God. Luke is not about to be formulating fourth- and fifth-century Christology and trinitarian doctrine in the first century, but he does articulate the disciples' relationship to Jesus and to God in the terminology of prayer: worship and praise. In our final section we will see how the early church prays to God through the power of Jesus and the promised Spirit. We will also learn that blessing God for the gift of Jesus can have its down side in persecution by the authorities and its positive side in faith-filled prayer that is answered by God's gifts of the Spirit and evangelical boldness.

PRAYER IN THE ACTS OF THE APOSTLES

In this section I will make some general comments about the prayer passages in Acts and then give more detailed comment on its one content-full prayer, Acts 4:23-31. It is at Ludger Feldkämper's scholarly door (1978, 306–32) that we must put the credit for noting and attempting to explain the telling parallels between the prayer passages in the Gospel and in Acts. His contentions are the following. Luke has constructed these parallels very carefully, using at times the same vocabulary. Further, these parallels are the carrier of Luke's subtle

Christology. Jesus at prayer was not only the teacher and model of prayer for his disciples, but he is also the enabler of their prayer. The community of disciples prays not only as Jesus prayed, but they also pray through Jesus. Let me list the nine parallels Feldkämper has detected and then explain his eighth one:

1. Jesus' prayer at baptism (Luke 3:21-22) and the church's prayer at its various inaugurations (Acts 1:14; 2:1ff.; 4:31; 8:15; 10-11).
2. Jesus' prayer and his powerful working in word and deed (Luke 5:16; 6:12) and Acts 3:1–4:31.
3. Jesus' prayer before choosing the Twelve (Luke 6:12) and Acts 1:15-26; 6:1-6.
4. Jesus' prayer and his acceptance of suffering (Luke 9:18ff., 28ff.) and Acts 9:11ff.
5. Jesus' cry of jubilation (Luke 10:21-22) and Acts 2:1-13; 10:44-48; 19:1-7.
6. Jesus' prayer and instruction to his disciples on prayer (Luke 11:1-13) and Acts 4:29-31; 5:12.
7. Jesus' prayer for Peter (Luke 22:32) and the church's prayer for him in Acts 12:1-17.
8. Jesus' prayer on the Mount of Olives (Luke 22:42) and Acts 21:14.
9. Jesus' prayer on the cross (Luke 23:34, 36) and Stephen's prayer in Acts 7:59-60.

The eighth parallel functions within the larger parallel that Luke draws between Jesus' life and that of Paul. Like Jesus who predicts his rejection and passion, so too does Paul (Acts 20:23). Both Jesus and Paul journey to their rendezvous with God's will in Jerusalem. Imprisonment is their reward for preaching the good news. And whereas Jesus says to his Father that "your will be done" (Luke 22:42), the disciples at Caesarea, unable to bend Paul from obedience to God's will, say: "The Lord's will be done" (Acts 21:14). This time "the Lord" involved is the risen Lord Jesus. But the message of the "will" remains the same, namely, continue to give testimony despite the cost. Neither Jesus nor Paul will bend from the divine will. Indeed, through his literary parallelism Luke shows that Paul goes his way in imitation of his Lord Jesus. And both Jesus and Paul offer role models for the Christian community. Let me put into my own two sentences Feldkämper's further but implicit argument. Through his prayer on the Mount of Olives Jesus accepted his Father's will that through suffering comes glory.

Now as the glorified Lord, Jesus calls and enables Paul to follow in his footsteps. I realize that Feldkämper has hinted at an explanation and has not produced an airtight argument. With my readers I lament this fact and raise my voice in supplication that someone give more attention to the parallels between the prayer passages in Luke's Gospel and Acts and show decisively how Jesus, the earthly intercessor, has become the heavenly intercessor who empowers missionaries like Paul.

In my assessment of the prayer passages in Acts, the one that now claims our attention, Acts 4:24-30, is the longest and is the only one with any content beyond a few words. From the very beginning of this chapter on prayer in Luke-Acts it has been my contention that the prayers in Luke-Acts are carriers of Luke's theology. With Acts 4:23-31 we are in the enviable position of making our point in spades. I will use the extraordinarily talented and insightful Joseph A. Fitzmyer (1998, 305–12) as my dialogue partner in assessing the significance of this passage. I make three points. First, if you go back to the beginning of this chapter and reread the prayer that Josephus composed from traditional materials and put into the mouth of Moses, you may be amazed to realize that Fitzmyer offers the same passage from Josephus, *Jewish Antiquities* 4.40-50 as "an interesting parallel," but does not specifically note any parallel except that of "an earthquake." In my mind the two main parallels include the similar address to God. Josephus has "Lord of all that is in heaven and earth and sea," and Acts 4:24 has "Lord, who made the heaven and earth, the sea and everything in them." The Greek would show even more clearly how similar these two addresses are. Perhaps, such similarity stems from the fact that the authors invoke the same source, Psalm 146:6. The second and more striking parallel is both authors' emphasis on divine providence. Josephus's very forceful statement of God's design reads: "Prove now once again that all is directed by your providence, that nothing befalls fortuitously, but that it is your will that overrules and brings everything to its goal." And Acts 4:28 articulates this theme in this wise: "to do whatever your hand and your plan had predestined to take place."

My second point recalls my earlier observation that the prayer that Josephus composes for Moses is not made out of thin air but contains traditional materials. I was happy to read what Fitzmyer (1998, 307) says about Acts 4:23-31: "This episode is one of Lucan composition, which may incorporate a few details inherited from a Palestinian tradition, such as the fact of the prayer and intervention of the Spirit and the mention of Herod and Pilate."

Finally, Acts 4:24-31 is Lukan theology in prayer form. Fitzmyer (1998, 306) is of the opinion that these verses are implicit thanksgiving, praise, and petition all rolled up in one. His point is well taken, but I would aver that these verses are Lukan theology of salvation history introduced by a prayer notice in 4:24 and concluded with a prayer notice in 4:31. I say this for a number of reasons. I ask you, my readers: Have you ever tried to say this "prayer"? Has the liturgy of any church taken it over into its daily prayer life as churches have Mary's *Magnificat*, Zechariah's *Benedictus*, and Simeon's *Nunc Dimittis*? Acts 4:24-31 doesn't work so well as prayer, but it is magnificent Lukan theology. Look at its opening confession of faith in the sovereignty of the Lord. Look at its "argument from Scripture" that what the powers-that-be did "against God's Messiah" and "against God's holy child Jesus, God's anointed" was in accordance with divine providence. And the final two verses issue the marching orders for the evangelizing church, whose activities Luke will narrate in the remainder of Acts. Through Peter, John, Philip, Stephen, Paul and Barnabas, bold preachers of God's word, that word, now filled to overflowing with the saving significance of the risen Lord Jesus, will spread from Jerusalem to Samaria and to the ends of the world. The mighty work, performed on behalf of the man who was lame from birth and was over forty years of age, is just the first of many to be performed in the name of Jesus. And all this, as the Little Pentecost of Acts 4:31 graphically demonstrates, is done through the gifts of the Holy Spirit, whom many consider the leading character of Acts.

Luke's Supposed Supernaturalism and Exaggerated Theology of Glory

Luke has been harshly criticized because he tells stories in which supernatural beings intervene to rescue his heroes from the pains of the cross of discipleship. It seems to me that this critique woodenly literalizes Luke's literary techniques. It turns Luke's evangelical entertainment or what Richard I. Pervo (1987) has fittingly called Luke's theme of "profit with delight" from stage props into major characters. Look at the "prison breaks" in Acts. I would warmly suggest that the story in Acts 5:17-42 of the apostles' angelic prison break and its aftermath is meant to be theologically entertaining as it narrates that God, not the Sanhedrin, is in charge of the Way. And look at Acts 12:1-17. While King Herod can kill James, the brother of John, he is unable to harm Peter, even though he imprisons him in the tightest security. It is with a deep faith in the God who saves and with a smile on his lips that Luke tells the story of how the members of the church, who are praying fervently to God for Peter's release, fail to recognize him when he appears on their doorstep, liberated in answer to their prayers. Peter's time to die for his Lord will come, but not now. Finally, there is the marvelous story in Acts 16:19-40 of Paul and Silas in the Philippian jail. In answer to their prayers, they are freed from their chains. And then they convert the jailer and his entire household. Of course, we know from the rest of Acts that Paul will be imprisoned again and sent to Rome, where he will arrive after escaping a great storm at sea and a viper bite on Malta. Indeed, Luke is a historian who knows how to get a smile out of his readers. But as any close reading of Acts, especially Luke's tales of Paul, will reveal, Luke has not erased the cross from the Way. Or in technical terms, Luke has not replaced a theology of the cross with a theology of glory. In a marvelous paragraph Charles Kingsley Barrett (1979, 84) brilliantly answers Luke's critics. Among other things he writes that Luke can still be a theologian even though his Christian cheerfulness keeps breaking in. "Like Paul, he [Luke] knows that nothing in heaven or earth, in life or in death, can separate the believer from the love of God, though he is apt to express the fact in such practical terms as release from prison or escape from shipwreck." And Luke's "practical theologia crucis is not contradicted by the fact that his pilgrims can 'shout as they travel the wilderness through.'"

Luke's critics also haul him to court for his use of angels (for prison breaks and other chores), visions, and dreams to convey God's will. From Luke's Gospel take the story of angel Gabriel and Mary of Nazareth (1:26-38) and of the angel who strengthens Jesus on the Mount of Olives (22:43). From Acts take Paul's vision at night of a man of Macedonia who pleads with him to come and help him (16:9). And recall Acts 23:11: "That night the Lord stood near Paul and said, 'Keep up your courage! For just as you have testified for me in Jerusalem, so you must bear witness also in Rome.'" What are we mere mortals and simple believers to make of these heavenly communications? If you're like me, they're not part of your daily routine. But this manner of speaking is part of the daily routine of historians and hagiographers. In my Franciscan heritage I'm used to hearing from hagiographer Thomas of Celano that St. Francis of Assisi saw the Lord Jesus in dreams and heard him talking from the cross at San Damiano. Further, Thomas of Celano tells us that the leper Francis aided and kissed turned out to be the Lord himself. Are these events literalistically true? I doubt it. But they are true on another, more powerful level. By using the hagiographer's stock in trade, Thomas of Celano was saying that Francis was convinced that he was following the Lord and that *the* turning point in his life was his care of the lepers. If we turn to Luke-Acts, Luke is using the standard literary equipment of his day to say that God did communicate with Mary of Nazareth and Paul of Tarsus, and both gave a generous and positive response. Did God's special revelation to them remove the cross from their lives? As we saw above in the case of persecuted Paul, Luke didn't think so. And with regard to Mary he describes her twice as trying to figure it all out (Luke 2:19, 52) and being told by Simeon that the sword of making a decision for or against God will pierce her soul (Luke 2:35).

In sum, I urge my readers to let Luke be Luke and Paul be Paul. Let each one describe the meaning of the cross in the life of Jesus and in the lives of his disciples in his own way. And just as we have learned to distinguish between newspaper editorials, cartoons, and front page news articles in our day and don't dump them all together in one category, let's try to separate out Luke's various genres. Such an endeavor will help us immensely in unraveling Luke's message from its historical wrapper of evangelical humor and heavenly concourse.

CONCLUSION

Perhaps, one of these days it will be my happy lot to teach a course on New Testament spirituality. In that course I would feature Luke-Acts in a prominent position, for Luke is a narrative theologian of prayer. He doesn't lecture us on the prayer of petition, the prayer of thanksgiving, the prayer of lamentation, and the prayer of praise. Nor does he expatiate in some abstract way about who God is and how deserving God is of our worship. Neither does he say in so many words that Jesus, our Messiah and Lord, is our intercessor at the right hand of the Father. How to persevere in prayer is not some dull tractate in Luke's hands. Luke tells stories and composes prayers out of traditional materials and rejoices in the faithful God whose will is gracious and will be done.

And if words merely teach whereas examples draw us out into action, Luke is the master historian of examples, especially those of Mary, Jesus, the early church, and Paul in prayer. And as Mary's *Magnificat* demonstrates in such a powerfully challenging way, Luke's narrative theology of prayer will force us out of cozy ecclesiastical confines onto the streets of justice. Take. Read. Enjoy and pray. Act.

FOR FURTHER READING

Balentine, Samuel E. 1993. *Prayer in the Hebrew Bible: The Drama of Divine-Human Dialogue.* Overtures to Biblical Theology. Minneapolis: Fortress.

Barton, Stephen C. 1992. *The Spirituality of the Gospels*, 71–112. Peabody, Mass.: Hendrickson.

Brown, Raymond E. 1993. *The Birth of the Messiah: A Commentary on the Infancy Narratives in the Gospels of Matthew and Luke.* New Updated Edition. The Anchor Bible Reference Library; New York: Doubleday.

Dunn, James D. G. 1975. *Jesus and the Spirit: A Study of the Religious and Charismatic Experience of Jesus and the First Christians as Reflected in the New Testament.* London: SCM Press.

Edmonds, Peter. 1980. "The Lucan Our Father: A Summary of Luke's Teaching on Prayer?" *The Expository Times* 91: 140–43.

Karris, Robert J. 1983. "Mary's Magnificat and Recent Study." *Review for Religious* 42: 903–8.

———. 1990. "The Gospel According to Luke." *New Jerome Biblical Commentary*, 675–721. Ed. Raymond E. Brown, Joseph A. Fitzmyer, and Roland E. Murphy. Englewood Cliffs, N.J.: Prentice Hall.

Snodgrass, Klyne. 1997. "*ANAIDEIA* and the Friend at Midnight (Luke 11:8)." *Journal of Biblical Literature* 116: 505–13.

Talbert, Charles H. 1988. *Reading Luke: A Literary and Theological Commentary on the Third Gospel.* Reading the New Testament Series. New York: Crossroad.

Terrien, Samuel. 1995. *The Magnificat: Musicians as Biblical Interpreters.* New York: Paulist.

Thurston, Bonnie. 1993. *Spiritual Life in the Early Church: The Witness of Acts and Ephesians*, 55–65. Minneapolis: Fortress.

3

Prayer in John's Gospel
and 1 John

THOSE OF YOU WHO ARE READING this book chapter after chapter
are going to be quite surprised when you come to the Jesus of
John's Gospel after seeing the historical Jesus and the Jesus of
Luke's Gospel. The divinity of Jesus, Son of God, shines forth in John's
Gospel so brightly that it almost blinds readers to Jesus' humanity.
This Johannine characteristic is what Ernst Käsemann (1968, 73)
referred to as John's consistent presentation "of Jesus as God walking
on the face of the earth." Thus, it will not be easy for me to draw
lessons for imitation from John's presentation of Jesus at prayer as I did
in the previous two chapters. My presentation will highlight the community's response to Jesus, Son of God, and thereby invite contemporary readers to imitate their forebears in the faith.

I presuppose a general division of John's Gospel into a Book of Signs
(chapters 1–12) and a Book of Glory (chapters 13–21). I acknowledge
my debt to C. K. Barrett, who has helped me to see John 4:19-26, which
occurs in the story of Jesus' encounter with a Samaritan woman, as a
statement of the evangelist's purpose in writing his Gospel. Barrett
(1982, 14) writes: "The Father himself seeks men who will worship
him in Spirit and in truth: this then was God's purpose in the incarnation, and John certainly wrote with the intention of furthering the
divine purpose. . . ." And from John 4:19-26 and Barrett's correct interpretation of these verses, I find that it is a short step to our theme of
prayer and worship in John. Let me quote Barrett again as he restates
his insight: "The figure of Jesus does not . . . make sense when viewed
as a national leader, a rabbi, or a *theios aner*; he makes sense when in

hearing him you hear the Father, when in looking at him you see the Father, and *worship* him" (1982, 16; emphasis mine).

So by relying heavily on the terminology of "worship" as well as "prayer," I have found more in John's Gospel and 1 John on this thematic than other commentators. I commence with what almost all scholars call a hymn—John 1:1-18. Then I deal with a category that John Painter (1993; 1996) has helpfully called the "quest stories." To me these stories represent humankind's quest for God or God's quest for men and women as worshipers. A section follows on the Johannine theme of how Jesus replaces Jewish feasts and allows us to glimpse John's community at worship. The subject of prayer in Jesus' name will provide entry into passages in John's farewell discourse and 1 John 5. Jesus' high priestly prayer in John 17 will offer further material for reflection. I conclude with the earthly Jesus' last words in John 19:28-30. And in what I write about the Gospel I presuppose the arguments of my earlier work (1990) that the Christian community finds itself being painfully separated from the Jewish community in which it was first wondrously nourished in the faith.

JOHN'S GOSPEL BEGINS WITH A HYMN (JOHN 1:1-18)

My best New Testament assignment in seminary was to write a paper on the topic "John's prologue is a summary of his entire Gospel." My classmates and I burnt the midnight oil and fought vigorously over who had the most convincing arguments. But in our frenzy to get the right answers we neglected to look at John 1:1-18 as a prayer. And I suppose that hundreds of seminary teachers over the years have never required their students to look at the first eighteen verses of John's Gospel as a hymn, psalm, song, or confessional statement. And books on prayer in the New Testament don't feature John's prologue either. Oscar Cullmann (1994, 89–111) is representative of this omission, for he does not treat John's prologue in his lengthy section on prayer in John's writings. Most scholars and teachers on John's Gospel seem content to repeat what Rudolf Bultmann (1971, 13) said many years ago: John's prologue is an "overture." Or they may update their terminology and quote Udo Schnelle (1992, 226): John 1:1-18 is a "programmatic introductory text." And even when scholars say that John 1:1-18 is a hymn, they are more apt to divide these verses into two piles than to show how the entire passage works as prayer. In one pile are the verses of the putatively original hymn, and in the other pile are the evangelist's modifications and/or corrections. Put in other words, there is little or no "performance tradition" of interpreting John 1:1-18 as a prayer. So I will have to take the risk of striking off on my own.

I follow, among others, R. Alan Culpepper (1981) and Francis J. Moloney (1998) and treat all of John 1:1-18 as a hymn. Furthermore, I march behind Rudolf Bultmann (1971, 14), who insightfully wrote the following about John's opening hymn: "so here from the beginning everything stands under this all-embracing 'We'. It is the community that is speaking! And in what way? In its form the Prologue is a piece of *cultic-liturgical poetry*, oscillating between the language of revelation and confession." I bypass Bultmann's conjectures (1971, 15–16, 78) that verses 6-8, 13, 15, 17-18 were interruptions and additions to an "original" hymn and adopt as my main parallel to John 1:1-18 *Odes of Solomon* 12, which, as Bultmann (1971, 14) suggested, moves between the language of revelation and confession. I quote Ode 12 in its entirety, so that we have something from the time of John's Gospel to guide our ideas of the prayers with which John and his contemporaries were familiar. The first three verses of Ode 12 serve as introduction and set the tone for what follows. Verses 6-12 contain the revelation, and verse 13 presents the community's confession. I have made some slight alterations to the translation of J. H. Charlesworth:

1. He has filled me with words of truth, that I may proclaim him.
2. And like the flowing of waters, truth flows from my mouth,
   and my lips declare his fruits.
3. And he has caused his knowledge to abound in me,
   because the mouth of the Lord is the true word, and the door of his light.
4. And the Most High has given me to his generations,
   which are the interpreters of his beauty, and the narrators of his glory,
   and the confessors of his thought, and the preachers of his mind,
   and the teachers of his works.
5. For the subtlety of the Word is inexpressible,
   and like his utterance so also is his swiftness and his acuteness,
   for limitless is his path.
6. He never falls but remains standing,
   and one cannot know his descent or his way.
7. For as his work is, so is his expectation,
   for he is the light and dawning of thought.

8. And by him the generations spoke to one another,
   and those that were silent acquired speech.
9. And from him came love and harmony,
   and they spoke one to another whatever was theirs.
10. And they were stimulated by the Word,
    and knew him who made them, because they were in harmony.
11. For the mouth of the Most High spoke to them,
    and his exposition was swift through him.
12. For the dwelling place of the Word is man,
    and his truth is love.
13. Blessed are they who by means of him have perceived everything,
    and have known the Lord in his truth. Hallelujah.

Let me highlight the salient points of this parallel for our analysis of John 1:1-18. First, we are moving in the same universe of discourse as the similar vocabulary indicates: Word, truth, light. Second, verse 13 is the explicit response of the community to the Lord's revelation. Third, verse 4 is expansive or "overloaded" just as John 1:13 is often judged to be. In this regard, verses 26-28 of the ninth hymn from cave one of Qumran (1QH 9:26-28) provide another example of how an author of a hymn can move from "simple" contrasts to an "over-loaded" statement: "for from darkness you make my light shine, to change my bruises to everlasting happiness, my weakness to wonder-ful force, the constriction of my soul to everlasting expanse. For you, my God, are my refuge, my protection, the rock of my strength, my fortress."

Before I quote the hymn that the community sings as it begins to read the good news about Jesus Messiah, Son of God, I lay before my readers my fundamental insights into the revelation and confession structure of this song. While Bultmann was certainly right in seeing *Odes of Solomon* 12 with its revelation-confession scheme as a paral-lel to John 1:1-18, he didn't adequately allow for the community's con-fessional response to the revelation. It is my contention that this response is not found first in verse 14 where the "we" of the commu-nity explicitly sounds forth. Rather the community's response is already found in verses 6-8. Moreover, verses 15 and 17-18 are not interruptions or additions, as Raymond E. Brown (1966, 22) and others contend, but further responses of the confessing community. Finally, the community singing this hymn is implicated in the responses of "the darkness," "his own," "the believers," and "we."

The translation that follows is my own. I have used italics to indicate most of the multiple "parallelisms" in this hymn, for example, from "word" one moves to its parallel "life" and from there to the next parallel "light." Also, through bold type I have marked off some of the words that direct those who pray this hymn in faith to get involved and to renew their commitment to God's revelation in the Word.

John's Hymn and the Community's Faith Response to It (1:1-18)

1. In the beginning was *the Word*, and *the Word* was *in God's presence*. And *the Word* was *God*. 2. He was in the beginning *in God's presence*.

3. All things *came about through him*. And without him not one thing *came about*. 4. What *came about* through him was *life*. And the *life* was *the light* for human beings. 5. And *the light* shines in *the darkness*, and *the darkness* did not overcome it.

6. There was a man, sent by *God*, whose name was John. 7. He *came to witness and to bear testimony* concerning *the light*, so that **all might believe** through him. 8. He was not *the light*, but came so that he *might witness* concerning *the light*.

9. *The true light*, which **enlightens every person**, was coming into *the world*. 10. He was in *the world*, and *the world came about through him*, and *the world* did not know him. 11. He came to *his own* home, and *his own* people did not *accept* him. 12. But to those who *accepted* him, he gave power **to become children of God, to those who believe in his name**, 13. who were born not from blood, nor from the will of the flesh, nor from the will of a husband, but from *God*.

14. And *the Word* became flesh and dwelt **among us**. And **we have seen** his *glory*, the *glory* as of the *only Son* from *the Father*, full of *the grace that is truth*. 15. John **witnesses** concerning him and **sounds forth the inspired cry**: This was he of whom I spoke, "The one coming after me ranks before me because he existed before me." 16. Now from his fullness **all of us have received**, and grace on top of grace. 17. For the law was given through Moses. *The grace that is truth* has *come about* through **Jesus Messiah**. 18. No one has ever seen *God*. The *only Son*, *God*, who is in the bosom of *the Father*, **has revealed him (to us)**.

Given the abundant "parallelism" in these verses, it is not surprising that R. Alan Culpepper (1981) and others have seen great unity in them. Whether Culpepper's analysis convinces the reader that this hymn manifests a chiastic structure or not, I personally am convinced of its well-structured unity. But its order is not chronological with its highpoint occurring in verse 14, for the incarnation is already referred to in verses 5 and 9-10, verses that occur before the pronouncement in verse 14 that the Word became flesh. Rather, the order is cyclic and is what we will find again and again in John. Or put in terms of Bultmann's scheme, the order consists of the interweaving of revelation and response. Relative to revelation, I mention these few items. Although the term "Word" occurs in the very first verse and refers to revelation, it is not until verses 14-18 that we learn that God's revelation or Word is a human being and stands as the fulfillment of Jewish expectations. Until that time, the composer teases the reader with references such as "the man sent from God, John, who witnesses to the light." Further, responses to God's revelation vary from that of "the darkness" (verse 5) to those of "his own" (verse 11) to those who accept the revelation and become children of God (verses 12-13) and finally to those who saw his glory (verse 14). Put another way, the composer uses the same motif of revelation and response again and again to draw readers into his prayer. The response occurs once and twice and then in its third occurrence in verses 14-18 is given full expression.

Seen from the perspective of the scheme of revelation and response, the so-called interruptions of John 1:6-8 and 15 provide another means for the composer to draw his confessing community into their song. For these singers are meant to identify with John, who bore witness and continues to bear witness to them of the incarnate Logos, preexistent and now glorified, and calls upon those who recite this hymn to deepen their faith in Jesus Messiah, incarnate Logos.

What I am saying here about John is really nothing new. For Morna Hooker (1969/70, 357) already made the telling point that the "interruptions" of verses 6-8, 15 are not about John at all: "They refer to the historical 'event' of Jesus Christ, that is, to the appearance of the Logos among men. Their importance lies in the fact that each refers to John as the witness who confirms the truth of what has just been said, that light is shining in the darkness, and that we have seen the glory of the incarnate Logos." I would develop Hooker's point even further. If one is reciting the hymn of the prologue as something "out there" and outside of one's own experience, then the references to John are interruptions. But if the believer is trying to enter into the existential meaning of the hymn, the references to the human being John are of immense help. First, we can imitate John whereas we can't imitate the Word.

Second, John is described as a witness thrice in verses 6-8 and once in verse 15. He witnesses to us, and we can be witnesses to the truth of this hymn, too. And as C. K. Barrett (1978, 167) sagely comments on the verbs "witnesses" and "cries out" in verse 15: "The tenses are remarkable. . . . [B]oth verbs speak of the testimony of John as having present significance." Yes, John is bearing witness to us who are presently praying this hymn. Finally, verse 7 alludes to the role John has had in leading believers, even those who are now praying this hymn, to faith.

Let me leave aside the hymn's motif of revelation and response and approach this magnificent hymn from another angle—its vocabulary. I make the following general points about how this vocabulary draws the believer turned pray-er into the meaning of the hymn. First, the language of this hymn is beguilingly simple. According to my count there are a mere 252 words in the Greek of John's prologue, exactly twenty less words than Abraham Lincoln used in his epochal "Gettysburg Address." "And" occurs 15 times, a fact that indicates most of the sentences are linked by a simple connective and not by words of "logic" such as "since" and "provided that." Technically, this style is called paratactic. The most common verb is "to be" (eleven times) followed by "to come about" (nine times) and "to come" and "to witness" (four times apiece). The most commonly used noun is "God" and "light" (six times apiece) followed by "world" and "grace" (four times apiece). Remarkably "Word" occurs only three times: twice in 1:1 and once in 1:14. The personal pronoun "him/his" occurs twelve times and helps forge links between verses. Such simple language makes this hymn appealing.

Second, as Norman R. Petersen (1993, 8–22) has shown, the hymn does wonders with its scant 252 words by taking everyday language and turning it into special language. Thus, the composer has taken such everyday words as God, word/communication, life, light, darkness, world, his own, accept, flesh, behold, glory, grace, truth, son, and father, and interpreted them in his own way. Our translations have caught on to the composer's language usage by capitalizing "word" and "son" and "father," thus turning them into Johannine special and sacred language. Those who recite John 1:1-18 are invited to assimilate in faith John's special vocabulary, which will recur in the Gospel. For example, Jesus is the light of the world (8:12) and the way, the truth, and the life (14:6).

Third, we can look at many of the ordinary words used in the hymn in a different way. Many of the everyday words are also religious words: God, word, life, light, darkness, world, his own. For example, various Gnostic systems of thought use "his own" as references to "the elite" or "enlightened," a usage quite different from that of the hymn. And these Gnostic systems, which despise material as evil, would never say that the Word became flesh and dwelt among believing men and women. Men and women of John's time could identify much of the language of his prologue as religious, but without faith it could not become their language.

Fourth, as Craig A. Evans (1993) has demonstrated and St. Bonaventure of Bagnoregio (1217–1274) saw over seven hundred years ago, the composer draws heavily upon Jewish tradition, especially language from its wisdom literature, whose key parallels I put into italics. For example, note how both Genesis and John begin with "In the beginning." And in Sirach 24:3, 8-9 Wisdom says this of herself: "*I came forth from the mouth of the Most High.* . . . My Creator said, '*Make your dwelling* in Jacob.'. . . Before the ages, *in the beginning*, he created me, and for all ages I shall not cease to be." Further, in Proverbs 8:22-23 Wisdom speaks thus: "The Lord created me *at the beginning* of his work, the first of his acts of long ago. Ages ago I was set up, *at the first*, before the beginning of the earth." Moreover, of Wisdom the book of Wisdom says: "For wisdom, *the fashioner of all things*, taught me. For she is a breath of the power of God, and a pure emanation of the glory of the Almighty . . . *she is a reflection of eternal light*, a spotless mirror of the working of God, and an image of his goodness" (7:22, 25-26). And it is also clear in these same wisdom traditions that not everyone accepts Lady Wisdom. Perhaps, this is described no more pithily than in Proverbs 8:34-35: "Happy is the one who listens to me, watching daily at my gates, waiting beside my doors. For whoever finds me finds life and obtains favor from the Lord; but those who miss me injure themselves; all who hate me love death." I think that it is clear how the image of Wisdom, who was with God at the beginning and who dwelt with God's chosen ones, flows behind our hymn. It is also clear that the rejection of wisdom for folly helps us to understand the rejection of the Word by his own. But it is also very clear that the hymn, while borrowing heavily from Jewish tradition, goes far beyond it, especially in declaring that God's revelation became flesh, dwelt among us in Jesus Messiah, who is the only Son of the Father. Can heirs of Jewish tradition move from their special language of Wisdom/Sophia as mediator of God's revelation to the composer's language of Jesus of Nazareth, God's Word, Son, and Anointed?

Finally, scholars as diverse as M.-É. Boismard (1993) and Norman R. Petersen (1993, 110–32) indicate that there is probably already in John's prologue a hint that Moses, although he mediated God's Law to God's people, did not see God. Believers in Jesus, God's Son, follow the one who has seen and been sent by the Father. In the Gospel Jesus' opponents identify themselves as "followers of Moses" (9:28) and may well represent the Jews in whose midst the Johannine community emerged and who subsequently expelled members of this Johannine community from their synagogue (see John 9:22; 12:42; 16:2).

As I stand back from my analysis of John 1:1-18, I realize that I am beginning a "performance tradition" of interpreting these verses as prayer. Some musicians may help us exegetes in seeing how these verses work as response to God's revelation. I think of the final section of Ralph Vaughan Williams's *Hodie*, where he uses verses from John 1:1-14 in his musical presentation of the meaning of Christmas. My confrere Robert M. Hutmacher has uncovered hymns that employ John's prologue. I mention the two most significant of these. The first two verses of John D. Becker's song "Alpha and Omega" pick up on John 1:1-3 and 1:18: "In the beginning was the Word, and through him all things came to be. And the Word was God. No man or woman has seen God. God's only Son, from God's right hand, has revealed God to us." And the first verse of the song "Christ Is the World's Light," with text from Fred Pratt Green, captures some of the themes from John 1:3-18: "Christ is the world's Light, he and none other. Born in our darkness, he became our Brother. If we have seen him, we have seen the Father. Glory to God on high." Perhaps, my readers know of other musical renditions that may help us exegetes establish a performance tradition of praying John's opening hymn as prayer.

In sum, the hymn's thematic of revelation and response appeals to those who pray this hymn in faith that they humble themselves before the revelation of God's Word made flesh and accept in joy and gratitude their new status as children of God. With this hymn still ringing in their ears, they are prepared to become lively participants in the story that follows. In and through this narrative the Son reveals his Father and draws men and women into the ranks of those who worship the Father in spirit and in truth.

HUMANITY'S QUEST FOR GOD AND
GOD'S QUEST FOR WORSHIPERS

I provide three guiding texts for this thematic. In John 4:23 Jesus tells the Samaritan woman, who has given up her quest for ordinary water and now seeks living water: "But the hour is coming, and is now here, when the true worshipers will worship the Father in spirit and truth, for *the Father seeks such as these to worship him.*" In John 6:44 Jesus tells those who are seeking life-giving bread: "No one can come to me unless *drawn by the Father* who sent me." Finally in John 12:32 Jesus responds to the request of the Greeks that they might see him: "And I, when I am lifted up from the earth, *will draw all people to myself.*" For me it is no exaggeration to say that John's Gospel is a story of quest: the Father's quest for men and women and humanity's quest for that which makes life and its fullness possible: water, bread, light, love, and God's Word.

And in my neck of the religious woods such human and divine questing resonates with people at the very deep level of communication with God. And whether John ever uses the terms "intercessory prayer" or "prayer of praise and gratitude" to denote these experiences of questing and being pursued, these experiences and John's references to them spell prayer with a capital P. I often hear people say that they feel that God is seeking them and calling them to a deeper prayer life. Or I hear people telling me that for years they tried to shut God out of their lives, but God kept knocking at their door, seeking them through dreams or in the words of friends, intruding into their consciousness when they thought they were most alone. Here is how Dorothy Day, Communist turned Christian and later cofounder of the Catholic Worker Movement, described her experience. She writes (1938, 8): "Through all my daily life, in those I came into contact with, in the things I read and heard, I felt that sense of being followed, of being desired; a sense of hope and expectation." And then there are those who perseveringly seek after God, trying to ascertain God's will. They pray and search with hearts restless for God.

A number of scholars have prompted me to investigate John's theme of human quest and divine pursuit. Raymond Collins (1976) first put me onto this train of thought with his study of "the representative figures" in the Fourth Gospel. Francis J. Moloney (1978; 1998) taught me to look closely at the Johannine characters who appear in and between the two signs in Cana of Galilee (2:1–4:54). L. William Countryman (1994, 139) has made the case that John's Gospel portrays "the believer's growth through a succession of stages: conversion, baptism, eucharist, enlightenment, new life, and union." But it is John Painter (1993; 1996) who has helped me most to see how various Johannine personages and signs function in John's tale of human and divine quests. I sample this thematic from three perspectives. First is the disciples' quest for Jesus in John 1:19-51. Next is Jesus' second sign in Cana of Galilee (John 4:43-54). I conclude with the figure of Nicodemus, who appears thrice (3:1-15; 7:50-52; 19:38-42). I remind my readers that the melody of the hymn of John 1:1-18 is still sounding: The Word of the Father seeks believers and wants to make them God's children and worshipers.

The Seeking of Jesus' First Disciples (John 1:19-51)

The Synoptic Gospels depict Jesus calling his first disciples. In Mark 1:16-20 Jesus calls Peter and Andrew, James and John: "Follow me and I will make you fish for people" (1:17). The two sets of brothers answer Jesus' call "immediately." In Luke 6:27-28 Jesus calls out to Levi, a tax collector, "Follow me." And Levi "got up, left everything, and followed" Jesus. Finally, Matthew 9:9 is streamlined and straightforward: "As Jesus was walking along, he saw a man called Matthew sitting at the tax booth; and he said to him, 'Follow me.' And he got up and followed him." To me Michelangelo da Caravaggio captured Matthew's amazingly direct story most powerfully in his extraordinary painting "The Conversion of St. Matthew."

These "call stories" in the first three Gospels predispose us readers of John's Gospel to think that the fourth evangelist will follow the same pattern: Jesus sees and calls, and the disciples follow. But a close reading of John 1:35-51 will reveal a different pattern. This pattern is that of seeking and finding. I will italicize the key words in my own rendition of John 1:37-39: "The two disciples heard John say this, and they *followed* Jesus. When Jesus turned and saw them following, he said to them: '*For what are you seeking?*' They said to him: 'Rabbi, *where are you staying?*' He said to them: 'Come and see.' They came and saw where he was staying, and *they remained with him* that day." This sequence seems so plain and ordinary as two disciples follow a new Rabbi to his place of study and teaching. However, as Raymond E. Brown (1966, 78–79), who was not easily given to spiritualizing exegesis, writes:

> Jesus' first words in the Fourth Gospel are a question he addresses to every one who would follow him. . . . This question touches on the basic need of man that causes him to turn to God. . . . Man wishes to stay . . . with God; he is constantly seeking to escape temporality, change, and death, seeking to find something that is lasting. Jesus answers with the all-embracing challenge to faith: "Come and see."

And John 1:40-51 is also informed with this pattern, as, for example, Andrew, now a follower of Rabbi Jesus, seeks after Peter, his brother, finds him, tells him that "we have found the Messiah," and brings him to Jesus, who gives him a new name.

In brief, John has transformed what may have been a traditional "call story" of Jesus' first disciples into a story of humankind's universal quest for a permanent dwelling with God. Also, it doesn't seem farfetched to suggest that in this passage John has put into his own theological language Jesus' directions on prayer that we treated in our last chapter: "Ask . . . seek . . . knock" (see Luke 11:9-10).

The Quest in the Second of Jesus' Signs (John 4:43-54)

Jesus' second sign at Cana in Galilee is doubly overshadowed by Jesus' first sign at Cana. His first sign there is unique in the evangelical tradition and deals with a marriage feast, Jesus' extraordinary encounter with his mother, and an abundance of unexpected and superb wine. Jesus' second sign is too similar to the accounts in Matthew 8:5-13 and Luke 7:1-10 to emerge from their shadows and shine on its own. Moreover, there is very little popular exegesis about this second sign. For example, the pilgrimage trade at Cana seems so taken up with promoting its local wine, which is far inferior to the 120 gallons of excellent wine that flowed at Jesus' word, that it gives nary a nod to Jesus' second sign at Cana. However impressive a healing at a distance may be, it can't be related to the common human experience of marriage nor can it be taken home as a souvenir for Aunt Maggie as a bottle of Cana wine can. As I bring John 4:43-54 out of the shadows, I am happily dependent on John Painter (1996) and glad to find that my earlier work (1990, 57–65) is still congenial.

The gentleman who is at center stage in this quest story is a

Galilean Jew who is an official in the employ of King Herod Antipas. In John 4:43-54 Galilee is mentioned six times to hammer home the point that this royal official is from Galilee. And from the dominant perspective of key characters in John's Gospel, to be from Galilee is to be marginalized. See John 7:41, where some of the crowd vehemently maintain that no Messiah can come from Galilee! And in John 7:52 leading Pharisees derogatorily reply to Nicodemus that no prophet can come from Galilee! And didn't Nathanael cast aspersions on Galilee earlier: "Can anything good come out of Nazareth?" (1:46). Such geographical marginalization is not unfamiliar to U.S. citizens. This southside Chicago native is reminded of how the lofty northsiders deride us. And now that I work in sparsely populated southwestern New York state I know firsthand that New York City slickers do not hold us as the apple of their eye. Will it surprise us that a marginalized person will be questing for life from Jesus and will not be deterred from his quest despite Jesus' rebuke in 4:48? But we are ahead of ourselves.

I paraphrase what Painter (1996, 357) has helpfully stated are the six elements in a quest story.

1. The quester makes a request, either explicitly or implicitly.
2. The quest dominates the story, and the quester is not merely a foil for Jesus.
3. The quester seeks something vital for human well-being. And in John something important at a physical level can become important for well-being at a deeper and spiritual level.
4. There is an objection or difficulty to be overcome, and this may redefine the quest's direction.
5. Jesus' pronouncement in a word or in an action is the key to the resolution of the quest.
6. The outcome of the quest is of crucial importance and must be mentioned in the quest story.

Let me correlate these six steps to the quest at hand. First, verses 43-46 set the stage for the Galilean royal official's request in verse 47 that Jesus come down to Capernaum and heal his son, who is near death. Second, it seems clear that the quest and the quester have leading roles in the story. Although Jesus is obviously the main character, without the royal official's request and quest there is no story. Third, rescue from death's door to life, while most welcome at the physical level, does not have its significance exhausted at that level. But to move from seeing Jesus as the giver of physical well-being to seeing him as the bestower of spiritual well-being takes faith. Surely, the objection found in verse 48 fits the fourth point, and it almost stops the quester in his tracks. But the quester faithfully persists and reveals that his son is young (verse 49). The fifth point of Jesus' pronouncement is so important that it is repeated thrice. "Go; your son will live" (verse 50) recurs in verse 53 and is at the base of the slaves' statement that "the child was alive" (verse 51). The evangelist mentions that the outcome of the quest, point six, took place on two levels. The quester had come to Jesus seeking life for his young little boy who was near death and had his request granted by Jesus' mere word. And in reality the quester also found life for himself, for that is what the reference to his belief in verse 53 means. In terms of the larger context of John's Gospel the outcast Galilean finds life in God's Word made flesh and professes that Jesus is his Savior and that of the whole world (see 4:42). He has faith to see through the "sign" (4:48) that Jesus is life and gives life. How many believers at John's time and our own find themselves on a similar quest?

Nicodemus Quests and Is Drawn
(John 3:1-15; 7:50-52; 19:38-42)

Nicodemus, a Pharisee and thus a member of the opponents in John's Gospel, has the rare distinction of appearing three times. His first appearance in 3:1-15 is his longest and is part of the sequence of stories of people seeking Jesus (2:1–4:54). This leader of the Jews comes to Jesus "at night" (3:2). Since we are already familiar with the hymn John used to begin his Gospel, we can easily recognize the allusion to 1:5-13. Will the Light of Jesus the Word be accepted by one of "his own," who comes to him in and out of the darkness? Before John uses Nicodemus's misunderstanding of the meaning of rebirth as a springboard for his teaching (3:3-15), he makes it clear that there is some incipient faith in Nicodemus and that his search is authentic: "Rabbi, we know that you are a teacher who has come from God, for no one can do these signs that you do apart from the presence of God" (3:2).

In the section that John largely devotes to Jesus' replacement of the feasts of the Jews (chapters 5–12), Nicodemus appears again. The passage is so short that it might be missed: "Nicodemus, who had gone to Jesus before, and who was one of the Pharisees, asked, 'Our law does not judge people without first giving them a hearing to find out what they are doing, does it?' They replied, 'Surely you are not also from

Galilee, are you? Search and you will see that no prophet is to arise from Galilee" (7:50-52). Has Nicodemus become a disciple of Jesus? Hardly. Is he still on the quest, searching for the true meaning of Jesus? Indeed, for his good heart wants justice and fairness for Jesus.

John's third and final reference to Nicodemus is unique in the Gospel tradition, for he appears, along with the familiar Joseph of Arimathea, to bury Jesus. I quote:

> Nicodemus, who had at first come to Jesus by night, also came with Joseph of Arimathea, bringing a mixture of myrrh and aloes, weighing about a hundred pounds. They took the body of Jesus and wrapped it with the spices in linen cloths, according to the burial custom of the Jews. Now there was a garden in the place where he was crucified, and in the garden there was a new tomb . . . and they laid Jesus there. (19:39-42)

To me the key verse for the interpretation of this passage from the thematic of questing is John 12:32: Jesus says: "And I, when I am lifted up from the earth, will draw all people to myself." Now Jesus has been lifted in the exaltation of his death, resurrection, and ascension and draws all to himself in the person of Nicodemus, one of the Pharisees and the marginalizers of the people of the land. I know that there are scholarly voices contrary to this opinion and refer readers, who want to sample the friendly opposition, to Jouette M. Bassler (1989) and Paul D. Duke (1985, 110). But I am still convinced of this viewpoint that I articulated earlier (1990, 96–101) and find great comfort that the magisterial Johannine commentator Raymond E. Brown (1994, 1268) is of the same opinion. He writes: "In 19:38-42 Joseph and Nicodemus have gained the courage to glorify Jesus publicly by a regal gift of spices and by the place in which they bury him. This is the fulfillment of Jesus' own words: 'When I am lifted up from the earth, *I shall draw all to myself'*" (12:31-34).

In summary, the figure of Nicodemus, who is given billing in major sections of John's Gospel, stands not only as quester but also as one who is ultimately drawn by Jesus. His persistent quest is a source of encouragement to all who are in pursuit of God's Word, and Jesus' drawing of him is a wellspring of hope.

I can provide no better conclusion to this section on questing for God than to quote John Painter (1996, 364), whose insights started me off on my search: "The diversity of questers seeking Jesus, as portrayed in John (the Baptist, disciples of the Baptist and their associates, the mother of Jesus, Nicodemus, a Pharisee, a ruler, Samaritans, a nobleman, a Galilean crowd, Mary and Martha, Greeks, and Mary Magdalene), reveals the universality of the quest: that all are questers, until they come to Jesus."

JESUS, GLORIFIED WORD OF GOD, TRANSFORMS JEWISH FEASTS

In any careful reading of the Fourth Gospel one begins to notice that the evangelist is exalting Jesus over various Jewish religious practices. Already in John 1:14 we read that the Word dwelt or set up his tabernacle among us. In the course of performing his first sign Jesus replaced the water in the six stone jars, set aside for Jewish rites of purification, with the abundant and best wine of Messianic fulfillment (2:1-11). When Jesus is in Jerusalem for Passover early on in his public ministry, he declares that his risen and glorified body is the new Temple (2:13-22). As we have seen earlier, Jesus tells the questing Samaritan woman that true worship will not take place on either the Samaritan or Jewish mountain, for the Father desires those who will worship him in spirit and in truth (4:21-24). That is, true worship occurs through the Spirit sent from the Father, who reveals the inner meaning of the truth that the Word revealed and is.

Gale A. Yee (1989) and R. Alan Culpepper (1998, 148–96) are among many interpreters who rightly contend that the final chapters of John's Book of Signs show how Jesus replaces the Jewish feasts. See also Charles H. Talbert (1993). As Culpepper (1998, 148) observes: "John 5–12 is marked by cycles of increasing hostility against Jesus set in the context of Jewish festivals. . . . At each festival Jesus does or says things that show that he is the fulfillment of what the festival celebrates." Thus, John 5:1 mentions "an unnamed festival," and the signs that take place in that chapter and in chapter 9 occur on a "sabbath," a day on which Jesus, like his Father, continues to give life (5:21). Chapter 6, which deals with the bread of life, occurs at the time of Passover (6:4), which commemorates, among other events, God's gift of manna in the desert. Chapters 7–8 are largely taken up with water and light themes from the harvest feast of Tabernacles/Booths (7:2). In this context Jesus cries out: "Let anyone who is thirsty come to me, and let the one who believes in me drink" (7:37-38). And in 8:12 he proclaims: "I am the light of the world. Whoever follows me will never walk in darkness, but will have the light of life." John 10:22 mentions the feast of Dedication of the Temple, which supplies the background for the teaching of God's Son "whom the Father has sanctified and sent into the world" (10:36). And John 12:1 indicates that the festival of Passover, or liberation from slavery, has rolled around again. Finally, it doesn't seem coincidental that the crucified Jesus, whom John had earlier declared to be the Lamb of God who takes away the sins of the world (1:29), dies when the Passover lambs are being slaughtered in the Temple.

What sense are we to make of this vast array of worship materials? What do they contribute to prayer and worship, the themes of this chapter? One important way to see their contribution is to locate them in the years after the physical destruction of the Jerusalem Temple in A.D. 70, when both Jews who believed in Jesus and those who did not were trying to continue their heritage of worship. We can define this situation further and view John 9:22, 12:42, and 16:2 as indications of the Jewish Christian plight of being cast out of their home in the Jewish synagogue for professing faith in Jesus and for compromising the traditional standards of election by welcoming into their midst the poor, Samaritans, Galileans, the physically disabled, those ignorant of the Law, and women. To me this tumultuous situation, where the combatants were acculturated to use sharp polemic, is reflected in John 5–12, where the motif of Jesus' replacement of Jewish festivals marches to a song that has biting and bitter words. I probe John 6:31-59 as a door to this situation and for the insights it may give us about what went on during a Jewish Christian worship service in the Johannine tradition.

As we saw above, what has come to be called John's treatment of the bread of life occurs when the Jewish feast of Passover was near (6:4). Moreover, the entire sequence from 6:31-59 is in reality an elaborate interpretation and polemical counter-interpretation of Exodus 16:15: "He gave them bread from heaven to eat" (6:31). Verses 32-34 interpret the first words of this quotation and change the subject and the tense of the verb, thus making it very clear that it is not Moses who gave the bread from heaven (manna), but it is Jesus' *Father* who *gives* the true bread from heaven for the life of the world. In 6:35-50 there is a lengthy exegesis of the meaning of "bread from heaven." In this section two points especially stand out. First, Jesus, God's bread as Wisdom, contrasts himself with God's bread, given to Moses, as the wisdom of the Law. See, for example, 6:35: "I am the bread of life. Whoever comes to me will never be hungry, and whoever believes in me will never thirst." Second, already in this section there are references to the

Eucharist, which is the dominant theme of 6:50-58. Note that in the verse I just quoted (6:35) there is reference to eating and drinking. So while being the bread from heaven as the Father's Word, Jesus is also bread at the Eucharist for those who believe in him. John 6:50-58 interpret the verb "to eat" in the passage "He gave them bread from heaven to eat." Verse 50 is a Janus-like verse that looks back to 6:35-49 and ahead to 6:51-58. But more important than this literary observation is the notion that verse 50 contains the Johannine form of "the words of institution": "And the bread that I will give for the life of the world is my flesh." Readers will recall that unlike the Synoptic Gospels John's version of Jesus' last hours has no account of his institution of the Eucharist. He puts his eucharistic formula here in a major division of his Gospel where he is depicting Jesus as the replacement of Jewish feasts. He puts it here where he is pitting Moses over against Jesus. He puts it here where he teaches that Jesus is not only Wisdom for his community, but also eucharistic food and drink for those who believe in him. And in 6:59, a verse that we can easily skip over, the evangelist says that Jesus' discourse on the bread of life occurred in the synagogue. This is not just any synagogue, but the one from which members of the Johannine community were cast out for their beliefs in Jesus, God's Word and Bread. It is also the synagogue in which they are worshiping now, reinterpreting the Scriptures in the light of Jesus, Glorified Word of God, singing hymns confessing their faith in the Word made flesh, and celebrating the Word's gift of his body and blood for the life of the world.

Let me make two quick points before we leave this thematic. For those readers who thought they heard echoes in John 6:31-59 from John's opening hymn, especially from John 1:14-18, your hearing is marvelous. God's gift of the Law to Moses has been surpassed in Jesus, who is the world's bread for life. Second, the fact that John presents Jesus as replacing the Jewish festivals should not lead us to think that he has thrown his Jewish heritage completely overboard. As we saw, he cherishes the Scriptures and plumbs traditional Jewish feasts to their core meaning and then reinterprets them by the Word, who is life, bread, water, light, and ultimate consecration to God. And this Word dwelt and dwells among us. Finally, he has not forgotten the Jewish religious norm of giving alms to the poor (John 12:5-8; 13:29). On this latter point, in the context of the larger thematic of the marginalized in John's Gospel, see R. Alan Culpepper (1998, 295–98).

PRAYER IN JESUS' NAME (JOHN 14:13-14; 15:7, 16; 16:23-27; 1 JOHN 3:22; 5:14-17)

John 13–17 contains Jesus' last will and testament to his disciples. Although Jesus will depart from them, he will still be present to them in the love they show to one another, through the gift of another intercessor, the Holy Spirit, through their bearing much missionary fruit, through his indwelling in their hearts, and through prayer in his name. From these various ways of Jesus' continued presence I select "prayer in his name." After discussing this promise, I will explore its thematic cousin in 1 John. In a subsequent major section I will focus on the last chapter of John's farewell discourse.

It seems worthwhile to quote the passages on prayer in Jesus' name, so that we can see how similar they are and recognize that they occur throughout John 14–16.

John 14:13-14: "I will do whatever you ask in my name, so that the Father may be glorified in the Son. If you ask me for anything in my name, I will do it."

John 15:7: "If you abide in me and my words abide in you, ask for whatever you wish, and it will be done for you."

John 15:16: "And I appointed you to go and bear fruit, fruit that will last, so that the Father will give you whatever you ask him in my name."

John 16:23-27: "On that day you will ask nothing of me. Very truly, I tell you, if you ask anything of the Father in my name, he will give it to you. Until now you have not asked for anything in my name. Ask and you will receive, so that your joy may be complete. . . . On that day you will ask in my name. I do not say to you that I will ask the Father on your behalf; for the Father himself loves you, because you have loved me and have believed that I came from God."

Let me make five observations about these passages and then illustrate them from Jewish tradition. First, notice the future tenses of the verbs, for example, "The Father will give you" (15:16). Jesus is talking about the future, but from the perspective of the evangelist this future has already arrived. Second, the word "name" in the phrase "in my name" refers to the reality of Jesus, that is, his power and relationship to the Father and now to his disciples. Put differently, the disciples are not praying as if their own persons and powers would bring about the object of their prayer. Third and closely related to number two, the image of Jesus the vine and the disciples as the branches conveys the intimacy of the disciples with Jesus and also their dependence on him (see 15:1-17). When they pray in Jesus' name, they are abiding in him as branches on the vine. Fourth, the relationship that the Son enjoys with his Father determines the flow of the disciples' prayer. They pray to the Father through the Son, and the Father grants the petitions. As Oscar Cullmann (1995, 111) says so well: "The way to the goal of any prayer, encounter with God, is opened to us through Jesus, the incarnate one, in whom God turns towards humankind." In a fifth point I highlight what is explicit in John 15:7 and implicit in the other passages: prayer must be in conformity with God's will and commandments.

I have found that a helpful way to approach these passages is to link them to the Jewish tradition that celebrates individuals who have intercessory power. In his commentary on 1 John, Hans-Josef Klauck (1991, 103, 327) presents many passages from this tradition. I take as my key passage one from a document contemporary with John's Gospel. In *4 Ezra* 7:102-115 prophet Ezra enumerates Abraham, Moses, Joshua, Samuel, David, Solomon, Elijah, and Hezekiah as powerful intercessors with God. To these names I would add Amos (Amos 7:1-6), Jeremiah (Jeremiah 37:3; 42:2), Isaiah (2 Kings 19:4), and the Maccabean martyrs (2 Maccabees 7:37-38; 4 Maccabees 6:28-29; 17:21-22). These individuals are the righteous who have prayed for the ungodly. They are the strong who have prayed for the weak. And God heard their prayer. This Jewish tradition seems echoed in the statement of the man born blind, who now sees physically because of Jesus and is coming to deeper insight into who Jesus is: "We know that God does not hear sinners, but does listen to one who worships him and obeys his will" (John 9:31).

With this Jewish tradition in mind I interpret the Johannine passages on prayer in Jesus' name in this way. God hears the prayers of those who believe in Jesus not because they are righteous nor because they are strong, but because they are united to Jesus, the vine, who has revealed the Father to them. Further, the passages in John 14–16 are not concerned with outstanding individuals interceding with the Father as is the case with patriarch Abraham or prophet Isaiah. Rather it is the community that intercedes. Moreover, the individuals who form the community may not have particular strengths of character like the Maccabean martyrs or leadership abilities like Moses, David, and Solomon. Nevertheless, they, too, have the power of intercessory prayer in Jesus' name.

Now that we have this background in mind, I think it will be somewhat easier to interpret the prayer passages in 1 John 3:21-22 and 5:14-17, which are cousins of those in John 14–16. The author of 1 John has at least a dual purpose. On the one hand, he is seriously warning his community about the dangers those who have seceded from them are posing to their faith in Jesus the incarnate Word. On the other hand, he is comforting them with the reality of their communion together and with the Father and with his Son Jesus Christ (see 1:3). And he reminds them: "If anyone does sin, we have an intercessor with the Father, Jesus Christ the righteous. And he is the atoning sacrifice for our sins, and not only for ours, but also for the sins of the whole world" (2:1-2). In 3:21-22 he focuses on the community's boldness in prayer: "Beloved, if our hearts do not condemn us, we have boldness before God. And we receive from God whatever we ask, because we obey his commandments and do what is pleasing to him." These verses resonate with those from John 14–16, especially as they exude confidence in God and show that the petitioning community lives in accord with God's will. But the new factor is the dimension of "sin": Believers can pray with boldness before God provided that they do not have sin in their hearts to condemn them.

1 John 5:14-17 make specific and present what the prayer passages in John's Farewell Discourse described in general and as future. That is, the community prays now in the present for those in its midst who have sinned, but not committed a sin until death. It is the common opinion among exegetes that "the sin unto death," mentioned in verse 16, is hatred of the brothers and sisters (3:15) and denial that Jesus Christ has come in the flesh (4:2-3). I quote David M. Scholer (1975, 246) as a representative of this exegetical consensus: "There is, of course, sin which *does* preclude membership in the believing community (i.e. murder = hatred of believers and lying = denial of Jesus); it is sin in the realm of death." So in 5:14-17 the author concludes his warning about the secessionists. And at the same time he takes his general teaching about the power of the community's prayer in accordance with God's will and makes it specific by applying it to the concrete situation of sin in the community. He comforts his community with their power of intercession for brothers and sisters who remain in the community but have committed sins that are not deadly. He writes: "If you see your brother or sister committing a sin which is not deadly,

you will ask, and God will give life to such a person" (5:16). In this context I remind my readers of the Jewish tradition of intercessors I referred to above. Most of the powerful Jewish intercessors, such as Abraham and the Maccabean martyrs, prayed for sinners. The entire Johannine community, and not just some extraordinarily blessed or talented individuals, continues in their intercessory footsteps.

I conclude my brief observations on prayer in Jesus' name with a hypothesis. From what we have seen so far about worship and prayer in John's writings I am of the opinion that community worship in John's community included the following components: singing of their lodestar hymn (John 1:1-18); interpretation of Scripture according to their belief in Jesus Messiah, Son of God; Eucharist; preaching, which may be the source of Jesus' extended discourses in the Gospel; prayers in Jesus' name for various needs and persons; and prayers for life/forgiveness for those who have sinned but have not sinned unto death. It would satisfy my curiosity immeasurably to find rituals from John's community's worship service and to see in particular how they went about detecting those who had sinned a nondeadly sin and how they prayed for that individual. But alas my prayers for this intention do not seem to be in accord with God's will and have not been granted. In any case, during our final chapter, which will deal primarily with James 5:13-18, we will return to the power of the community's prayer for sinners. But now we must give some consideration to Jesus' extended prayer in the last chapter of his Farewell Discourse.

JESUS' REVELATION AS PRAYER IN JOHN 17

In this section I will first make some literary observations about the twenty-six verses that constitute Jesus' prayer and then make some general comments. I draw inspiration partly from Ernst Käsemann (1968, 5), who has reminded me that Jesus' prayer here is not really a supplication but revelation to and instruction for his disciples. He writes: "This is not a supplication, but a proclamation directed to the Father in such manner that his disciples can hear it also. The speaker is not a needy petitioner but the divine revealer and therefore the prayer moves over into being an address, admonition, consolation and prophecy." And Gérard Rossé (1988, 159–60) has taught me to look deeply into the reasons why the evangelist uses a prayer for Jesus' final discourse and revelation: "The community must not lose sight of the reality that its own life and proper identity are a gift from God. . . . The prayer, therefore, orients believers towards God and invites them to find in God insight into their own identity. And because John 17 is a prayer *of Jesus* (and not of the disciples), it is to be understood that it will be heard. For 'I knew that you always hear me' (John 11:42)."

My first literary observation directs our attention back to the very first section of this chapter, for a good case can be made that Jesus' prayer in John 17 forms a literary inclusion with the prayer of John 1:1-18. Here is the evidence for my position. These two prayers have expressions in common that are found nowhere else in John's Gospel. "Jesus Christ" occurs only in John 1:17 and 17:3. "The world did not know" occurs only in John 1:10 and 17:15. The expressions "before the world existed" (17:5) and "before the foundation of the world" (17:24) are synonymous with the statements, "he was in the beginning with God" (1:2) and "because he was before me" (1:15). And these expressions and statements only occur in these two prayers. While it is common Johannine coin that the world opposes God's revelation, there is a high concentration of this thematic in these two prayers (1:10-13; 17:9-16). Further, both are programmatic prayers. John's Prologue sets the prayerful and faith-filled mode in which the rest of the Gospel is to be read and provides an advance summary of its contents. John 17 is Jesus' prayer as he looks back over his ministry, prays for his own, and prays for those who will come to believe because of his disciples' missionary activity. Finally, both are prayers of the community. Surely, John 1:1-18 comes from the community. And as Marie-Eloise Rosenblatt (1988), among others, has indicated, Jesus' prayer in John 17 is not his own, but that of the community who reflects back upon his revelation and prays for the future through his voice.

If what I am saying about John 17 as an inclusion is true, then this prayer casts thematic light back on previous chapters. Its function would be similar to that of the inclusion of Jesus' second sign at Cana in Galilee (4:43-54) that shed its spotlight back through prior episodes to Jesus' first sign at Cana in Galilee (2:1-11) and brightly illumined other characters such as Nicodemus and the Samaritan woman who, like the Galilean royal official, were also in pursuit of Jesus and his gifts of life. I suggest that the thematic light that John 17 shines back upon Jesus' ministry can be seen specially in two places: (1) in verses 4, 6-8, 25, and (2) in verse 19. John 17:6 sums up well the meaning of the first set of verses : "I have made your name known to those whom you gave me from the world. They were yours, and you gave them to me." While the primary focus of this verse may be Jesus' disciples, it also refers to those who were questing after Jesus and were being drawn and given to him by the Father. The other key verse is John 17:19; it reads: "And for their sakes I make myself holy, so that they also may be made holy in truth." There is no doubt that the designation of John 17 as Jesus' "high priestly" prayer stems from verse 19. This designation helps us to see how Jesus' prayer relates back to the earlier theme of Jesus as the replacement of Jewish feasts. Through Jesus, and not through feasts commemorating God's gift of manna or life-giving water for the harvest, believers approach the Father as the giver of life. In this connection Francis J. Moloney (1998, 468–69) is absolutely right in not tying holiness to festivals and sacrifice, but to conformity with the will of the holy God and Father and to separation from the world. Moloney (1998, 469) writes of Jesus: "Addressing God in the presence of the disciples, he commits himself to a final act of holiness for their sake (*hyper auton*), so that in his total self-gift, making known the love of God, he makes known to them the holiness that must be theirs (v. 19)." Although Rudolf Bultmann (1971, 489) did not think that John 17 made sense at the end of the Farewell Discourse and placed it after 13:1-30, it makes eminent sense to me where it is as an inclusion to the prayer with which the evangelist commenced his Gospel and as a summary of the themes on prayer and worship contained in 1:19–12:50. I ask my readers to accept my position as sensible.

My second literary observation deals with the structure of John 17. Rossé (1988, 44–62, 182–88) has detailed various attempts to analyze the structure of Jesus' prayer. I offer his own analysis (1988, 156) as a starting point for my subsequent discussion.

Verses 1-5 situate the prayer at *the* hour and under the thematic of the glorification of Father and Son.

Verses 6-11a are transitional. Verses 6-8 make explicit the content of Jesus' ministry, which was merely alluded to in verse 4. And verses 9-11a prepare for the prayer proper by presenting the situation of the community within the world.

Verses 11b-23 constitute the heart of the prayer. Verse 11b presents the theme: "*Holy* Father, *protect* them in your name that you have given me, so that *they may be one* as we are one." The depths of this theme are plumbed in verses 12-16 (protect), verses 17-19 (make holy), and verses 20-23 (may be one).

Verses 24-26 form a double conclusion. Verse 24 functions as an inclusion with verses 1-5, especially verse 5, and brings out the transcendent nature of the community. Verses 25-26 resume verses 6-11, 20-23 and put the entire prayer under the banner of the love of the Father and the presence of Christ.

While we might quibble with some aspects of Rossé's structural analysis, for example, seeing verses 6-11a as transitional, I believe that he is fundamentally correct in seeing John 17:11b-23 as the heart of Jesus' prayer. Notice that four times in this section the evangelist describes Jesus praying: "Protect them" (17:11); "I ask you to protect them from the evil one" (17:15); "Make them holy in the truth" (17:17); "I ask not only on behalf of these, but also on behalf of those who will believe in me through their world, that they may all be one" (17:20-21). On these notions of protection, holiness, and oneness I make the following brief commentary, drawing freely on the previous insights of Käsemann and Rossé.

It seems to me that one of the foremost messages for the community who listens in on Jesus' core prayer is that of consolation, for Jesus prays for their protection from the world and from the evil one (17:14-15). If there is an echo here from the "deliver us from evil" petition of the Lord's Prayer, it has been rephrased in John's dualistic thought that the world is opposed to God's revelation. And John 16:2, in the immediate context of John 17, makes John's general dualistic thought much more specific. In the Johannine community's continuation of Jesus' mission it, too, will be hated: "They will put you out of the synagogues. Indeed, an hour is coming when those who kill you will think that by doing so they are offering worship to God."

While there is consolation present in Jesus' second petition, there is also considerable challenge and admonition in it for his disciples: "Make them holy in the truth. Your word is truth. As you have sent me into the world, so have I sent them into the world" (17:17-18). As I insisted above in my quotation from Francis J. Moloney on Jesus' holiness, we are moving in a universe of discourse different from the common one about what constitutes holiness. Sacrifice and ritual purification do not remove the filth that separates us from God. Holiness comes from God and God's revelation and doing God's will. The Father's gift of the communication of his will in his Word is the communication of his "truth." And just as the Father sent his Son into the world that was turned against him, so too does the Son send his disciples into that same world to communicate his gift of life and light, water and bread.

Jesus' third petition is perhaps the most profound and has been adopted by ecumenical movements throughout the world: "I ask not only on behalf of these, but also on behalf of those who will believe in me through their word, that they may all be one. As you, Father, are in me, and I am in you, may they also be in us, so that the world may believe that you sent me" (17:20-21). I make two points. First, John's Gospel, unlike the Synoptic Gospels, does not depict Jesus sending forth his twelve apostles (see Mark 6:7-13) or seventy-two disciples (see Luke 10:1-12) on mission. Granted there are some glimpses of the community's future mission in the Book of Signs, for example, 4:34-38; 10:16; 12:20-23, it is only in the Book of Glory that missionary work comes to the fore. See John 15:16–16:11 and especially 20:21. Now in his final petition Jesus, Son of God, prays explicitly for the missionary work of his disciples and for those whom they will lead to belief in "the only true God and Jesus Christ whom you have sent" (17:3). In this regard Käsemann is right to call John 17 prophecy.

Second, and as Rossé rightly notes, Jesus' third petition reveals the gift nature and the profundity of the community's identity. It is one because and as the Father and Son are one. While the community may mistakenly seek unity through bureaucracy and edict, in its heart of hearts it acknowledges that its unity is a gift to be gratefully accepted and a challenge to be met daily. Furthermore, the community's unity becomes witness to the world as the repetition in 17:21 and 23 stresses: "so that the world may believe that you have sent me." And if the community is to live the unity of Father and Son, its mission is to continue the works that Jesus, in union with his Father, performed (see 14:12), and to be water, bread, light, and life for the world and especially for its marginalized.

In summary, Jesus' high priestly prayer bids us readers to look back over Jesus' ministry and to see how the Word of God has sought and succeeded in gaining worshipers for his Father. It points us ahead, as it presents admonition and consolation for the future. It admonishes believers that the world is turned against them just as it was turned against the Word. Consolation comes to disciples who believe that God always hears Jesus' prayer and that consequently the Father of Jesus will protect them, make them holy, and keep them one as they are sent forth into the world. In the words that Jesus spoke right before this prayer: "Take courage. I have conquered the world" (16:33).

Jesus' Last Words from the Cross
(John 19:28-30)

I provide my own translation of these key verses: "After this Jesus, knowing that all was now finished, in order that the Scripture be fulfilled, says: 'I thirst.' There was a vessel there filled with water laced with vinegar. So having placed a sponge filled with the water laced with vinegar on a hyssop branch, they brought it to his mouth. When he had taken the water laced with vinegar, Jesus said: 'It is finished.'"

First, in dependence on R. Alan Culpepper (1998, 228–38) I want to view these verses in their context of John's version of Jesus' crucifixion. Second, I will interpret these verses in the context of the thematic I have been developing in this chapter and make explicit what is often left implicit by the commentators. That is, Jesus' last words contain a prayer.

It is our common human tendency to homogenize the account of Jesus' passion contained in the four Gospels to the point that we have difficulty identifying what comes from what Gospel. To simplify matters, allow me to compare the passion account of Luke, whose Gospel was featured in our last chapter, with that of John. Let me describe their differences in two waves. In the first wave we find that in Luke's account Simon of Cyrene helps Jesus carry his cross. In John, Jesus carries his own cross. In Luke, Jesus is mocked thrice on the cross. In John there is no mockery. Luke conveys much of his theology of God's mercy to sinners through his account of the "good thief." In John's Gospel the two others, crucified with Jesus, are not identified as criminals nor do they talk. Luke describes darkness at Jesus' crucifixion. John does not. In John there is no rending of the veil of the Temple. In Luke there is. In Luke the centurion confesses that Jesus was truly a righteous and innocent person. In John there is no centurion and consequently no confession.

A second wave of differences between the accounts of Jesus' passion found in Luke and John has these elements which are arguably symbolic. Only John mentions Jesus' seamless tunic that was woven from the top (19:23-24). In the interpretation of Culpepper (1998, 232): "Metaphorically, through the description of the seamless tunic, John ties the death of Jesus to the theme of unity. When he draws all people to himself, he draws them into one body, one communion." My readers might also want to refer to the "unbroken net" of 21:11. Moreover, only John mentions that Jesus' mother and the beloved disciple were present at the cross (19:25-27). And through his words to them Jesus constitutes a new family of mother and son, which is the beginning of the community of believers. Only in John is Jesus given a drink of water laced with vinegar on a hyssop branch. I will have more to say about that hyssop branch subsequently, but it directs the readers' attention to Passover. Due to its chronology John's Gospel is the only one that implies that Jesus dies at the same time that the lambs were being slaughtered in the Temple for Passover. Jesus' last words are not the Lukan "Father, forgive them, for they know not what they are doing" and "Father, into your hands I commend my spirit." Rather as we saw above, they are: "I thirst" and "It is finished." To these last words we will return shortly. Only in John is it said that Jesus' side is pierced with a lance and that from his pierced side blood and water flowed. The symbolic reference is to the life-giving power of blood and water, now released through Jesus' death. Finally, only in John does the author mention that the soldiers did not break Jesus' legs and thus fulfilled Scripture. One likely candidate for the Scripture to which the author refers is Exodus 12:46 and its description of the Passover lamb: "You shall not break any of its bones."

As we move to our second point, I suggest that the two waves of material I have just presented should alert us to at least two things. John's presentation is rather unique and operates on a symbolic level that takes the literal meaning, for example, of a seamless tunic, to another, deeper level. In applying these insights to John 19:28-30, I underscore three points about verse 28. From his giving himself over to the soldiers in the garden, through his sovereign trial and carrying of his own cross Jesus has shown that he is in command. The words "knowing that all was now finished" indicate that Jesus, the Good Shepherd, is about to hand over his life on his own accord. Despite what his crucifixion might indicate, he is not forced to do anything, but gives his life freely. Second, while all the evidence points to the fact that a crucified person in Palestine at the time of Passover would be thirsty, Jesus' words, "I thirst," go beyond their literal meaning. In John's Gospel terms such as "food," "hunger," "eat," "drink," and "thirst" are carriers of deeper meaning. Recall the role that water played in Jesus' conversation with the Samaritan woman in 4:4-42. In 4:14 Jesus says: "Those who drink of the water that I will give them will never be thirsty." And in this same story Jesus responds to his disciples, who have returned from town with food that they offer to him:

"My food is to do the will of him who sent me and to finish his work" (4:34). And from an earlier discussion I recall Jesus' words about bread and drink: "I am the bread of life. Whoever comes to me will never be hungry, and whoever believes in me will never be thirsty" (6:35). Jesus' words as Wisdom are food and drink for hungry and thirsty men and women. But perhaps the closest passage to Jesus' words in 19:28 are Jesus' words in 18:11: "Am I not to drink the cup that the Father has given me?" Jesus thirsts to do the Father's will and to finish the work the Father has given him. Just as a person needs drink to sustain life, so too does Jesus need obedience to and communion with his Father to sustain his life and his life's work. Jesus is needy to do the Father's will.

Finally, there is a passage of Scripture behind Jesus' "I thirst." L. Th. Witkamp (1996) sees Psalm 69:21 fulfilled in Jesus' thirst and the giving of water laced with vinegar: "For my thirst they gave me to drink water laced with vinegar." By alluding to this psalm text, John assimilates it into his own text and context. What may have been a real physical thirst in the situation envisioned in Psalm 69:21 is now a symbolic thirst: the thirst to do God's will to its nth degree and to drink the cup the Father has set out for him. As Witkamp (1996, 509) writes: "If we read the words of the psalm in the context of John's own use of the metaphors of eating food and drinking water, we seem to have no option left except to interpret the word *I thirst* not in a literal sense as the context of Psalm 69 itself would suggest but in a spiritual sense as Jesus' thirst to drink the cup the Father has given to him—that is, to complete the Father's work in laying down his life and to return to his sender." If Psalm 69:21 is indeed the reference point or even if Psalm 22:16 is as Raymond E. Brown (1994, 1069–78) argues, Jesus is depicted as dying with a prayer on his lips. Indeed, it is a prayer of just one word in Greek, but it says so much. And it is perhaps the one prayer of the Johannine Jesus with which his disciples can most easily identify. Jesus is resolute to the end to his Father's will in freely laying down his life for his sheep (10:17-18) and in giving an example to his disciples of selfless service until death (13:1-20).

From John 19:29 I single out the "hyssop branch." Commentators are almost unanimous in pointing out that the weak hyssop branch could not support a sponge soaked in water. And many commentators look for another, deeper level of meaning. John's use of symbolism previously in his Gospel and in his passion account and his play on the theme of Passover throughout his Gospel lead many interpreters to see Exodus 12:22 as background for the mention of hyssop in John 19:29:

"Take a bunch of hyssop, dip it in the blood [of the slaughtered Passover lamb] that is in the basin, and touch the lintel and the two doorposts with the blood in the basin." Jesus, the lamb of God who takes away the sin of the world (1:29), sheds his blood which preserves his own from woe just as the blood on the hyssop branch preserved the Israelites from woe of old. And in terms of our thematic, Jesus thereby fulfills the inner meaning of liberation and salvation celebrated in the feast of Passover.

Jesus' final words, "It is finished," in 19:30 recall a host of themes in John's Gospel. From those I have not mentioned so far, I single out the following. John 13:1 speaks of Jesus' enduring love for his disciples: "Now before the feast of the Passover, Jesus knew that his hour had come to depart from this world and go to the Father. Having loved his own who were in the world, he loved them to the end." Jesus has completed his work as the incarnate Word to reveal his Father (1:18). Lifted up on the cross, Jesus now draws all people to himself (3:14; 8:28; 12:32). He has completed his work of showing forth the glory of God through signs and works, words and discourses, and loving death for others (13:31-32).

CONCLUSION

In many ways John's Gospel presents Jesus as the Son of God striding across the face of the earth, almost untouched by human concerns. Sure, we find some passages like his weeping over Lazarus's death that graphically show his humanity. With such a high Christology we would not expect the fourth evangelist to dwell long on Jesus' prayer life. Rather the evangelist underlines the Revealer's otherness and our human dependence. Jesus is word, light, life, water, bread, resurrection, and truth, holding out to women and men what they need for authentic life. But at the same time the evangelist stresses God's search for men and women through the Word and their search for God. I have dwelt much on these aspects of John's theology and Christology, for they are the basis for Christian prayer and worship in the Johannine community.

Recently a colleague, knowing that I am fond of mystery stories, put me on to Henning Mankell's *The White Lioness.* It didn't take me long to realize that the Swedish detective inspector Kurt Wallander was not only searching for clues to solve a murder but was also questing for the meaning of life. The author had dropped too many clues along the way for me to think that he was telling his story on one level only. In this chapter I have followed many of the clues that the fourth evangelist has given us about the meaning of life in the Word. Hopefully I have rephrased these clues, especially those concerning "prayer and worship," in such a manner that they will aid my readers along the way to the truth that is Jesus, God's Word.

FOR FURTHER READING

Brown, Raymond E. 1998. *A Retreat with John the Evangelist: That You May Have Life*. Cincinnati: St. Anthony Messenger Press.

Countryman, L. William. 1994. *The Mystical Way in the Fourth Gospel: Crossing Over into God*. Rev. ed. Valley Forge, Pa.: Trinity Press International.

Cullmann, Oscar. 1995. *Prayer in the New Testament*. Overtures to Biblical Theology. Minneapolis: Fortress.

———. 1995. *Prayer in the New Testament*, 89–111. Overtures to Biblical Theology. Minneapolis: Fortress.

Culpepper, R. Alan. 1981. "The Pivot of John's Prologue." *New Testament Studies* 27: 1–31.

———. 1998. *The Gospels and Letters of John*. Interpreting Biblical Texts. Nashville: Abingdon.

Dowd, Sharyn E. 1993. "Toward a Johannine Theology of Prayer." In *Perspectives on John: Method and Interpretation in the Fourth Gospel*, 317–35. Ed. Robert B. Sloan and Mikeal C. Parsons. The National Association of Baptist Professors of Religion Special Studies Series 11. Lewiston, New York: Edwin Mellen.

Karris, Robert J. 1990. *Jesus and the Marginalized in John's Gospel*. Zacchaeus Studies: New Testament. Collegeville, Minn.: Liturgical Press.

Klauck, Hans-Josef. 1991. *Der erste Johannesbrief*. Evangelisch-Katholischer Kommentar zum Neuen Testament 33/2. Zurich: Benziger; Neukirchen-Vluyn: Neukirchener Verlag.

Moloney, Francis J. 1998. *The Gospel of John*. Sacra Pagina Series 4. Collegeville, Minn.: Liturgical Press.

Painter, John. 1996. "Inclined to God: The Quest for Eternal Life—Bultmannian Hermeneutics and the Theology of the Fourth Gospel." In *Exploring the Gospel of John: In Honor of D. Moody*

Smith, 346–68. Ed. R. Alan Culpepper and C. Clifton Black. Louisville: Westminster John Knox.

Rossé, Gérard. 1988. *L'ultima preghiera di Gesù dal Vangelo di Giovanni.* Rome: Città Nuova.

Rosenblatt, Marie-Eloise. 1988. "The Voice of the One Who Prays in John 17." In *Scripture and Prayer: A Celebration for Carroll Stuhlmueller, C.P.,* 131–44. Ed. Carolyn Osiek and Donald Senior. Wilmington, Del.: Michael Glazier.

Talbert, Charles H. 1992. *Reading John: A Literary and Theological Commentary on the Fourth Gospel and the Johannine Epistles,* 172–78. Reading the New Testament Series. New York: Crossroad.

———. 1993. "Worship in the Fourth Gospel and in its Milieu." In *Perspectives on John: Method and Interpretation in the Fourth Gospel,* 337–56. Ed. Robert B. Sloan and Mikeal C. Parsons. The National Association of Baptist Professors of Religion Special Studies Series 11. Lewiston, New York: Edwin Mellen.

Witkamp, L. Th. 1996. "Jesus' Thirst in John 19:28-30: Literal or Figurative?" *Journal of Biblical Literature* 115: 489–510.

Yee, Gale A. 1989. *Jewish Feasts and the Gospel of John.* Zacchaeus Studies: New Testament. Wilmington, Del.: Michael Glazier.

4

Paul on Prayer

INTRODUCTION OR HOW I'VE COME TO WHERE I'M GOING

I BEGIN AT THE BEGINNING and share with my readers my research journey in writing this chapter. In his bibliography on prayer James Harding (1994, 213–26) lists an impressive 212 items on Paul and his epistles. How was I going to master such a welter of titles? But as I sifted through the titles, I breathed a sigh of relief as I realized that about 70 percent of this bibliography dealt with four Pauline hymns: 89 titles on Philippians 2:6-11; 31 on Colossians 1:15-20; 16 on the hymns in Ephesians, especially Ephesians 1:3-14, and 10 on 1 Timothy 3:16. And I had already published a book (1996) on many of these and other hymns and thus had taken into consideration much of Harding's bibliography. And my publishers didn't want me to repeat pages of my earlier work here, even though, in my humble opinion, it is a good and well-written study.

Of the other books and articles mentioned by Harding I have taken into consideration those listed under "For Further Reading" at the end of this chapter and have learned much from them, especially from the brief study by Krister Stendahl. But I didn't just want to repeat what P. T. O'Brien (1975) and Louis Monloubou (1982) had said so well about the apostolic nature of Paul's prayer. In the 1970s, two superb studies appeared on prayer in Paul. I did not see it as my task to summarize the wonderful presentation of Paul's "intercessory prayer passages" by Gordon Wiles (1974) or the painstakingly thorough and insightful monograph by David M. Stanley (1973). I thought that recent massive studies on Paul would be my salvation. I generally found in them, however, only brief notices about important topics such as the role of the Spirit in prayer. Perhaps this lack of recent material on prayer in Paul should not have surprised me when I reflected that Paul presupposes his prayer life and rarely talks about it in his letters. As a matter of fact, we have to infer from his intensely Pharisaic orientation and from Jewish practices of his time that he said the *Shema Israel* twice a day and some form of the Eighteen Benedictions thrice a day, frequented the synagogue weekly, and prayed the psalms of praise and lament found in Israel's psalter. For the content of the *Shema,* the Eighteen Benedictions, and other Jewish prayers, I invite interested readers to consult the appendix at the end of chapter 1, "Prayer and the Historical Jesus."

In this bibliographical quandary I fought off temptations to succumb to writer's block. In a moment of serendipity I decided to try to link Paul's prayer with his stories and thus hitch the Karris wagon of interpretation to those contemporary stars of Pauline interpretation who were telling me and many others that Paul's stories lie at the heart of his theology. But I was not going to lose my head up with the stars and try to do all of Paul's letters, or just the so-called seven genuine ones (Romans, 1 and 2 Corinthians, Galatians, Philippians, 1 Thessalonians, and Philemon). I took comfort in the fact that David G. Peterson (1990) had limited his study of "Prayer in Paul's Writings" to one letter, Romans, and narrowed my choice to Philippians because it is relatively short and therefore manageable, theologically and narratologically meaty, and close to my heart. In brief, I will take the plunge into a narrative approach to Paul, determine what stories Paul refers to in Philippians, and see how his prayers or experience of prayer correspond to these stories. For better or for worse, mine will be a presentation of what contemporary Pauline scholarship on Paul's stories can contribute to our understanding of Paul's prayer. Or to change my imagery, in this chapter I want to function as a contemporary museum curator who displays familiar paintings and artworks in a new way, so that even regular patrons of the museum will see them in a new and inspiring light. My goal is to turn a head or two in God's and Christ's direction by phrasing a common insight on prayer in a slightly different way.

What Are Paul's Stories?

What are Paul's stories? According to James D. G. Dunn (1993, 36–46) Paul's stories are two: "the Story of Israel" and "the Story of the Christ." In the view of N. T. Wright (1992, 409) Paul's story is "the Israel-story, fulfilled, subverted and transformed by the Jesus-story, and now subverting the world's stories." Wayne Meeks (1993, 196) cites Paul's story in one long sentence:

> The pivotal story for Paul was simple and astounding: God's son and anointed one was the very Jesus who was most shamefully crucified, dead, and buried, but whom God then raised from the dead, exalted to share his own throne and very name in heaven, to sit at God's right hand as Lord until all things would be subjected to him and God alone would reign in righteousness over all his people and creation.

In passing, I call my readers' attention to the fact that at the heart of Meeks's reconstruction of Paul's story is the hymn of Philippians 2:6-11.

For our purposes I prefer the way Ben Witherington III (1998, 230–53) describes Paul's story as actually a fivefold one: the story of God; the story of humankind; the story of God's people; the story of Christ; the story of Paul and of Christians. We will use Witherington's more complete description of Paul's stories in our analysis of Philippians but will not promise that it is always possible to separate these stories so cleanly from one another that there is no interconnection. Further, my description of these stories, especially the story of God's people, will necessarily be brief and may put at a disadvantage those readers whose acquaintance with the Hebrew Scriptures is hoary or fleeting.

Philippians as an Integral Letter

I have resisted my previous academic training which gave a siren call to focus immediately on such obvious prayer passages as Paul's thanksgiving in 1:3-11 and the liturgical hymn that Paul quotes in 2:6-11. For I am being convinced that one must set these important passages in the larger context of the four chapters that constitute Philippians and in the even larger context of Paul's theological stories.

The title that Ben Witherington III (1994) gave to his book on Philippians suggests what this letter is all about: *Friendship and Finances in*

Philippi. Indeed, in this letter, written toward the end of his missionary activity while he is in jail, Paul is thanking the Philippians for their financial gifts, which have facilitated his ministry and are indicative of their *koinonia* in faith and friendship. But Paul has other fish to fry and is concerned about unity and harmony in the Philippian community. An outline of Philippians may capture some of Paul's designs.

1:1-2	Opening
1:3-11	Thanksgiving, which suggests the gist of the rest of the letter
1:12-26	"Here's what's going on in my life" or what is technically called the *narratio*
1:27-30	The argument of the letter for unity, expressed briefly in what is technically called the *expositio*
2:1–4:3	The "proof" of Paul's argument, technically called the *probatio*
4:4-20	Concluding remarks or what is technically called the *peroratio*
4:21-23	Farewell

If you read Philippians carefully, you will note that Paul mentions certain people, for example, Timothy and Epaphroditus; Euodia and Syntyche; the dogs and evil workers; Paul and Christ. Paul refers to these people, himself included, as positive and negative examples of unity. In Philippians 1 we find Paul as a positive example (verses 12-14 and 18b-30) and the "rival preachers" as negative examples (verses 15-18a). In Philippians 2 there are the positive examples of Christ (verses 5-11), Timothy and Epaphroditus (verses 19-30) and the negative example of the crooked and depraved generation (verse 15) and the lack of harmony in the Philippian community itself (verses 1-4). Philippians 3 provides the positive example of Paul (verses 5-17 and 20-21), which is contrasted with the sharply depicted negative example of the Judaizers or dogs (verses 2-6, 18-19). Finally, in Philippians 4:2-3 there is the appeal for unity between Euodia and Syntyche, who serve as positive and negative examples, positive as community leaders, negative as needing reconciliation. The reconciliation of these two influential, female community leaders will be a great boon to the unity of the community.

I make my own the conclusion of Witherington (1994, 19): "Overall it appears to me that this letter is about positive and negative examples on which the Philippians must pattern themselves or which they must shun, and is thus a largely deliberative argument for *concordia*." While this opinion is not the common one, I invite those who maintain that Philippians is a composite letter to peruse the detailed and convincing presentation for the integrity of Philippians offered by Ralph Brucker (1997, 280–346).

In any case, the skeleton of Paul's integral letter to the Philippians is set before us. Let's embark on our pursuit of Paul's fivefold story.

The Story of God

As we begin this story, I remind my readers that it may not be possible to keep all five stories in neat and separate boxes, for there is understandably considerable overlap.

If you're like me, you probably read Philippians time after time without averting to the fact that the word "God" appears twenty times. Rather than discuss all of these passages for what they might say about God, I will limit myself to three key passages.

In Philippians 1:2 Paul greets the believers at the Roman colony of Philippi with "Grace and peace to you from God our Father and the Lord Jesus Christ." God is Father, but not in the same way that non-Christians at Philippi might say that Zeus is their Father. As we saw in our chapter on prayer and the historical Jesus, God is father of the human race and also father of the Jewish people, whom he brought forth from slavery to new life, from being no-people to being God's people. At the very beginning of his letter to the Philippians Paul reminds them and himself that their God is the God of Abraham, Isaac, and Jacob and the God of election and grace. "It is God who is at work in you, enabling you both to will and to work for his good pleasure" (2:13).

In the second stanza of the hymn in Philippians 2:6-11 there are two references to God. God has exalted Jesus, who was obedient until death on the cross, and has made all things subject to him. And all this happens for the glory of God the Father. Here we see clearly that it is almost impossible to separate out in a clear and neat way the various components of Paul's fivefold story. God is not just God, but the Father of a people and the God who exalted the crucified Jesus and gave him the name that is above every other name.

Finally, in Philippians 3:3 Paul writes: "For we are the circumcision, those who worship by God's Spirit and boast in Christ Jesus and place no confidence in the flesh." Here God's story joins hands with the story of Paul and the Christians. While it is only in Romans 8 that Paul will spell out in great detail how Christians live by God's gift of the Spirit, here the briefest of outlines presses itself upon our consciousness. We make contact with God in worship, thus showing our dependence upon God, and do so not by our own powers, but through the bestowal of God's Spirit. Through this same Spirit the believers cry out "Abba, Father" (Romans 8:15; Galatians 4:6). And it is this same Spirit who makes intercession for believers in their weakness and in accordance with God's will (Romans 8:26-27).

In sum, through allusions to the story of God Paul makes it clear to his communities that their God is not a remote creator God. Their God comes to them in the present through the Spirit, with a history of benefaction, and with a future of hope.

To me the Pauline prayer that intertwines with God's story is that of Philippians 1:9-10. I give my own translation to capture more of the nuances of this rich prayer: "And this is my prayer: that your love may increase more and more in knowledge of God's revelation in Christ and every kind of practical insight, so that you may discern what really matters." On a rhetorical level this part of Paul's thanksgiving telegraphs the rest of his letter, for Paul wants the Philippians to show greater love for one another and will motivate them to do this by his own example of self-sacrificing love and especially that of the crucified slave, Jesus Christ. Further, Paul will tell the Philippians that external signs of election such as circumcision and observance of certain food laws are not what really matter, as he gives them "practical insight." But on the level of spiritual theology this is an awesome prayer wish for those who turn it into their prayer and say: "God, increase my understanding of what you have revealed in Christ Jesus and may it make my life more loving, whatever the cost. Help me to lay aside things that are really trash. Give me insight into what you consider vital."

The Story of Humankind

This is the bleakest of the five stories, for it deals with the rule of flesh, sin, and death in the lives of men and women. While Paul doesn't deal with this story and its implications in the profound way that he does, for example, in Romans 5–8, this story is still present in Philippians. Let me touch on the highlights.

The first three verses of the hymn in Philippians 2:6-11 contrast the disobedience, arrogance, and self-aggrandizement of the first Adam with the obedience, humility, and selflessness of the second Adam. And the effects of the first Adam's fall are still operative. As a matter of fact, if they were not, we wouldn't even have Paul's letter to the Philippians, whose theme is unity. Yes, Paul champions unity amidst the following effects of sin: envy and rivalry (1:15), selfish ambition (1:17), selfishness and vainglory (2:3), pursuit of one's own interests (2:4, 21), to say nothing of the problems raised against unity by the Judaizers in chapter 3.

In their situation of alienation from God and subjection to the reign of sin, the Philippians had gladly received the gospel of God's grace that Paul preached to them. And that is one of the main reasons why Paul is continually rejoicing in this letter and encouraging the Philippians to do the same. Paul joins with the Philippians in celebrating the exaltation of their Lord, Jesus Christ, over all heavenly and earthly powers and even those under the earth (2:10). And Paul directs their eyes in a hope-filled gaze toward their savior, who will transform their bodies, subject to corruption, to be like his glorified body (3:20-21).

Indeed, in Philippians Paul's message comes across loud and clear that he wants the believers to be blameless at the coming of the Lord Jesus and to beware of this "crooked and perverse generation" (2:15). And this wish forms the second part of the prayer wish we discussed at the end of our treatment of Paul's story of God. The full prayer wish of Philippians 1:9-11 reads: "And this is my prayer, that your love may overflow more and more with knowledge and full insight to help you determine what is best, so that in the day of Christ you may be pure and blameless, having produced the harvest of righteousness that comes through Jesus Christ for the glory and praise of God." Paul is confident that he and the Philippians can reach the goal of meeting the Lord Jesus at his coming without stumbling in the faith because of what God has done already for them. As Paul says in 1:6: "I am confident of this, that the one who began a good work among you will bring it to completion by the day of Jesus Christ." And in Philippians 3 Paul emphasizes that his and the Philippians' right standing with God does not come from their own slavish moral practices but from Jesus Christ. And their righteousness is not for their own honor and glory but "for the glory and praise of God."

The Story of God's People

If contemporary Pauline studies have shown us anything these past fifteen years, it is that Paul is thoroughly Jewish and takes with utmost seriousness God's promises to Israel. But at the same time Paul fights to the point of being alienated from Peter, James, and Barnabas to maintain a law-free gospel for Gentile converts. While it is true that Paul's telling of the story of God's people within the story of the Messiah Jesus is more developed in Galatians and Romans, it is also present here in Philippians.

There is continuity between the story of God and the story of God's people, for it is the same God and Father who has worked in the past, works now, and works toward the culmination of God's creative purpose. Jesus is called the Messiah, a Jewish term for the anointed one, the Christ, whom God has highly exalted and given the name that is above every name. But there is also discontinuity between the story of God's people and the story of the Messiah and the Messiah's people. As Philippians 3 shows in an especially clear light, Paul and other Jewish Christians differ on certain key points of observance of God's Law and do so with the vehemence that only first-century polemic can muster. Food laws ("the belly") and circumcision ("the mutilation") and works of righteousness ("evil workers") are not necessary for Gentiles who have turned to faith in Jesus the Messiah. And Paul can even tout his high status in Judaism and then toss it aside as so much rubbish: "circumcised on the eighth day, a member of the people of Israel, of the tribe of Benjamin, a Hebrew born of Hebrews; as to the law, a Pharisee; as to zeal, a persecutor of the church; as to righteousness under the law, blameless. Yet whatever gains I had, these I have come to regard as loss because of Christ" (3:5-7).

From this polemic and the longer, comparable one that flashes like a brushfire through Galatians one might surmise that Paul had hit the delete button with regard to the story of God's people, Israel. But that is definitely not the case, as can be seen from Paul's most full consideration of these matters in Romans. Allow me to conclude this section by smuggling in some thoughts and prayers from Romans. In Romans 11:26 and 29 Paul makes two lapidary statements: "And so all Israel will be saved" and "For the gifts and the calling of God are irrevocable." How these statements correspond with Israel's disobedience remains a mystery to Paul, who concludes his impassioned argument with a prayer that I invite us to make our own.

> O the depth of the riches and wisdom and knowledge of God! How unsearchable are his judgments and how inscrutable his ways! "For who has known the mind of the Lord? Or who has been his counselor?" "Or who has given a gift to him, to receive a gift in return?" For from him and through him and to him are all things. To him be the glory forever. Amen. (Romans 11:33-36).

Sometimes we don't know the answers and hold on for dear life to the certainties we have, and for the rest we struggle to let God be God. And we do this in the happy realization of God's initiative in our regard, for as Paul says elsewhere: "Now that you have come to know God or rather have come to be known by God" (Galatians 4:9).

The Story of Christ

When I began to study Paul's fivefold story, I read through Philippians many times. One of those times I decided to note the frequency of Paul's references to God, Christ, and Spirit. The count for Christ was forty-eight. With some exaggeration I would say that there is hardly a verse in Philippians that fails to mention Jesus Christ. And for many proponents of Paul's stories the key elements of the story of Christ are found in the hymn of Philippians 2:6-11. This hymn has two stanzas. Philippians 2:6-8 form the first stanza, and 2:9-11 form the second stanza. Allow me to quote this hymn in its entirety in a translation I published earlier (1996, 42–43):

6. Who, though he was of divine status,
        did not regard being like God
        something to take selfish advantage of.
7. Rather he made himself powerless,
        assuming a slave's status,
        being born as a human being.
        And while existing in human appearance,
8. he further humbled himself
        by being obedient unto death,
        even death by crucifixion.
9. Wherefore God highly exalted him
        and bestowed upon him the name
        which is above every name,

10. so that at the name of Jesus
     every knee should bend
     of those in heaven, on earth, and under the earth;
11. and every tongue should confess
    that Jesus Christ is LORD
    to the glory of God the Father.

Richard B. Hays (1996, 27–32), among others, has done an excellent job in showing how this story of Christ's obedient giving of himself for the sake of others in the first stanza functions as an example. If the Philippians would take to heart Christ's story, then there would be less self-interest and more care for their brothers and sisters in Christ. But Paul's use of this hymn does not stop at the first stanza, for Paul picks up the second stanza's theme of exaltation in Philippians 3:20-21. Christ was not exalted just for himself but also for those who believe in him. For Christ has a determinative role in their future: "But our citizenship is in heaven, and it is from there that we are expecting a Savior, the Lord Jesus Christ. He will transform the body of our humiliation that it may be conformed to the body of his glory, by the power that also enables him to make all things subject to himself." In other words, believers are called upon to make both parts of this two-stanza hymn their own. The first part will inform their gathering of a harvest of righteousness by being united in their faith community (Philippians 2:1-4). And the second part will inform their hope that the story of flesh, sin, and death will not overwhelm them, but that their future is intimately tied to that of their Savior and Lord, Jesus the Messiah. And as liberation theologians have been reminding us during the last two decades, to confess that Jesus, and not Caesar or Mammon, is Lord may cost the disciple dearly. Christians have only one Lord and will not serve Mammon or its puppets.

As we come to the end of this brief consideration of the story of the Messiah, there seems to be no need to cite any prayer from Philippians other than that of 2:6-11. But citation or recitation of this hymn is not enough, for it must become the lodestar of believers' lives. And that, perhaps, is the prime message of the New Testament stars who have been championing Paul's stories. These stories, confessed in faith, have profound ethical consequences when Christians pattern their lives on that of their Lord Jesus and have "the same mind that was in Christ Jesus" (Philippians 2:5).

Finally, this hymn is evidence that Martin Dibelius, one of the founders of form criticism, was off target some seventy years ago when he contended that the sermon stood at the fountainhead of Christian literature. Rather a stronger case can be made that at the beginning of the Christian movement the hymn was mightier than the sword in winning souls for Christ. The early Christians took very seriously the admonition given voice in Colossians 3:16: "And with gratitude in your hearts sing psalms, hymns, and spiritual songs to God" (see also Ephesians 5:19-20) and composed many hymns. Romans 8:31-39, Colossians 1:15-20, Ephesians 2:14-16, 1 Timothy 3:16, 2 Timothy 2:11-13, and Titus 3:4-7 are just a few examples from the Pauline tradition of this hymn-making. And happily contemporary Christian composers and full-voiced choirs and congregations joyfully continue this tradition of faith-filled celebration. For a far more detailed discussion of the role of hymn composing and singing in the first Christian communities I refer my readers to the "Liturgy Past" section of my chapter "The Prayer of the Hymns in Revelation."

The Story of Paul and of Christians

As we saw earlier in this chapter, Philippians is shot through with positive and negative examples for the Philippians to emulate or shun. And Paul, especially in Philippians 3, is one of the good examples. His story becomes paradigmatic for all Christians. This persecutor of the church of God now regards "everything as loss because of the surpassing value of knowing Christ Jesus." For Christ Paul has "suffered the loss of all things and regards them as rubbish, in order that he may gain Christ" (3:7-8).

What was the turning point in Paul's life story? In chapters 9, 22, and 26 of the Acts of the Apostles Luke tells the story of Paul's "change" thrice to emphasize how important it was. Paul's call was so signal that he himself refers to it a number of times: 1 Corinthians 9:1; 15:8-9; Galatians 1:13-17. What happened to Paul? Basing myself on the work of Alan Segal (1990) and C. R. A. Morray-Jones (1993), I highlight two passages in Paul as I search for an answer. In Galatians 1:14 Paul claims: "I advanced in Judaism beyond many among my people of the same age, for I was far more zealous for the traditions of my ancestors." In what ways did Paul advance? Did he fast more? Did he interpret the Scriptures more insightfully than his peers? Did he pray more frequently and compose new psalms as the covenanters at Qumran did? Did he have more intense mystical experiences?

I contend that Paul advanced so greatly beyond his contemporaries because he had "greater" mystical experiences than his peers. That Paul was a mystic seems clear from 2 Corinthians 12:1-4, where Paul is compelled to engage in honest boasting:

> It is necessary to boast; nothing is to be gained by it, but I will go on to visions and revelations of the Lord. I know a person in Christ who fourteen years ago was caught up to the third heaven—whether in the body or out of the body I do not know; God knows. And I know that such a person—whether in the body or out of the body I do not know; God knows—was caught up into Paradise and heard things that are not to be told, that no mortal is permitted to repeat.

I do not equate this mystical experience with Paul's "conversion" experience, but it gives us a vital clue from within Paul's own letters about the nature of the experience of his "call." Like other Jewish mystics Paul was wont to contemplate two "fiery" visions. The first is the vision of Isaiah 6:1, 6: "I saw the Lord sitting on a throne high and lofty; and the hem of his robe filled the temple. . . . Then one of the seraphs flew to me, holding *a live coal* that had been taken from the altar with a pair of tongs." And in Paul's mystical repertoire were also the visions of Ezekiel 1, especially 1:26-27:

> And above the dome over their heads there was something like a throne, in appearance like sapphire; and seated above the likeness of a throne was something that seemed like a human form. Upward from what appeared like the loins I saw something like gleaming amber, something that looked *like fire* enclosed all around.

I have read *1 Enoch* 14:8-25 before. But when Morray-Jones (1993, 202–3) quoted it in the context of his argument about Paul's mystical experience, my eyes almost jumped out of my head and I shouted: "What an insightful parallel!" As I quote this vision of Enoch, the biblical personage who was transferred to heaven alive, note the series of three (marble wall and two houses) and the endless mention of fire:

> [8]And behold I saw the clouds. And they were calling me in a vision. And the fogs were calling me, and the course of the stars and the lightnings were rushing me and causing me to desire. And in the vision, the winds were causing me to fly and rushing me high up into heaven. [9]And I kept coming (into heaven) until I approached a wall that was built of white marble and surrounded by tongues of fire, and it began to frighten me. [10]And I came into the tongues of fire and drew near to a great house that was built of white marble. And the inner wall(s) were like mosaics of white marble, the floor of crystal, [11]the ceiling like the path of the stars

and lightnings between which (stood) fiery cherubim and their heaven of water, [12]and flaming fire surrounded the wall(s), and its gates were burning with fire. [13]And I entered into the house, which was hot like fire and cold like ice, and there was nothing inside it; (so) fear covered me and trembling seized me. [14]And as I shook and trembled, I fell upon my face and saw a vision. [15]And behold there was an opening before me (and) a second house which is greater than the former and everything was built with tongues of fire. [16]And in every respect it excelled (the other)—in glory and great honor—to the extent that it is impossible for me to recount to you concerning its glory and greatness. [17]As for its floor, it was of fire and above it was lightning and the path of the stars; and as for its ceiling, it was flaming fire. [18]And I observed and saw inside it a lofty throne—its appearance was like crystal and its wheels like the shining sun; and (I heard) the voice of the cherubim. [19]And from beneath the throne were issuing streams of flaming fire. It was difficult to look at it. [20]And the Great Glory was sitting upon it—as for his gown, which was shining more brightly than the sun, it was whiter than any snow. [21]None of the angels was able to come in and see the face of the Excellent and the Glorious One, and no one of the flesh can see him—[22]the flaming fire was round about him, and a great fire stood before him. No one could come near unto him from among those that surrounded the tens of millions (that stood) before him. [23]He needed no council, but the most holy ones who are near him neither go far away at night nor move away from him. [24]Until then I was prostrate on my face covered and trembling. And the Lord called me with his own mouth and said to me, "Come near to me, Enoch, and to my holy Word." [25]And he lifted me up and brought me near to the gate, but I (continued) to look down with my face.

My suggestion is that on a mystical journey similar to that which Enoch experiences in *1 Enoch* 14 Paul was indeed "caught up," that is, he was not in control of the situation. And contrary to any expectations he might have had from previous mystical journeys into God's fiery throne room, Paul did not see "the Excellent and Glorious One" seated on the throne. Rather he saw Jesus the Messiah seated on that throne! What a shock to see enthroned Jesus, who should have been cursed by God because he hung on a tree (Galatians 3:13). Such an astounding experience helps us make sense of what Paul says of his call and God's revelation of his Son to him, and why he insists mightily in Philippians 3 that he counted all that had gone before as so much dung. Such a revelatory experience would surely knock Paul off his high horse of persecuting Jesus' followers.

And Paul's mystical shock of finding Christ seated on God's throne should advise us that mystical journeys were not a frolic in the park.

Rabbinic tradition is clear that engaging in mystical contemplation of God's fiery throne room or entering into Paradise was risky business. As the Jerusalem Talmud says: "Four men went into *pardes*: One looked and died. One looked and was stricken (with madness). One looked and cut the shoots (committed apostasy). In peace one went in and came out in peace" (modified text from Morray-Jones, 1993, 210). Paul is lucky to escape from such an experience of "flaming fire" with his life intact, but he did have to suffer the consequences of "a thorn in the flesh, a messenger of Satan to torment him" (2 Corinthians 12:7). Morray-Jones (1993, 282–83) seems to be correct when he argues that Paul may be referring to the demonic angels who guarded the pathways along the mystical journey and inflicted, among other things, "nervous illness" or maddening headaches to contemplatives. Even though Paul asked the Lord thrice for relief, the Lord would not remove the consequences of mystical experience, but did console Paul with the message "my grace is sufficient for you, for power is made perfect in weakness" (2 Corinthians 12:9). David Stanley (1973, 59–60) is correct to parallel Jesus' prayer in the Garden of Gethsemane, whose threefold nature is clear in Matthew 26:36-46 and also found in Mark 14:32-42, to Paul's threefold prayer here. As Stanley (1973, 60) says so well: "Like Jesus also, Paul is led by persevering petition to recognize and accept the divine answer to his prayer, although it was so very different from what he had envisaged it might be." What a lesson is here for all of us when we think that our mission has to go the way we had it planned! God's will be done! May God's plans be implemented.

If I am at all correct in my interpretation of Paul as a mystic, then we indeed have further material for our reflections on prayer. Will all Christians have the same mystical experiences as Paul had? Should all? Are such ecstatic experiences a desirable goal for all? Such a gift does not seem to be among those gifts of the Spirit listed by Paul in 1 Corinthians 12:4-11. But since the one body of Christ rejoices in the gifts of its members, we might minimally accept the view of Krister Stendahl (1984, 159): "We can rejoice in ecstasy, our own and that of others."

What messages on prayer does Paul have for ordinary Christians, who may not feel drawn to mystical experiences? Let me tease out some reflections from Philippians. Nonecstatic Christians may get on Paul's wavelength in Philippians 3 by recalling their own "conversion" experience or when they, as mature believers, assimilated into their own lives the faith their godparents articulated for them during their infant baptism. They repeat time after time with Paul: "I want to know Christ and the power of his resurrection" (3:10). And Christians who are not drawn to flights of ecstasy and have their hands full with quotidian cares may take courage from the exhortations to prayer that Paul gives in Philippians 4:6-7. These exhortations show that God cares for all believers, not just contemplatives: "Do not worry about anything, but in everything by prayer and supplication with thanksgiving let your requests be made known to God. And the peace of God, which surpasses all understanding, will guard your hearts and your minds in Christ Jesus." And implied in the friendly *koinonia* Paul enjoyed with the Philippians, but not explicitly stated, are their prayers for one another. Romans 15:30 expresses this intercessory give-and-take well: "I appeal to you, brothers and sisters, by our Lord Jesus Christ and by the love of the Spirit, to join me in earnest prayer to God on my behalf. . . ." There are many things that we believers, mystics or not, need to pray for as we all imitate Paul: "Forgetting what lies behind and straining forward to what lies ahead, I press on toward the goal for the prize of the heavenly call of God in Christ Jesus" (Philippians 3:13-14). And as Paul reminds us so well and so often in Philippians, we press on with joyful hearts, rejoicing in the God who has called us into fellowship, given us to drink of the Spirit, and will keep us blameless until the day of Christ Jesus. I conclude this section of exposition by paraphrasing Paul and praying: "And may our God fully satisfy your every need according to his riches in glory in Christ Jesus" (Philippians 4:19).

CONCLUSION

It seems to me that the same methodology I presented above can be applied to the other six genuine Pauline letters. I would recommend that interested readers start with 1 Thessalonians or Philemon and then move to Galatians. Finally, move on to 1 and 2 Corinthians and Paul's longest letter, Romans. Ferret out Paul's fivefold stories and see how they are related to his prayer wishes, doxologies, and exhortations on prayer. And advanced students might feel compelled to apply the same methodology to other letters in the Pauline tradition: Ephesians, Colossians, 2 Thessalonians, 1 and 2 Timothy, and Titus, especially to the hymns embodied in these letters which are too frequently neglected in New Testament surveys and courses on Paul.

As I look back over what we have done in these pages, I suppose I might be criticized by some for being too theological. Or to change the image, my readers might say that they wanted a "plug-and-play" approach, and I gave them a minicourse on the inner workings of a computer system. But as the New Testament stars have been telling us, we may miss the point if we don't get the story. Let me give an example.

In their wisdom our better politicians saw that citizens of the United States would become rugged individualists and substitute their individual stories for the story of the nation. So there are national holidays such as Memorial Day to remind us of the high price the men and women of our armed services paid to preserve our nation's freedom. And there's Independence Day on July 4th to make all rugged individualists remember that they stand on the shoulders of those who fought tyranny and oppression for their and our liberation. And Thanksgiving is set aside to drum into the thickest head of the most rugged individualist that we are dependent on others, especially on God, for the largess we enjoy in this land. Indeed, those of us who have been socialized into rugged individualism will miss the point if we do not allow national holidays to draw us back into the stories of our founding. And so with the fivefold story that Paul tells us. We must get into contact with the story of God, lest we forget our dependence on God and God's love for us. The story of humankind should bring us to our knees as we acknowledge publicly and privately how much our lives are dominated by flesh, sin, and death. And God knows how easily we can forget the story of God's people and remove the "Judaeo" portion of our Judaeo-Christian tradition. So easy it is to sing of Christ's humiliation and exaltation, put the hymnal back in its place, and forget that that hymn has anything whatsoever to say about either our humbling ourselves for others or Christ's saving transformation of us or our obedience to Jesus as our Lord. Finally, we should be reminded that we need interconnection with our brothers and sisters in the faith and might even support mystics like Paul who risk their necks to bring back from the flaming heights their insights into God's love and design for us.

For those of you who still think that I'm ethereal and want a more direct approach to prayer in Philippians or Paul in general, I invite you to take one of Paul's letters. Study it for a day or for a week at your leisure. Read through it carefully, noting on a piece of paper or in your word processor Paul's statements about prayer. Try to put his prayer wishes into your own words. Make them your prayer. Take his admonitions on prayer to heart and sing a hymn or pray for fellow believers in a faraway country. And if you ever are desirous of knowing what makes Paul's prayers or Paul himself tick, I invite you to shake hands with Paul's fivefold stories. And as you embrace Paul's stories, you might ask yourself the telling question: What stories govern my life? How can I make room for Paul's theological stories in the stories that control my life?

FOR FURTHER READING

Cullmann, Oscar. 1995. *Prayer in the New Testament,* 69–88. Overtures to Biblical Theology. Minneapolis: Fortress.

Karris, Robert J. 1996. *A Symphony of New Testament Hymns: Commentary on Philippians 2:5-11, Colossians 1:15-20, Ephesians 2:14-16, 1 Timothy 3:16, Titus 3:4-7, 1 Peter 3:18-22, and 2 Timothy 2:11-13,* 42–62. Collegeville, Minn.: Liturgical Press.

Monloubou, Louis. 1982. *Saint Paul et la prière: Prière et évangélisation.* Lectio Divina 110. Paris: Cerf.

Morray-Jones, C. R. A. 1993. "Paradise Revisited (2 Cor 12:1-12): The Jewish Mystical Background of Paul's Apostolate." *Harvard Theological Review* 86: 177–217, 265–92.

O'Brien, P. T. 1975. "Thanksgiving and the Gospel in Paul." *New Testament Studies* 21: 144–55.

Osiek, Carolyn. 1988. "Paul's Prayer: Relationship with Christ?" In *Scripture and Prayer: A Celebration for Carroll Stuhlmueller, C.P.,* 145–57. Ed. Carolyn Osiek and Donald Senior. Wilmington, Del.: Michael Glazier.

Peterson, David G. 1990. "Prayer in Paul's Writings." In *Teach Us To Pray: Prayer in the Bible and the World,* 84–101, 325–28. Ed. D. A. Carson. Grand Rapids: Eerdmans.

Segal, Alan F. 1990. *Paul the Convert: The Apostolate and Apostasy of Saul the Pharisee,* 34–71. New Haven, Conn.: Yale University Press.

Stanley, David M. 1973. *Boasting in the Lord: The Phenomenon of Prayer in Saint Paul.* New York: Paulist Press.

Stendahl, Krister. 1984. *Meanings: the Bible as Document and Guide,* 151–61. Philadelphia: Fortress Press.

Wiles, Gordon P. 1974. *Paul's Intercessory Prayers: The Significance of the Intercessory Prayer Passages in the Letters of St Paul.* Society for New Testament Studies Monograph Series 24. New York: Cambridge University Press.

Witherington, Ben, III. 1994. *Friendship and Finances in Philippi: The Letter of Paul to The Philippians.* The New Testament in Context. Valley Forge, Pa.: Trinity Press International.

5

The Prayer of the Hymns
in Revelation

I**N THIS CHAPTER** we move from the familiar territory of Jesus, the
Gospels, and Paul to the unfamiliar terrain of the Revelation of
John the Divine. To aid our understanding of this challenging and
oft-neglected writing I commence by making connections between our
previous chapters and this one. I will also indicate how Revelation has
influenced some of our religious songs. My goal is to make my readers
more comfortable with the unknown by relating it to what they do
know.

In our treatment of Paul we mentioned that Paul had been trans-
ported to heaven. John the Seer has the same experience, and the
transport happens on a Sunday. We further probed the theological significance of Paul's stories. What Paul says so briefly in Philippians
about "the end" of the story is also covered in the stories and/or
visions of Revelation, and often in great detail. For example, in Philippians 2:6-11 Paul describes Jesus' story as one involving humiliating
death on the cross, exaltation, and the obedient submission rendered
him by all in heaven, on earth, and under the earth. The prophet John
will cover much of the same theological and christological territory in
Revelation 5, especially 5:13 where every creature in heaven, on earth,
under the earth, and in the sea give glory and praise to one seated on
the throne and to the slaughtered Lamb. And Revelation 21–22 with
their detailed description of the New Jerusalem fill out wondrously
Paul's brief statement about Christian hope: "But our citizenship is in
heaven, and it is from there that we are expecting a Savior, the Lord
Jesus Christ" (Philippians 3:20). Finally, almost all of Revelation 4–22

may be seen as a graphic and anticipatory depiction of Paul's conviction that death has been swallowed up in the victory that is ours through our Lord Jesus Christ (1 Corinthians 15:54-57).

Our discussion of prayer in Luke-Acts sought to ascertain the relationship between prayer and God's plan for creation and redemption. The Revelation of John the Divine drinks from the same theological spring but employs different imagery and terminology. In Revelation 5 it is only the slaughtered Lamb who is worthy to open the scroll, written both inside and on its back and sealed with seven seals. Once this scroll is opened John sees the fulfillment of God's plan and describes it in the remainder of his revelation. As David E. Aune (1997, 374) says so well:

> The scroll represents the final and fully predetermined stage in God's redemptive purpose for the world, which will unfold between the heavenly exaltation of Christ following his death and resurrection and the final inauguration of the eternal reign of God. The scroll and its contents therefore include the entire eschatological scenario extending from 6:1 through 22:9.

Our discussion of some of the symbolism in John's Gospel has prepared us for the myriad of symbols in John's Revelation. For example, John's Gospel used the symbol of water to describe Jesus' power to give life through his revelation and death. That same symbol recurs in Revelation and is transposed to heaven: "Then the angel showed me the river of the water of life, bright as crystal, flowing from the throne of God and of the Lamb, through the middle of the street of" the New Jerusalem (22:1-2). Also in John's Gospel we noted that Jesus is crucified and dies at the time that the Passover lambs were being slaughtered in the Temple. Indeed, Jesus is the Lamb of God who takes away the sins of the world. In John's Revelation the slaughtered Lamb who conquers becomes a dominant symbol of Jesus' life-giving power over death and destruction.

Also, we began our treatment of prayer and worship in John's Gospel with an examination of its opening hymn (1:1-18). The pattern of "revelation and response" I detected there is analogous to the antiphonal singing of the hymns in Revelation as one group after another responds in praise to the revelation of the "one seated on the throne" and to "the slaughtered Lamb."

Finally, one of the most powerful images in the teaching of the historical Jesus and in the Synoptic Gospels is that of God's kingdom. It is God's rule for peace and salvation and against evil, death, and sin. In

Revelation we can read many stories of how God's kingdom has come as it conquers the powers of death. We move from the Hallelujah Chorus of "The Lord our God the Almighty reigns" (19:6) to listening to the loud voice from the throne proclaiming, "Death will be no more. Mourning and crying and pain will be no more" (21:4). And also note the refrain on "conquering" in the conclusions of each of the seven letters in Revelation 2–3 which introduce Revelation. For example, the last letter ends with "To the one who conquers I will give a place with me on my throne, just as I myself conquered and sat down with my Father on his throne" (3:21).

Are there any connections between Revelation and some familiar religious songs? There are quite a few. I concluded my first discussion of "from the known to the unknown" by referring to God the King's conquest of evil. The Greek verb *nikan*, which I translated above by "to conquer," can also be rendered as "to overcome." And in that rendition it became the rallying song of the civil rights movement: "We shall overcome someday." Many spirituals draw inspiration and words from Revelation. Take the powerful "Ride on, King Jesus" that draws freely upon Revelation 19:11-16. Yes, indeed, no man can hinder King Jesus, who rides on "a white horse" and is "King of Kings and Lord of Lords." And each time the Christmas season rolls around there are frequent performances of G. F. Handel's oratorio *The Messiah*, which was first performed in Dublin, Ireland, on April 13, 1742. No. 44 concludes Part II, is sung by the chorus, and bears the title "Hallelujah!" Its text is taken from Revelation 19:6, 11:15, and 19:16: "Hallelujah! for the Lord God omnipotent reigneth. The kingdom of this world is become the kingdom of our Lord, and of His Christ; and he shall reign for ever and ever. King of Kings, and Lord of Lords. Hallelujah!" And No. 53 concludes Part III and the entire oratorio, is sung by the chorus, and bears the title "Worthy is the Lamb that was slain." Its text comes from Revelation 5:12-13: "Worthy is the Lamb that was slain, and hath redeemed us to God by His blood, to receive power, and riches, and wisdom, and strength, and honour, and glory, and blessing. Blessing and honour, glory and power, be unto Him that sitteth upon the throne, and unto the Lamb, for ever and ever. Amen." And in Lutheran and Roman Catholic traditions Richard Hillert's hymn "This Is the Feast of Victory" is a favorite during the Easter season. With organ and trumpet accompaniment it is an exhilarating version of the joyous message of Revelation 5. And I'm sure that my readers can identify other songs and hymns in their religious and American heritage that stem from Revelation.

In conclusion, there are significant connections between Revelation and our earlier chapters. And religious songs have transmitted to us a certain amount of Revelation's message. I will build upon these bits and pieces of knowledge by examining the life setting, literary form, content, and purpose of Revelation and by brief analyses of its many hymns. After that I will examine the literary context of these hymns in Revelation and their role in liturgy, past and present.

THE LIFE SETTING OF REVELATION

In considering Revelation's life setting, I will proceed from the general to the specific. And there will be two variations of the specific. Dating Revelation to the last decade of the first Christian century is generally accepted. And there is a general tendency in the scholarly community to see the situation behind Revelation not as systematic persecution by Emperor Domitian but as sporadic harassment in the province of Asia for merely being a Christian. Early expression of what has become the general tendency came from Adela Yarbro Collins (1984, 77): "There is insufficient evidence to warrant the conclusion that Domitian persecuted Christians as Christians." And this general tendency received most recent articulation from Thomas B. Slater (1998, 254): "I propose a socio-religious setting for the Revelation to John in which Asian Christians experienced local harassment, ridicule, discrimination and oppression in the early 90s for their religious beliefs and customs." In this connection almost all commentators refer to the letter that Pliny the Younger wrote to Emperor Trajan (A.D. 98–117) when Pliny was governor of Bithynia, a province that borders the area of the seven churches in the province of Asia addressed in Revelation 2–3. Although Pliny's *Letter 96* from book 10 of his *Letters* dates from ca. A.D. 112, it is held to be reflective of a situation and policy that obtained at least twenty years earlier and in a wider area than just Bithynia.

Here are the pertinent passages from Pliny's letter in a translation modified somewhat from that in the Loeb Classical Library:

> For the moment this is the line I have taken with all persons brought before me on the charge of being Christians. I have asked them in person if they are Christians. And if they admit it, I repeat the question a second

and third time, with a warning of the punishment awaiting them. If they persist, I order them to be led away for execution. For, whatever the nature of their admission, I am convinced that their stubbornness and unshakable obstinacy ought not to go unpunished. . . . (10.96.2-4)

Christians who have recanted

all did reverence to your statue and the images of the gods in the same way as the others, and reviled the name of Christ. They also declared that the sum total of their guilt or error amounted to no more than this: they had met regularly before dawn on a fixed day to chant verses alternately among themselves in honor of Christ as if to a god, and also to bind them- selves by oath, not for any criminal purpose, but to abstain from theft, robbery and adultery, to commit no breach of trust and not to deny a deposit when called upon to restore it. After this ceremony it had been their custom to disperse and reassemble later to take food of an ordinary, harmless kind (10.96.7).

Finally, Pliny notes the widespread influence of the Christians and hopes that his policies will hinder this "wretched cult":

I think, though, that it is still possible for it to be checked and directed to better ends. For there is no doubt that people have begun to throng the temples that had been almost entirely deserted for a long time. The sacred rites that had been allowed to lapse are being performed again. And flesh of sacrificial victims is on sale everywhere, though up till recently scarcely anyone could be found to buy it. It is easy to infer from this that a great many people could be reformed if they were given an opportunity to repent. (10.96.9-10)

Trajan's response to Pliny (*Letter 97*) approves of Pliny's procedure and states: "These people must not be hunted out. . . .But pamphlets cir- culated anonymously (with the names of Christians in them) must play no part in any accusation."

The following points stand out in Pliny's *Letter 96* and *Letter 97*: (1) Individual Christians are reported to Pliny. Neither Trajan nor Pliny orders a blanket persecution of Christians. (2) Christians neither wor- ship the emperor or the nation's gods nor eat of meat sacrificed to these gods. (3) The Christians, who do not recant, are seen as stubborn and contumacious and are punished. (4) Pliny provides a description of Christian worship that includes, among other things, antiphonal singing of praise to Christ "as to a god." To this last point we will return in due time.

While the correspondence between Pliny the Younger and Emperor Trajan provides some general background for the life setting of Revelation, the letters to the seven churches of Asia provide more specific background. As Charles H. Talbert (1994, 25) assesses these seven letters: "the Revelation to John . . . seems addressed, for the most part, to complacent, spiritually anemic Christians. They seem to be concerned mostly with making an accommodation to the larger pagan society so as to share in its economic prosperity and to avoid the social sanctions of pagans and Jews." Granted Talbert's interpretation, how does worship or the singing of hymns fit in? Talbert observes (1994, 40): "From the point of view of the prophet John, if saints want to make an ultimate difference in the world, the most important thing they can do is to worship, joining their earthly praise and intercession with the whole company of heaven." And after his discussion of the hymn of Revelation 15:3-4 and in response to his question of why worship is the most important and significant thing Christians can do, Talbert says: "It is because just and lasting change in the world ultimately is God's doing" (1994, 70).

From analyses of Revelation's seven letters and from what it has to say about the rule of the Beast and the Whore Babylon, other commentators specify the life setting of Revelation somewhat differently. In his lengthy and worthwhile discussion of Revelation's attitude to imperial Rome Walter E. Pilgrim (1999, 145–80) moves from his initial assessment of Rome and its emperors as unworthy objects of worship to an assessment of them as perpetrators of injustices and oppressors of the poor. Towards his conclusion Pilgrim writes (1999, 176–77): "For Revelation addresses persons experiencing innocent suffering and grave injustice. It speaks from the underside of history, from the vantage-point of the marginalized and dispossessed. Accordingly, 'the outcry of Revelation for justice and judgment can be fully understood only by those who hunger and thirst for justice.'" In his last sentence Pilgrim quotes from one of the foremost exponents of this justice viewpoint, Elisabeth Schüssler Fiorenza (1991, 139).

And Richard B. Hays (1996, 181–84) is helpful in articulating how an analysis of the hymns of Revelation might accord with this justice interpretation of Revelation. While acknowledging that the nonviolent resistance given by the members of the U.S. civil rights movement as they sang "We shall overcome someday" is not exactly "exegesis" of Revelation in the strict sense, Hays does maintain that "it illustrates the social posture from which the text is appropriately to be read" (1996, 184). Further, Hays (1996, 184) maintains that singing the "Hallelujah Chorus" of Revelation 11:15 "is a political act, and the political power of the act is the greater because it is sung, for others can join the chorus and fix it in aural memory." Hays (1996, 184) concludes his insightful chapter on Revelation's contribution to Christian ethics with these words: "Despite the strangeness and obscurity of Revelation at the level of linear reason, its imaginative vividness has made it a perennial source of art and liturgy in the church and has thereby supplied the power to sustain countercommunity in a world feverishly worshiping the Beast."

The analyses of Slater, Talbert, and Pilgrim, and the scholarly colleagues who share their views provide the parameters of our discussion of the hymns of Revelation. I might summarize the results of their view of Revelation's life situation in this way. Slater has set forth the general social, religious, and political situation without too much theological speculation about its significance. Talbert has offered one theological assessment of this general situation, one ultimately founded on the First Commandment and God's injunction that the faithful worship no other god. There is no compromise possible. And accommodation is just a weasel word for idolatry. Pilgrim, Schüssler Fiorenza, and Hays argue theologically that the ultimate question involved in Revelation is one of justice. God's just judgments will win out. God will vindicate those who suffer injustices. And yes, believers and singers of Revelation's hymns must be actively involved in the cause of justice.

I move now to a treatment of the literary form, content, and function of Revelation, some aspects of which have already surfaced in previous paragraphs.

THE LITERARY FORM, CONTENT, AND FUNCTION OF REVELATION

One of the more sobering realizations in dealing with Revelation is that we cannot read its twenty-two chapters straight off as we would a history book. In order to understand Revelation, we have to go back to school and learn new vocabulary. Speaking of new vocabulary, I recall that during my years in Rome dealing with mandates from Roman Catholic Congregations I happily learned that "immediately" meant within a week, "soon" meant within a month, and "in a short time" meant within three months. Can you imagine a child in an American school being told to go to the principal's office immediately and showing up a week later? But then again, Italians and canon lawyers don't compute time the way we Americans do. Nor did John the Divine compute time the way we do. See, for example, the very first verse of Revelation: "to show his servants what must *soon* take place." These days it seems that all of us, young and not so young, are going back to school to learn some new vocabulary or new meanings of familiar words, for instance, that "default" means two different things on a tennis court and in a computer program. So it should not surprise us that revelation means something different when applied to deep sharing between friends and to the Revelation of John the Divine. And as we all know from the hard knocks of our schooling, learning is not always easy. As my Italian confreres would say: *Coraggio, caro!* "Dear friend, hang in there!"

Having gotten us on the alert for new vocabulary, I gratefully acknowledge my dependence on David E. Aune (1997, lxxxii) and say that the *literary form* of John's Revelation is an apocalypse (Greek for "revelation") in a first-person prose narrative. Let me explain the various components of this definition. Recall Revelation 1:9-10: "*I*, John . . . was on the island of Patmos. . . . *I* was in the spirit on the Lord's day." As you read through Revelation, you will note again and again: "I saw" or "I heard." And Revelation has largely a narrative structure whose "plot" displays various episodes that consist of revelatory visions often mediated to John by a supernatural revealer. Take, for example, the episode of the throne-room visions of Revelation 4–5 where John sees the one seated on the throne and the slaughtered Lamb. And it was "the first voice" that said to him: "Come up here, and I will show you what must take place after this" (4:1). And the narrative structure of Revelation leads to a central revelatory message (chapters 19–22) that God has conquered the beasts, evil, and death; the bride is prepared for the Lamb; and the time for the New Jerusalem has come. See 21:2: "And I saw the holy city, the New Jerusalem, coming down out of heaven from God, prepared as a bride adorned for her husband." And finally, what is unique about the form of Revelation is that the narrative of its visions and auditions is framed by a narrative of prophecy (1:1–3:22 and 22:8-21). Put in different terms, whereas the visions and auditions give the distinct impression that everything is so black and white that the unrighteous will never repent, the very nature of prophecy is to persuade people to repent, a factor that is very evident in the letters to the seven churches.

Aune (1997, lxxxii) defines the *content* of Revelation as "the communication of a transcendent, usually eschatological, perspective on human experiences and values." John the Divine, who describes himself as one who shares with his fellow believers the persecution and the kingdom and the patient endurance (1:9), invites the Christians of Asia to take a heavenly and end-time look at their experiences of sporadic harassment for the name of Jesus, of fellow believers who have too willingly sold their souls in exchange for Babylon's values, and of their own temptations to flee their faith for physical comfort and safety. Yes, John comforts his readers with various visions of how God will finally triumph over the forces of death and evil and vindicate those who have suffered, are suffering, or will suffer for their faith. Thomas B. Slater (1998, 250–51) uses slightly different terminology but makes the same point: "John placed a regional repression of Christians on a cosmic scale in order to explain the plight of his fellow Christians within the wider perspective of the divine plan." As we will see momentarily, John uses the hymns that populate his Revelation to convey his vision of ultimate reality to his readers and to allow them to participate now, through worship, in end-time vindication.

Finally, Aune (1997, lxxxii) defines the *function* of Revelation as threefold: "(a) to legitimate the transcendent authorization of the message, (b) by mediating a reactualization of the original revelatory experience through a variety of literary devices, structures, and imagery . . . , so that (c) the recipients of the message will be encouraged to continue to pursue, or if necessary to modify, their thinking and behavior in conformity with transcendent perspectives." Let me take each one of these three aspects of Revelation's function in turn. It is obvious from the beginning to the end of Revelation that John the Divine is not conveying his own message, but God's word. Take, for example, John's words in 22:6: "And he (the angel) said to me: 'These words are trustworthy and true, for the Lord, the God of the spirits of the prophets, has sent his angel to show his servants what must soon take place.'"

John has the further goal of trying to get his readers and audience to experience the heavenly visions and insights he has been granted. In this light John's goal is similar to that of the artist, be he or she playwright, musical composer, poet, or novelist, that is, to take the participant away from ordinary time and space into another time and space where the transcendent can be glimpsed with fear, trembling, and joy, where ordinary meanings are seen in the light of eternal ones. Some of John's literary devices and images may indeed be strange to us in the third millennium and may tax our imaginations to quick exhaustion. But others, while at first strange, have been made familiar to us through dramatic music with soloists and large chorus. I refer again to the familiar Handel's *The Messiah* and its famous choruses of "Hallelujah" and "Worthy is the Lamb." The spiritual "Ride on, King Jesus" captures so well for us the power of the Lord over evil that we can easily assimilate the imagery of his white horse, his eyes like a flame of fire, and the sharp sword that issues from his mouth. Or can the person who has been part of a large group of people marching for social justice and singing "We Shall Overcome Someday" fail to experience, at least for a fleeting but precious moment, that evil has had its day and that God's plan for good will overcome? Charles H. Talbert (1994, 3–4) makes the same point: "Revelation is a script for an oral performance in a ritual setting. . . . By means of an oral enactment, the auditors entered into another universe and experienced a new reality. Revelation's power continues to be felt best when it is heard." A colleague of mine tells me that the public reading aloud of Revelation by his students in class takes sixty-four minutes and is a wonderful and fantastic experience. Could such a public reading become the content of a Lenten evening service and a means of strengthening the community's life of faith and discipleship?

The third aspect of Revelation's function moves in the realm of thought and behavior modification. This is, indeed, the proof of the pudding. John's visions, prophecies, and hymns have as their goal to lead his beleaguered readers in Asia to be steadfast in the faith, to abandon their inclinations to assimilate Babylon's values, and to take comfort from the Lamb, who, though slaughtered, has triumphed. In this regard note how often the author of Revelation calls for "patient endurance" or gives examples of those who have testified faithfully to Jesus. I ask my readers to look up Revelation 1:9; 2:2-3, 19; 13:10; 14:12; 19:10; 20:4. Seen from the perspective as a call to faithful discipleship, Revelation is very much like the Gospels and their appeal to patient discipleship and taking up the cross of Jesus.

THE HYMNS OF REVELATION

For the sake of more easy comprehension of wondrous materials, I investigate the hymns of Revelation from four angles: their number and nature; content; context in Revelation; context in the liturgies of the Christian communities, past and present.

Number and Nature of the Hymns in Revelation

I give my readers an advance idea of the large number of hymns in Revelation by quoting from four authors. Reinhard Deichgräber (1967, 44-59) counts thirteen hymns: 4:8; 4:11; 5:9-10; 5:12; 5:13; 7:10; 7:12; 11:15; 11:17-18; 12:10-12; 15:3-4; 16:5-6; 19:1-8. David E. Aune (1997, 315), by dividing 19:1-8 into four distinct hymns, arrives at the number of sixteen hymns: 4:8c; 4:11; 5:9b-10; 5:12b; 5:13b; 7:10b; 7:12; 11:15b; 11:17-18; 12:10b-12; 15:3b-4; 16:5b-7b; 19:1b-2; 19:3; 19:5b; 19:6b-8. He further avers that "with the exception of the single independent hymn in 15:3b-4, they are arranged in seven antiphonal units (4:8-11; 5:9-14; 7:9-12; 11:15-18; 16:5-7; 19:1-4, 5-8)." While mentioning the same hymns that have been detected by Deichgräber and Aune, David R. Carnegie (1982, 243 n. 1) adds 1:5b-6, 13:4, and 18:20 to the pool of hymns in Revelation. Finally, Charles M. Mountain (1996) arrives at eighteen hymns by counting the sixteen found in Aune as well as 13:4 and 14:3. Mountain (1996, 46) also suggests that there are other possible hymns in Revelation, to wit, the hymn of lament found in 18:2, 10, 14, 16, 17-20 and the "Prophetic Proclamation in the Form of a Hymn of Praise" in 7:14-17. While not arguing the point in this context, I believe that scholars should cast a wide net in counting and analyzing the hymns in Revelation. In my subsequent analysis I will follow Carnegie's listing of Revelation's hymns.

Counting the number of hymns in Revelation presupposes that we know the nature of a hymn and can spot its presence. In their efforts over the years to detect the presence of a preexistent hymn that a New Testament author may have incorporated into his writing, scholars have come up with two general criteria. As Peter T. O'Brien (1991, 188–89) writes:

> Recent scholarship has drawn attention to two criteria for discerning hymnic material in the NT: (a) *stylistic*: a certain rhythmical lilt when the passages are read aloud, the presence of *parallelismus membrorum* (i.e., an arrangement into couplets), the semblance of some metre, and the presence of rhetorical devices such as alliteration, *chiasmus*, and antithesis; and (b) *linguistic*: an unusual vocabulary, particularly the presence of theological terms, which is different from the surrounding context.

As scholars have employed these criteria to hymnic passages in Revelation, it is clear that these passages generally meet the first criterion, especially through their extensive use of *parallelismus membrorum*. But as Deichgräber (1967, 58–59) has contended, they fail the test of the second criterion. For these hymns are closely linked to their contexts, for example, 5:9-10. Second, their vocabulary is that of the author. Note, for example, that 11:17-18 uses the Greek *pantocrator* (Almighty), which also occurs in 1:8; 4:8; 15:3; 16:7; 19:6 and 21:22, for a total of seven times. However, Deichgräber does concede that the author, in composing his hymns, may have used liturgical forms that were employed in the Christian communities he knew, such as "Hallelujah!" and "Holy, Holy, Holy." I direct those readers interested in a contrary view to consult the article by John J. O'Rourke (1968).

So the hymns in Revelation are indeed hymns because they fit the first criterion determined by the scholarly community. And John the Divine has taken appropriate steps to make sure that readers would spot his hymns by introducing sixteen of them with the verb "saying" and setting them in a context of worship of God and/or the slaughtered Lamb.

As I have worked through the hymns of Revelation, I have discovered that their nature is diverse. There are acclamations, doxologies, judgment doxologies, songs of victory, and one thanksgiving song. While this diversity suggests the richness of worship, it also suggests to me the inexhaustible nature of the object(s) of worship. Use all the forms of worship you possibly can, and still you won't begin to plumb the depths of God, creator and redeemer. As we work through the hymns of Revelation, I invite my readers to tally the different ways in which the composer of the hymns of Revelation tells us about God. Is such diversity haphazard or, like so many other features of Revelation, theologically purposeful?

Theological Content of the Hymns in Revelation

In examining the content or theology of these hymns, I follow the leads of Leonard Thompson, Richard Bauckham, and Josephine Massyngbaerde Ford. Thompson (1973, 468) makes the following important observation: "hymns express the *fides quae creditur*, and they are a means of evoking the *fides qua creditur*." That is, the hymns give voice to the objective faith that Christians believe, but they can also lead to and convey a subjective experience of these objects of faith, God or the Lord Jesus Messiah. Bauckham (1993a, 35) says: "The issue of true and false worship is fundamental to John's prophetic insight into the power-structures of the world his readers lived in." And relative to the Christology of Revelation, Ford (1998, 212) makes the helpful suggestion: "Although the hymns may not be in chronological order, one can trace a developing Christology through these hymns if one considers them in the light of the various eschatological figures anticipated by different Jewish groups in the second-temple period." So while the visions of the seven seals, trumpets, and bowls show God's power and judgment in action, it is the hymns of Revelation that largely convey its theology and Christology. And it is to these teachings, as they occur in Revelation's hymns, that we now turn.

Revelation 1:5b-6

Of the four authors I cited above it was only David Carnegie (1982, 249–50) who listed 1:5b-6 as one of Revelation's hymns. I provide my own translation, for contemporary translations that aim at smoothness often mask the roughness of this hymn. I start with verse 5: "And from Jesus Christ, the witness, the faithful, the first born of the dead and the ruler of the kings of the earth. To him who loves us and who freed us from our sins by his blood, and he made us a kingdom, priests to his God and Father, to him be glory and power forever and ever. Amen." At base we have a doxology here: "to him . . . be glory and power forever and ever. Amen." But this doxology has been doubly expanded through narrative. The first expansion consists of the two participles "loves us" and "freed us." The second expansion is a full sentence whose verb is not a participle: "And he made us a kingdom, priests to his God and Father." And David E. Aune (1997, 45) increases our sense of the strangeness of these verses when he astutely observes: "No other doxology incorporates such a brief narrative into its structure. Further, this doxology is addressed to Christ, while Christian doxologies are almost exclusively addressed to God." The criteria I mentioned above for the detection of preexistent hymnic material were stylistic and linguistic. While being generally helpful, these criteria may be too narrow. In this instance the expansive eleven criteria of Markus Barth (1974, 6–8) are very helpful. Barth's third criterion fits our verses quite well: "Specific deeds of God or Christ are with preference described either by the (aorist) participle of a verb, or by relative clauses" (7). In the instance at hand we have the two participles: "who loves us and freed us." Also Barth's fourth criterion applies: "Those who benefit from God's mighty acts speak in the first person plural" (7). In 1:5-6 Jesus Christ is not proclaimed as some abstract person and ruler but as one who has touched "our" lives. Finally, the content of what Jesus has done—loves, freed, created a kingdom and priests— seems traditional or borrowed, that is, it is prepackaged and does not come from the author. It echoes with three other New Testament passages which seem couched in traditional terminology. I refer to Galatians 2:20: "And the life I now live in the flesh I live by faith in the Son of God *who loved me and gave himself for me.*" And Ephesians 5:2 has: "And live in love, as *Christ loved us and gave himself up for us.*" And behind Revelation 1:6 there seems to be a interpretation of Exodus 19:6 similar to that of 1 Peter 2:5 and 10: Christians are a holy priesthood and offer spiritual sacrifices acceptable to God through Jesus Christ.

In brief, my point is that at the beginning of his Revelation John the Divine has quoted a traditional hymn/creed upon which he will expand in what follows. Just as the Jesus Christ he will portray in the hymns that follow is witness, faithful, first born from the dead, and ruler of the kings of the ages, so too does this Jesus love those he has freed from their sins by the shedding of his blood and made them a kingdom and priests for his God and Father. Here we have theology, Christology, and ecclesiology neatly combined. This opening hymn/ creed is so important to John that he virtually absorbs it in the new song sung to the slaughtered Lamb in 5:9b-10: "Because you were slaughtered and purchased for God by your blood from every tribe and tongue and people and nation. And you made them a kingdom and priests for our God, and they shall reign on the earth." Further, the thought of this opening hymn makes its appearance at the end of Revelation, thus forming a literary *inclusio:* "And the servants of God and of the Lamb will reign forever and ever" (22:5).

I leave off consideration of Revelation 1:5b-6, knowing that it is not quite the same as the other hymns in Revelation, for it is not antiphonal nor is it introduced by a verb of "saying" nor is it sounded in a throne-room scene nor is it included in the heart of Revelation where all the other hymns are. Yet judged by criteria that have been used to ascertain the presence of other preexistent hymns and creeds in the New Testament, it stands a good chance of being a hymn/creed.

Revelation 4–5

Five of the hymns detected by scholars occur in Revelation 4–5. The first section of this throne-room vision constitutes chapter 4 and deals with God. The author uses antiquity's symbol for power, to sit on the throne, to describe God (4:2-3). And it is this God who is professed in the hymn of 4:8 to be transcendently above and beyond all (Holy, holy, holy!), who is *Pantocrator* (Almighty), and who always was, is, and will always be. In traditional terms these are God's attributes: transcendent, almighty, eternal. And the next hymn (4:11) is an acclamation of God's worthiness, for God alone is creator. The "for" clause of this acclamation expresses the faith of the community in lovely parallelism, "for you created all things. And by your will they existed and were created."

All of Revelation 5 comprises the second section of John's inaugural throne-room vision and deals with the Lion of the tribe of Judah, who in actuality is the slaughtered Lamb. He is the only one able to open the sealed scroll and set into motion the final accomplishment of God's will and plan. The first hymn in honor of the Lamb is found in 5:9-10 and is an acclamation in the "you" style used earlier in the acclamation to God in 4:11. This "new song" is similar to that sung by Moses and Miriam in Exodus 15 for God's liberation from Egyptian slavery through the blood of the Passover lamb and confesses the universal dimensions of the Lamb's ransoming activity: "from every tribe and language and people and nation." And important for our theme is that the ransomed people are "priests" (5:10) in praise and worship of their God (see 1:6 and Exodus 19:6). The second acclamation of Revelation 5 is found in verse 12, is in the third person, and carries the christological thought of this chapter forward significantly. For it attributes to the slaughtered Lamb what the earlier acclamation in 4:11 had attributed to God: "glory and honor and power," as well as wealth and wisdom and might and blessing. And the final hymn in 5:13 is a doxology to both the one seated on the throne and to the Lamb, both of whom are to receive "blessing and honor and glory and might forever and ever."

From our angle of vision the five hymns in Revelation 4–5, two to God and three to the Lamb, are truly remarkable for what they say about the content of Christian faith. In the words of Richard Bauckham (1981, 331):

> The conjunction of God and the Lamb (cf. 7:10; 11:15; 14:4; 20:6; 22:1) in this verse (5:13) illustrates how John, while holding Christ worthy of worship, remains sensitive to the issue of monotheism in worship. Christ cannot be a second object of worship alongside God, and so the specific worship of Christ (5:9-12) leads to the joint worship of God and Christ, in a formula in which God retains the primacy.

And this is the faith that Christians in Asia are willing to die for. And it is the faith sung by every creature in heaven, on earth, under the earth, and in the sea and by all that is in them. And to this song of faith the four living creatures say: "Let it be. Amen," and the twenty-four elders fall down and worship (see 5:13-14). Indeed, this faith is acknowledged to be universally true.

Revelation 7:10-12

Between the opening of the sixth and seventh seals two hymns are sung antiphonally in the heavenly throne room. In the first hymn an uncountable multitude from every nation, tribe, people, and language stand before the throne and before the Lamb and sing "a short cry of victory": "Victory belongs to our God who is seated on the throne and to the Lamb." The two closest parallels to this "short cry of victory" are Psalm 3:9 and Jonah 2:9 (2:10 in the Hebrew Bible). And the context of Revelation indicates that the Greek word *soteria* means "salvation" as deliverance from and victory over persecution. It is a celebration of the victory of both God and the Lamb and puts into song the Pauline theme of "grace alone" (*sola gratia*).

The doxology that follows in 7:12 is sung in worship to God by all the angels who are standing around God's throne. The seven predicates of this doxology are almost identical to those sung of the Lamb in the hymn of 5:12: "Blessing and glory and wisdom and thanksgiving and honor and power and might be to our God forever and ever! Amen." Thus, the human and angelic realms give praise and glory to God and to the Lamb for salvific victory over persecution and death.

Revelation 11:15-18

The next set of antiphonal hymns occurs in 11:15-18 after the seventh angel blew his trumpet. The first hymn comes from loud voices in heaven and is somewhat difficult to categorize. Although Deichgräber considers it a "song of victory," Klaus-Peter Jörns is rightly hesitant. It seems rather to be a proclamation of fulfillment of the promise of God's reign (see Micah 4:7) and adds an important dimension to the faith being transmitted by Revelation's hymns. Not only creation and redemption come from the one seated on the throne and from the Lamb, but also the final and complete conquest of all powers that stand against the divine will. In anticipation, but with firm belief, this first hymn proclaims: "The kingdom of the world has passed over to the rule of our Lord and of his Christ. And he will rule forever and ever" (11:15). And the twenty-four elders worship God, and in response to the proclamation of 11:15 sing a thanksgiving song that celebrates God's judgment upon the saints, all who fear God's name, and the raging nations (11:17-18). Using expressions with which we are already familiar from the early hymns of Revelation 4–5, the thanksgiving song begins: "We give you thanks, Lord God *Pantocrator*, who are and who were, for you have taken your great power and begun to reign" (11:17).

Revelation 12:10-12

At first blush, the hymn of 12:10-12 is quite different. Unlike the hymns we have studied so far, it is not an antiphonal hymn. And so we are not given two or more voices singing two or more hymns to guide us in our interpretation. But there is guidance of another sort, for the "accuser" or "devil" is the element that unifies the three verses or strophes of this hymn. In 12:10 God and the Messiah have expelled the "accuser" from heaven. In 12:11 the saints have conquered the devil by the blood of the Lamb and by their selfless testimony. In 12:12 a woe is uttered upon the earth, for the devil has come down to it. Thus, the content of this hymn also expresses the faith of the communities in Asia. As the martyrs have shown, God is *Pantocrator* to cast the "accuser" out of heaven, and the blood of the Lamb conquers the devil. While this hymn may be merely a variation of the faith expressed in the antiphonal hymn of 11:15-18, it adds a cosmic dimension to the trials and temptations of faith and the victory of God and his Messiah. As Ford (1998, 223) says, "the victory and authority of the Anointed One are not limited to victory over Satan but are also a victory over the first and second death. Importantly, this hymn shows that close union of the martyrs, the church, with the Christ: Their victory should be celebrated by the entire universe."

Let me take the opportunity of the hymn of 12:10-12 to make a point that probably has become clear to my astute readers. The hymn of 12:10-12 is a perfect example of the contention of Jörns (1971, 163) that many of the hymns in Revelation display a mixed form. That is, they may not, for example, be pure "doxologies" or "short cries of victory." While Jörns' summary analysis of the hymns of Revelation (1971, 162–63) may be slightly atomistic, it is nonetheless instructive. Run a careful eye over 12:10-12 and detect how the composer uses parallelisms such as you find in many of the Old Testament psalms. For example, in 12:11 the phrase "by the blood of the Lamb" is set in parallel to the phrase "by the word of their testimony." And note how 12:12 balances a "cry of rejoicing" with a "cry of woe." And for Jörns, 12:10 is mixed indeed as it combines the Old Testament "short cry of victory" with the predicates of a "doxology," before moving to the "for" clause which, in turn, uses the hymnic "participial" style in "who accuses." While the composer's literary finesse comes across especially in the Greek text, enough shines through even in English translation for us to appreciate it.

Revelation 13:4

Most commentators do not include 13:4 among the hymns, for it is largely in narrative style. But I agree with David R. Carnegie (1982, 254) that it needs to be considered in any discussion of the hymns of Revelation and the motif of true and false worship. Carnegie writes: "There is an obvious and intended contrast between the heavenly worship of God and the Lamb in Revelation 4 and 5, and the earthly worship of the beast in Revelation 13. It is particularly noteworthy that the worship of the beast is set in the form of a hymn (Revelation 13:4b) corresponding to the hymns of praise offered to God and the Lamb." Who can read 13:4 after studying the earlier hymns and not miss the brutal parody: "They worshiped the dragon, for he had given his authority to the beast. And they worshiped the beast, saying: 'Who is like the beast, and who can fight against it?'" The succeeding chapters will give a dramatic theological answer to this question. For not only can the Lamb fight against the beast, but the Lamb will also conquer it.

Revelation 15:3-4

The hymn of 15:3-4 is remarkable in a number of ways. First, it is not antiphonal. Second, it is sung in heaven, but not by the four living creatures nor by the twenty-four elders nor by myriads of angels, but by those who have conquered the beast. Third, as any annotated Bible will indicate, it contains so many biblical allusions that it is unique in this regard among the hymns of Revelation. Finally, the universality of salvation celebrated in this hymn is extraordinary in a book that seems to champion the destruction of one's enemies. David Aune (1998, 873–74) is correct in calling these verses a descriptive hymn of praise in the "you" style and in noting that 15:3-4 lack the typical introduction of a descriptive hymn of praise, that is, a call to praise in the imperative.

It is to the credit of Richard Bauckham (1993a, 98–102; 1993b, 296–307) that he has made good sense of the rationale behind the Old Testament allusions in this hymn where others have just seen a pastiche of biblical allusions. The following verses from the Song of Moses in Exodus 15:11-14 are key. I underline Exodus 15:11: "Who is like you, O Lord, among the gods? Who is like you, majestic in holiness, awesome in splendor, doing wonders? You stretched out your right hand. The earth swallowed them. In your steadfast love you led the people whom you redeemed. You guided them by your strength to your holy abode. The peoples heard and trembled" (Exodus 15:11-14). Thus, God's uniqueness, liberating power, and the establishment of God's people are celebrated. The non-Israelites are in awe.

But how does John the Divine get from Moses' song in Exodus 15 to the note of universality in the new song of the Lamb in Revelation 15:3-4? He does so by using a principle from Jewish exegesis, that is, passages in which the same words or phrases occur can be used to interpret each other. And there are three major Old Testament passages that do contain some of the same words that Exodus 15:11 does. And because this is so, the interpreter can illumine Exodus 15:11 by the passages that are not the same. I underline those passages quoted in Revelation 15:3-4 and matched in Exodus 15:11. The first passage is Jeremiah 10:6-7a: "There is none like you, O LORD. You are great, and your name is great in might. Who would not fear you, O King of the nations? For that is your due." The second passage comes from Psalm

86:8-10: "There is none like you among the gods, O Lord, nor are there any works like yours. <u>All the nations</u> you have made <u>shall come, and prostrate before you,</u> O Lord, <u>and shall glorify your name.</u> For you are great and <u>do wondrous things</u>. <u>You alone are God</u>." Finally, there is Psalm 98:2: "O sing to the Lord a new song, <u>for he has done wondrous things</u>. His right hand and his holy arm have gotten him victory. The LORD has made known his victory. He has <u>revealed his righteous acts</u> in the sight of the nations." Through his exegetical method the composer of 15:3-4 does indeed have the victorious witnesses sing a new song of liberation, but it is also the Song of the Lamb. Victory comes through death, but now not only for the victors, but also for those who wielded the sword. As Bauckham (1993b, 306) writes: "The vindication of the martyrs is the victory of God celebrated in the song of the Lamb, corresponding to the wondrous deeds done by Yahweh at the Red Sea. Just as the latter led to the awed recognition of his deity by the nations who heard of them (Exod 15:14-16), so the former leads to the repentance and worship of all the nations (Rev 15:4). "

If my readers have been checking off what items of the creed are being celebrated by the various hymns, the hymn of 15:3-4 invites you to put a big check mark alongside "salvation of all." A further tick might be put alongside "liberation/deliverance." For just as God delivered Israel from the rule of its oppressors, so too does God now liberate the faithful from an oppressive regime. And just as Moses and Miriam celebrated Israel's deliverance in song, so too do these faithful, in their turn, celebrate their deliverance with the new song of the slaughtered Lamb.

Revelation 16:5-7

It seems that scholars give little attention to the hymn in Revelation 16:5-7. For example, although Carnegie (1982) lists it among the hymns of Revelation, he does not discuss it at all. And in an extensive article on Revelation's hymns Ford (1998, 225) devotes merely four lines to 16:5-7. And contemporary lectionary and breviary eschew this hymn like the plague.

I begin my analysis of this largely neglected hymn by quoting what David Aune (1998, 885–86) says about its literary form. Although many scholars refer to this hymn as a "judgment doxology," Aune considers it "a declarative hymn of praise." He writes: "The 'judgment doxology' is in fact a more specific form of the *declarative hymn of praise*, in which the focal issue is the justice of God's punitive actions. In OT hymns the glorification of Yahweh as judge occurs more frequently than the celebration of Yahweh as creator or king. . . ." In brief, this antiphonal hymn is about God's justice for and vindication of God's persecuted and martyred "saints and prophets."

Revelation 16:5-7 is related to the hymn of 15:3-4 in three ways. First, "the angel of the waters" prays it after the third bowl of plagues had been poured forth. These plagues are modeled after the ten plagues that God visited on Egypt through Moses as part of God's liberation of his people. The hymn of 15:3-4 comes from this same general context of Exodus and liberation and is introduced as "the song of Moses, the servant of God, and the song of the Lamb." Second, the vocabulary of these two hymns is strikingly similar. Note, for example, how "For you alone are holy" (15:4) is paired with "You are just, O Holy One" (16:5), and "Just and true are your ways" (15:3) is paired with "Your judgments are true and just" (16:7). Finally and closely related to the previous point, there is the theological clash between God's will to universal salvation in 15:3-4 and God's justice in 16:5-7. As Adela Yarbro Collins (1977, 372–73) has shown, the vocabulary of the hymn in 16:5-7 is that of John the Divine. That is, he didn't borrow a traditional hymn, whose theology, although distasteful, had to be swallowed. No, he composed this hymn with his eyes wide open. It is as if through the hymns of 15:3-4 and 16:5-7 John is saying: God wills universal salvation, but God is also just and against sin and will vindicate his faithful servants. And it seems that the author even wants to accentuate how untidy his theology is, for he writes in 16:9 and 11 that the fourth and fifth bowls were meant to bring people to repentance and were thus not strict punishments.

How does the hymn of 16:5-7 fit into the creed? Is it part of "to judge the living and the dead"? How does it fit into your creed?

Revelation 18:20

The materials in Revelation 18 are generally passed over in analyses of the hymns of Revelation. I note three exceptions. Charles Mountain (1996, 46) lists Revelation 18:2, 10, 14, 16, 17-20 as a "hymn of lament" and includes this hymn in his appendix under the category of "other possible hymns in Revelation"; but he gives virtually no commentary on it. Josephine M. Ford (1998, 225–27) titles the hymn of

Revelation 18:2-3, 4-8, 10, 14, 16, 19-23 "The Destruction of Babylon" and provides a helpful initial commentary on this hymn of lament. She rightly observes that this hymn, unlike others in Revelation, is not a hymn of praise nor does it occur in a worship setting. Finally, in a long footnote (1998, 226 n. 91) she makes a point that is very helpful for any contemporary retrieval of the meaning of Revelation and its hymns. She writes: "I should be prepared to follow the argument of C. H. Hunzinger, who sees Babylon as the symbol of a decadent society in general. . . ." Finally, David Carnegie lists Revelation 18:20 as a hymn but then gives it a slight commentary of three lines in a footnote (1982, 252 n. 38).

For the purposes of my thematic of true and false worship I focus on the hymn of Revelation 18:20, which technically is "a call to rejoice." It is a call for the entire universe and for the persecuted and murdered saints, apostles, and prophets to rejoice in the justice God is meting out to Babylon. And why is Babylon receiving her just deserts? From the laments of Revelation 18 it seems that she is being punished for her luxury, false worship, and arrogance toward God. For greater detail on Babylon's punishments I recommend the excellent article by Adela Yarbro Collins (1980, 200–3) on Revelation 18 as "funeral dirge." Babylon is described as wallowing in wealth, as 18:3 says: "And the merchants of the earth have grown rich from the power of her luxury." Babylon has been unfaithful to God and committed fornication with false gods, as 18:9 puts it: "And the kings of the earth . . . committed fornication and lived in luxury with her." And Babylon's arrogance towards God comes across very strongly in 18:6-7: "As she glorified herself and lived luxuriously. . . . Since in her heart she says: 'I rule as a queen. I am no widow, and I will never see grief.'" But as the final verse of this chapter, verse 24, makes clear, Babylon is also being punished for her persecution and killing of the saints: "And in her [Babylon] was found the blood of prophets and of saints and of all who have been slaughtered on earth."

Although the words of Richard Bauckham (1993a, 35) are written with the worship scene of Revelation 4 in mind, they can also apply to Revelation 18: "In the end, the book is about the incompatibility of the exclusive monotheistic worship portrayed in chapter 4 with every kind of idolatry—the political, social and economic idolatries from which more narrowly religious idolatry is inseparable." To this point I will return in my section on liturgical contexts, past and present, for the hymns of Revelation.

Revelation 19:1-8

I think that it may be of great significance that John the Divine, who is known for his literary techniques, began to use hymns in earnest with the five hymns in Revelation 4–5 and now concludes his use of hymns with the four in Revelation 19:1-8. Even if you tally the hymns in Revelation at eighteen, 50 percent occur in Revelation 4–5 and 19. It seems that the composer of hymns is also the composer of a literary inclusion whereby themes first announced in the hymns of chapters 4–5 are picked up once again and given wondrous development in the hymns of 19:1-18. Let's examine these hymns and their themes now.

Revelation 19:1-8 is easily divided into two sections. Revelation 19:1-4 takes place in heaven and concludes the theme of God's just destruction of Babylon (18:1-24). The second section, while introduced from heaven, encompasses those on earth and celebrates the nuptials of the Lamb and his bride. Thus, theology, Christology, and ecclesiology come together in the final hymns of Revelation.

Revelation 19:1-2 describes John's audition of the hymn of a great multitude in heaven. This hymn seems to be a combination of a judgment doxology and a victory cry. Note that it begins with "Hallelujah!," which means "Praise Yahweh!" Notice also that the reasons for giving God praise revolve around God's judgments: "His judgments [against Babylon] are true and just. He has judged the great whore . . ." (19:2). Further, glory (*doxa*) is given God for God's victory (salvation) over Babylon (19:1) in avenging God's servants. This judgment theme is continued in the short hymn of 19:3, which picks up words from 18:9 ("when they see the smoke of Babylon's burning") and praises God (Hallelujah). And the "Amen. Hallelujah!" of the twenty-four elders and the four living creatures in 19:4 is their confirmation of God's judgment as they fall down and worship God seated on the throne.

The final antiphonal hymns of Revelation occur in verses 5-8 and consist of a hymn of praise. In 19:5 the voice from the throne issues an invitation to all God's servants and all those who fear God from whatever walk of life to praise God (and not Babylon). And the great multitude responds with a voice "like the sound of mighty thunderclaps" and celebrates God's reign over Babylon and evil and the arrival of the marriage of the Lamb and his bride's readiness. As with so many events in Revelation, the Lamb's marriage and the saints' preparedness for that marriage is announced in anticipation of the complete enactment of God's plan and in anticipation of what John the Divine will describe in Revelation 21–22.

Conclusion on the Content of the Hymns of Revelation

In my brief treatments of the hymns of Revelation I have primarily stressed the faith that they impart (*fides quae creditur*). To bring another voice into the analysis of this "objective" faith, I call upon Esther Yue L. Ng (1990, 122–28). She argues well that the contents of the creed of the hymns of Revelation comprise the following elements: a fundamental assertion of God's transcendence; God as Creator; Christ as Redeemer; Christ as Executor and Revealer of God's Plans for Humanity; God as King and Judge; God as the Guarantor of Salvation; Christ as the Bridegroom and Coming One; God the Father and the Lamb as Worthy Recipients of Worship.

Let me build upon the objective creed of Revelation's hymns by picking up another one of their functions. That is, the hymns are meant to lead to faith (*fides qua creditur*). Klaus-Peter Jörns (1971, 174) says well:

> So we can describe the teaching of Revelation's hymns as "the hymnic Gospel." The fact that these hymns were sung of heavenly fulfilled promises (up until 19:6b-8) legitimizes their message. The fulfilled promises (sung of in the liturgy) provide assurance for the faith of the community that the things promised them will come to fulfillment. The "hymnic Gospel" is simultaneously comfort, exhortation, and a cry of jubilation, and it is part and parcel of the ambiguous time of waiting for the coming of God and God's Christ in salvation for believers and its opposite for the ungodly.

With these sentences that come from the conclusion of Jörns' book, which bears the title *The Hymnic Gospel*, we are at the doorstep of our next sections. For Jörns is alluding to the composer's placement of the hymns in Revelation and how they function liturgically.

The Literary Context of the Hymns in Revelation

In my brief analyses of Revelation's hymns I have tried to situate them in their literary and thus theological context(s). Space restraints prevent me from making more than a few important general observations at this point. A detailed outline of Revelation such as that of David Aune (1997, c–cv) would show how the hymns of Revelation occur in the major sections of Revelation 4–19 and that many of them occur in the heavenly throne room, for example, Revelation 4–5; 7:10-12. Klaus-Peter Jörns (1971, 174) views the literary positioning of Revelation's hymns from yet another angle: "the hymns occur either at the beginning (4–5; 12; 15) or at the end (7:11; 16; 18; 19) of larger sections in the overall structure of Revelation." That is, the fulfillment of God's salvific plan commences with or results in worship. And Leonard Thompson (1969, 342) has perhaps thematized this literary observation best: "heavenly worship is the literary form by means of which the seer realizes the kingship of God and his just judgment prior to the realization of these realities in the dramatic narrative form."

In my final section I want to probe the significance of Thompson's observations some more. Suffice it to say at this juncture that Revelation's hymns and its narrative episodes of divine visions are in literary cahoots to convey the composer's theology

The Role of Revelation's Hymns
in Liturgy, Past and Present

Liturgy Past

As I begin this section, I realize that the style of John the Divine has captivated me. For I, too, will be repeating what I said earlier, but from a different slant to engender greater insight. After giving a very broad description of early Christian worship from various sources, I will return to the liturgy of Revelation.

Earlier I argued that the author of Revelation did not borrow pre-existent hymns but created his own hymns. Yet that opinion need not mean that the hymns of Revelation or Revelation itself did not have their origin in early Christian worship services. Although it is hard to come across a blueprint of early Christian worship, we do have some helpful sketches of the important role that singing hymns played in liturgy. I start with Paul and the Pauline tradition. In 1 Corinthians 12–14 Paul has much to say about the spiritual gifts and their place in worship. I limit myself to a few pertinent points. Paul was familiar with male and female prophets and their prophecies. And does not Revelation call itself a book of prophecy (1:3)? The Pauline worship service also consisted of "apocalypses" or "revelations" (14:6). Could the revelation of one of John the Divine's visions, all of which came to him on a Sunday (1:10), have been presented first at a worship service? And there was the singing of praise (14:15).

Moving to the Pauline tradition, I note that Colossians 3:16 reads: "Let the word of Christ dwell in you richly. Teach and admonish one another in all wisdom. And with gratitude in your hearts sing psalms, hymns, and spiritual songs to God." And Ephesians 5:18-20 has something quite similar: "be filled with the Spirit, as you sing psalms and hymns and spiritual songs among yourselves, singing and making melody to the Lord in your hearts, giving thanks to God the Father at all times and for everything in the name of our Lord Jesus Christ." It does not seem to me that the authors of these two Pauline letters were talking about ideals but about the realities of worship in their communities. It was worship with many, many songs of various types. And in the opinion of Leonard L. Thompson (1990, 71): "Singing involves a double movement. It is a movement from the human to the divine, a human act of praise; but it is also a movement from the divine to the human, a making present of the God. Hymns can be sung only if the Spirit impells [sic]."

While works such as Edgar Krentz (1995) provide marvelous materials about the rich hymnody of antiquity that quite likely informed Christian worship, Philo of Alexandria, a contemporary of Paul, provides a concrete example of the wealth of these hymnic resources in a Jewish context. Would not the Christian communities of Asia Minor addressed by John the Divine have had similar rich resources? In his *On the Contemplative Life* Philo provides a description of the banquet that the members of an ascetic Jewish community of men and women called the Therapeutae or healers celebrated every seven weeks. Their banquet or worship service had much music. I quote from *On the Contemplative Life* 10.80 in the translation of David Winston:

> Then the president rises and sings a hymn composed in honor of the Deity, either a new one of his own composition, or an old one by poets of an earlier age. For they have bequeathed many meters and melodies, iambic verse, hymns suited for processions, libations, and the altar, odes sung by the chorus when either stationary or dancing, well arranged metrically for its various evolutions. After him the others too sing in their places and in proper order while all the rest listen in deep silence, except when they need to chant the choral refrains, for then they all sing out, men and women alike.

Philo is an excellent witness of how skilled singers combined traditional hymnody with new creations and how these men and women singers chanted choral refrains. Could one want a more powerful parallel to the "new song" of Revelation 5:9-10?

To this evidence from "believers," I turn to evidence I produced earlier in this chapter in "The Life Setting of Revelation." In his interrogations of Christians the nonbeliever Pliny the Younger discovered a number of important things about Christian worship. Am I stretching my readers' imaginations if I ask them to think that what Pliny turned up about A.D. 112 was part of Christian worship in Asia some twenty years earlier and may apply to Revelation? Pliny's *Letter 96* to Trajan has: "They [the Christians] also declared that the sum total of their guilt or error amounted to no more than this: they had met regularly before dawn on a fixed day to chant verses alternately among themselves in honor of Christ as if to a god. . . ." Were these Christians chanting verses, on alternate sides, of hymns such as Philippians 2:6-11 or Colossians 1:15-20? Or some hymns similar to the hymns we studied in Revelation 5?

Assembling the various pieces of evidence I have outlined above does not constitute proof that the hymns of Revelation were actually used in any worship service anywhere in Asia. But they inform my imagination of how John the Divine and the communities in Asia may have come to worship in hymns the one sitting on the throne and the Lamb that was slaughtered.

And Revelation and its hymns provide other evidence of how these hymns helped Christians to combat the allure of Babylon and endure harassment for their faith. It is the opinion of David E. Aune (1983) that John the Divine may have composed some of his hymns and their settings to counter and even parody "Roman Imperial Court Ceremonial." Aune's observations fall short of proof, but they are suggestive. First, the primary responsibility of the Roman emperor from the time of Julius Caesar on was to render justice. People came from far and wide to the emperor for justice. Is it just happenstance that the primary role of God in Revelation is to dispense justice and that God is praised for exercising justice in the "judgment doxologies" of Revelation? Also there is evidence that conquered foreign rulers appeared before the emperor and worshiped him. Further evidence indicates that people gave golden crowns to the emperor as a sign of obeisance. And what do the twenty-four elders do except despoil themselves of their golden crowns in obedience to the one seated on the throne (4:10)? And there is some late evidence of acclamations given to emperors and other rulers. Take, for example, this acclamation to an Augustus: "Our hope is in You. You are our salvation!" which was repeated twenty-six times. And acclamations to God and to the Lamb abound in Revelation. Finally, it could quite well be that what is proclaimed of the one seated on the throne in Revelation 4:11 is directed against what Emperor Domitian claimed for himself: "Our Lord and God" (see David Aune [1997, 311–12]).

From these scraps of evidence I am of the opinion that the worship services or prayer meetings in John the Divine's time were quite lively and largely composed of Spirit-filled singing and were directed to and guided by their experiences of local persecution for the faith. And it is through this worship and singing that they experienced God's powerful presence and God's will to conquer the forces of evil, be these of individual or governmental nature. It seems to me that the imagery of the seven seals, trumpets, and bowls could just be wishful thinking and pie in the sky. But the communities in the province of Asia addressed by the prophecy of John knew that this imagery spoke the truth because during their worship they experienced the power and judgment of the one sitting on the throne and the slaughtered Lamb. The reality of this worship experience made John's visions and auditions real. The faith they experienced at worship led to and deepened their faith in the final judgment of their God over whatever evils they faced. Finally, their faith, enlivened and emboldened by worship, looked forward to worship in the New Jerusalem where there is no temple. "For its temple is the Lord God *Pantocrator* and the Lamb" (21:22). Indeed, the angel's words to John ring true: "Don't worship me. Worship God!" (see 22:9).

Liturgy Present

After I have typed and retyped and retyped the previous pages about Revelation's hymns, I come to the end of it all and ask: Do Revelation's hymns make an actual difference in the life of the church? Do Christian communities find nurture in these sixteen or so hymns? Would Christians take to the streets in civil disobedience and in protests against oppressive powers after singing hymns modeled after those of Revelation? It seems that the responses will differ. Charles M. Mountain (1996, 41) notes that one recent denominational hymnal contains at least eighty hymns based on Revelation. Hopefully, individual communities will take advantage of this largess and nourish their faith from Revelation's hymnody. But sadly the observation of Esther Yue L. Ng (1990, 119) is probably a better indicator of the actual situation in the churches: "apart from the first three chapters and certain hymnic portions, the book of Revelation is seldom preached from the pulpit, sung in church, or read in quiet devotions in some circles." What a shame! But rather than shame others, I should direct shame against my own high church tradition where Revelation is kept in the sacristy except for a paltry annual ration of two servings. Every third year in Cycle C (1998, 2001, etc.) regular churchgoers will find that the second reading for the Second through Sixth Sundays of Easter comes from Revelation. I note that only one hymn (5:1-14) is found in these five lections and that hardly a priest in the land will base his homily on the second reading.

Those whom piety and schedule prompt to attend daily Eucharistic liturgy will discover that Revelation occurs every other year (2000, 2002, etc.) as the first reading for the last two weeks (thirty-third and thirty-fourth) of the liturgical year. Four of these twelve selections contain hymnic materials: 4:1-11; 5:1-10; 15:1-4; 19:1-3, 9. For those who say the breviary or Divine Office, ten of the sixteen hymns listed by David E. Aune (1997, 315) occur with great frequency. Revelation 4:11 and 5:9, 10, 12 are used at evening prayer every Tuesday. Revelation 11:17-18 and 12:10b-12a occur at evening prayer every Thursday. Revelation 15:3-4 is featured at evening prayer every Friday. Finally, Revelation 19:1-2a, 5, 6b-7 is part of evening prayer every Sunday. But if people would compare the wording of these hymns in the breviary with their wording in a standard translation, they would realize that these hymns have been taken out of context and trimmed of their antiphonal components and "offensive" words.

In summary of the Roman Catholic Church's use of Revelation for liturgy, I judge that the devout and observant attendee at weekly liturgy will be exposed to some of the richly symbolic teaching of Revelation over the course of three years. Those who say the breviary or Divine Office will experience most of the splendid hymns of Revelation on a weekly basis in an adjusted version. But ordinary churchgoers, who number in the millions, will hardly hear a verse from Revelation and would be startled if a homilist would actually preach from Revelation. I am pleased to acknowledge kindred thoughts in a recent article by Petros Vassiliadis (1997, 112), who concludes thus: "The reintegration of the book of the Apocalypse into the entire liturgical cycle of the Church . . . remains one of the most urgent 'desiderata' of contemporary Orthodoxy."

In accordance with the time honored principle of *ecclesia semper reformanda est* (the church always has to be reformed), I, for one, think a reform is in order. And as with many reforms, it may be wise to start the reformation with the clergy, nuns, and monks. If the hymns from Revelation used four times a week at Vespers could be recited in a form that looks more like their original selves, then the transformative power that these hymns had at the time of John the Divine and at crucial times since then might work its way into the hearts and minds of those who pray and sing them. And this transformative power might in turn be shared with laity and others who fear God. Might it be too quixotic to think that those monks, nuns, and clergy who recite the full hymns of Revelation at Vespers four times a week would be led to some countercultural activity against idolatrous economic, political, and social powers? And as in the days of Pliny the Younger, what contemporary temples, cultural rituals, and recreational facilities would be abandoned by Christians whose worship is directed solely to the one seated on the throne and the slaughtered Lamb?

FOR FURTHER READING

Aune, David E. 1983. "The Influence of Roman Imperial Court Ceremonial on the Apocalypse of John." *Biblical Research* 28: 5–26.

———. 1997–1998. *Revelation 1–5, 6–16, 17–22.* Word Biblical Commentary 52A, B, C. Nashville: Thomas Nelson.

Barth, Markus. *Ephesians: Introduction, Translation, and Commentary on Chapters 1–3.* Anchor Bible 34A. Garden City: Doubleday.

Bauckham, Richard. 1981. "The Worship of Jesus in Apocalyptic Christianity." *New Testament Studies* 27: 322–41.

———. 1993a. *The Theology of the Book of Revelation.* New Testament Theology. New York: Cambridge University Press.

Carnegie, David R. 1982. "Worthy Is the Lamb: The Hymns in Revelation." In *Christ the Lord: Studies in Christology Presented to Donald Guthrie,* 243–56. Ed. Harold H. Rowden. Leicester: Inter-Varsity Press.

Ford, Josephine Massyngbaerde. 1998. "The Christological Function of the Hymns in the Apocalypse." *Andrews University Seminary Studies* 36: 207–29.

Howard-Brook, Wes, and Anthony Gwyther. 1999. *Unveiling Empire: Reading Revelation Then and Now*, 197–202. The Bible and Liberation Series. Maryknoll, New York: Orbis. This book arrived too late for me to consider its chapter on Revelation's hymns.

Mountain, Charles M. 1996. "'Glory and Honor and Blessing': The Hymns of the Apocalypse." *The Hymn* 47: 41–47.

Ng, Esther Yue L. 1990. "Prayer in Revelation." In *Teach Us To Pray: Prayer in the Bible and the World*, 119–35, 332–35. Ed. D. A. Carson. London: Paternoster; Grand Rapids: Baker Book House.

O'Brien, Peter T. 1991. *The Epistle to the Philippians. A Commentary on the Greek Text*. New International Greek Testament Commentary Series. Grand Rapids: Eerdmans.

O'Rourke, John J. 1968. "The Hymns of the Apocalypse." *Catholic Biblical Quarterly* 30: 399–409.

Pilgrim, Walter E. 1999. *Uneasy Neighbors: Church and State in the New Testament*. Overtures to Biblical Theology. Minneapolis Fortress.

Schüssler Fiorenza, Elisabeth. 1991. *Revelation: Vision of a Just World*. Proclamation Commentaries. Minneapolis: Fortress.

Slater, Thomas B. 1998. "On the Social Setting of the Revelation to John." *New Testament Studies* 44: 232–56.

Talbert, Charles H. 1994. *The Apocalypse: A Reading of the Revelation of John*. Louisville: Westminster John Knox.

Thompson, Leonard. 1969. "Cult and Eschatology in the Apocalypse of John." *Journal of Religion* 49: 330–50.

———. 1990. *The Book of Revelation: Apocalypse and Empire*. New York: Oxford University Press.

Yarbro Collins, Adela. 1984. *Crisis and Catharsis: The Power of the Apocalypse*. Philadelphia: Westminster.

6

Prayer in the Letter of James

W HY DEVOTE A CHAPTER to prayer in the Letter of James? Haven't we gotten more than sufficient information and challenge about prayer in the previous chapters? Yes and No. Yes, we learned much about prayer and have been consoled as we studied Jesus' teaching on prayer, Jesus at prayer, and the lessons on prayer given us by Luke, John, Paul, and John the Divine. No, we have learned too little about prayer and sickness. Or put another way, we have learned much, especially from our last chapter on the hymns in Revelation, about the psalms of praise; but largely absent from our curriculum so far have been the psalms of lament. I want to take a somewhat different look at James 5:13-18, focusing on 5:14: "The sick should call for the elders of the church and have them pray over them and anoint them with olive oil in the name of the Lord." But before we get to that passage, we have to do considerable homework.

WHAT IS THE LETTER OF JAMES?

At first sight James is far easier to understand than Revelation or even Paul. It hasn't the multiplicity of symbols and images of Revelation that can exhaust one's imagination and buoy up one's faith. And absent from it are Paul's involved and lapidary arguments about faith and sin, righteousness and circumcision, Jew and Gentile, God's fidelity to promises and how the Lord Jesus Christ, crucified for our sins and raised from the dead, relates to all of the above. Half of the verbs in the

163

Letter of James are imperatives. Whether we take to heart what James commands or pay mere lip service to his imperatives, it is clear that he is giving directions, for example, James 5:13: "Someone is experiencing difficulties. Pray!" But the problems for interpretation and understanding begin to arise when we try to see how James has arranged his imperatives over the course of five chapters. That is, what is the literary form of the Letter of James? What holds together the different thoughts on prayer present in James 5:13-18?

Simply put, the literary form of the Letter of James is exhortation (technically: paraenesis) in the format of a letter. Perhaps, we may get a better understanding of the literary form of James by looking very briefly at the more familiar passage of exhortation found in Romans 12:9-21, which occurs at the end of Paul's most theological letter to communities mainly unknown to him. I invite my readers to turn to this passage in their Bibles. First, I want you to rest with your first impression. Is your first impression that this passage lacks order? If you have seen disorder, allow me to guide your rereading of this passage, so that you can begin to see its order and its logic. As you read through this passage again, note that the word "good" occurs at its beginning and end, forming a literary inclusion and suggesting that this section is not put together haphazardly and will deal with various aspects of doing "good." Next I call your attention to verses 13 and 14 and suggest that Paul has linked the disparate contents of these verses together via the Greek catchword *diokein*. In verse 13 this catchword can be translated as "to pursue hospitality," whereas in verse 14 its meaning is "those who pursue you" or "persecutors." I invite my readers to direct their attention now to verse 11 and its command "serve the Lord." Does "Lord" here refer to Jesus or God or both? It is hard to give a dogmatic interpretation. Finally, note the dual possible meanings of "lowly" (Greek: *tapeinois*) in verse 16. The NRSV translates "Do not be haughty, but associate with *the lowly*," and it has this footnote: "Or *give yourself to humble tasks*." In our normal logic we need an answer: Is the reference to humble people or humble tasks? For surely it cannot mean both. But paraenesis argues and tries to persuade people in its own way. It has its own logic. For those who seek clarity, it often offers plurality of meaning and delights in theological playfulness with words.

If we were to take my sketchy analysis of the paraenesis of the more familiar Romans 12:9-21 and apply its principles of analysis to all five chapters of the Letter of James, we would find that these five chapters are indeed exhortation and are linked via literary inclusions and catch-words. And as we will see in James 5:13-18, words such as "olive oil" and figures such as "Elijah" have multiple referents. Indeed, the chapters that constitute the Letter of James do not consist merely of one exhortation on one subject followed by another exhortation of yet another theme. There is considerable organization and thematic unity to the Letter of James.

I ask my readers' indulgence for an aside at this juncture. On a recent sabbatical I studied the twenty-eight admonitions that St. Francis of Assisi (d. 1226) gave to his brothers. For months I immersed myself in these medieval exhortatory materials. It took me some time, but gradually I began to detect the unity within each admonition. Take for example admonition 6:

> 1. Let us all attend, brothers, to the good shepherd, who endured the passion of the cross to save his sheep. 2. The sheep of the Lord have followed him in tribulation and persecution, shame and famine, in infirmity and temptation, and all other suffering. And for these things they received from the Lord eternal life. 3. Whence it is a great shame for us servants of God that the saints performed works and that we, by reciting them, want to receive glory and honor.

In my book on Francis's admonitions (1999, 87–92) I have argued that behind verse 1 there is an allusion to John 10:10-11 and that verse 1 is linked to verse 2 via the catchword "sheep." Behind verse 2 are allusions to Matthew 10:16 and Romans 8:35-36, for in both passages reference is made to "sheep" and to various trials. Verse three connects to verse 2 via the linkword "shame" and functions as a "zinger" as it slaps the brothers on their cheeks and gets their moral attention. And while this admonition can truly stand on its own, it is connected to other admonitions in vocabulary and theme. For example, through the words "attend/pay attention," "glory," and "cross" and through the "we" style, it is linked to admonition 5.

And as I studied the connections between all twenty-eight of Francis's admonitions, I began to detect the large thematic or organizing principle that held them all together. I worded that organizing principle thus: "Give glory to the All Good God who gives good gifts to all. And since God has been so good to you, what are you going to do about it?" Although Francis of Assisi never explicitly refers to the Letter of James, his thought is not far removed from James 1:17: "Every generous act of giving with every perfect gift is from above, coming down from the Father of lights." And it goes without saying that Francis of

Assisi is heir to the paraenetic tradition, witnessed also in the Letter of James, as he demands that action follow belief. While the Admonitions of St. Francis date to the thirteenth century, they are still valid witnesses to the nature and unity of paraenetic literature and may help us appreciate the Letter of James that at first blush may seem so disorganized.

For our purposes I adopt the analysis of the literary structure of the Letter of James put forward by Luke Timothy Johnson. In Johnson's view the paraenetic materials, called aphorisms, in James 1:1-27 serve as the "overture" or "table of contents" for James 2:1-5:18. For our purposes I limit my discussion to the theme of prayer and quote Johnson (1995, 14–15) on this point: "It has often been observed that the same topics treated by maxim in the first chapter reappear in the form of essays later. Thus, the prayer of faith in 1:5-7 is advocated more elaborately in 5:13-18." Lest my readers think that I am quoting an idiosyncratic analysis to foster my agenda, I ask them to take a look at what Richard Bauckham (1999, 61–73) says about the literary structure of James. You will find that Johnson and Bauckham are in basic agreement. So I'm building my interpretive house on a solid foundation.

And what is the overarching principle James has used to organize the various components of paraenesis into the letter that bears his name? Among many scholarly suggestions I select three. The title of Robert W. Wall's book, *The Community of the Wise* (1997b), expresses his view of the goal of the Letter of James. Wall (1997b, 250) writes: "The deeper logic of James's message, then, is that wisdom, if presently practiced, forms the eschatological community that will triumph with the Lord at his *parousia*." Thus through the wisdom that the Letter of James imparts, believers dispersed throughout the world will be formed into a community ready to meet the Lord at his second coming. Wall is especially adept at interpreting the eschatological dimensions of the Letter of James.

Luke T. Johnson (1995, 14) moves at another level of abstraction and phrases the organizing goal of the Letter of James differently. He writes:

> an important organizing (and selecting) principle in James is a central set of convictions concerning the absolute incompatibility of two construals of reality and two modes of behavior following from such diverse understandings. This "deep structure" of polar opposition between "friendship with the world" and "friendship with God" undergirds the inclusion and shaping of James' material.

Johnson's proposal becomes clearer if my readers check James's description of Abraham, whose faith was active along with his works: "And Abraham was called a friend of God" (2:23). And James 4:4 pointedly describes the opposite of "friend of God": "Adulterers! Do you not know that friendship with the world is enmity with God? Therefore, whoever wishes to be a friend of the world becomes an enemy of God."

Richard Bauckham (1999, 177) shows the richness of James's presentation as he proposes that completeness "is not just one important theme, but the overarching theme of the whole letter, encompassing all the other major concerns." Bauckham's justifiably lengthy analysis of this theme begins with vocabulary as he notes that the words "complete/perfect" (*teleios*) and "to complete/perfect" (*teleioun*) occur a significant seven times: (1:4 (twice); 1:17; 1:25; 2:8; 2:22; 3:2. Is it pure coincidence that seven is the symbolic number for completeness? More important, though, in Bauckham's view (1999, 178–83) than mere vocabulary are the five ways this theme is used and how it is contrasted with its opposite, "double-mindedness." These five ways are integration, exclusion, completion, consistency, and divine perfection. Three of these ways can be handled rather quickly. Bauckham (1999, 181) gives "completion" and "consistency" a paragraph apiece and shows that believers must "complete" their faith in deeds and must eat a complete meal of the commandments and not pick and choose. Further, in all dimensions of their life they must show that their actions are consistent with their hearing. By "exclusion" Bauckham (1999, 179) means excluding what is incompatible with one's belief: "People can either be friends with God (4:4), like Abraham (2:23), or they can be friends with 'the world' (4:4), but the choice must be made. The distinction cannot be fudged." So what is key for Johnson has become one aspect of a much larger thematic in Bauckham's analysis.

I will give more space to Bauckham's points about "divine perfection" and "integration," because they are important in themselves and vital for our treatment of James 5:13-18. Bauckham (1999, 181) writes of "divine perfection": "God is wholly good: he tempts no one to evil and cannot himself be tempted to evil (1:13). He is consistently good, never wavering from his steadfast purpose of giving good gifts to his creation (1:17). Moreover, his giving is single-minded and wholehearted (1:5: *haplos*), just as people's response should be." And what God gives are perfect gifts, especially the complete or perfect law (1:25) and complete wisdom (3:17). And these two gifts "make possible the wholeness of human life lived according to God's complete law and informed by the complete wisdom from above" (Bauckham 1999, 181). It is to this God that one prays for health in body and spirit in James 5:13-18.

By now my readers can well imagine how Bauckham (1999, 178) will describe "integration," which "is concerned with the harmonious wholeness of the individual person and of the community." The individual believer is not to waver, doubt, or be double-minded. Tongue and heart should be in harmony. And very important for our later consideration of James 5:13-18 is what Bauckham (1999, 178) says about physical and spiritual health: "Salvation is restoring health to both body (5:15) and soul (or life: 1:21; 5:20), while physical healing may be accompanied by forgiveness of sins (5:16). Thus the whole life of an individual is integrated or included in the total dedication of the person to the service of God." And what Bauckham (1999, 178-79) says about the communitarian aspects of wholeness aids our pre-understanding of James 5:13-18: "Loyalty to God and to each other should unite individuals in a community characterized by peaceable, gentle, considerate, caring and forgiving relationships (2.13; 3.13, 17; 4.11-12; 5.16, 19). . . . The poor above all must be encompassed in the wholeness of the community (1:27), just as the person who errs should be restored by love (5:19-20)."

As we come to the end of discussing the viewpoints of Wall, Johnson, and Bauckham about the organizing principle of James's paraenesis, we may feel that our minds are operating at a fifth level of abstraction where the air is very thin indeed. Does James 5:13-18 say anything explicitly about "wisdom"? Where, you might ask, in James 5:13-18 does the author say anything about "friendship with God" as opposed to "friendship with the world"? Finally, the word "complete" or "perfect" is absent from James 5:13-18, isn't it? Or if my readers don't want to pick on Wall, Johnson, and Bauckham, they can pick on me. As you reread Francis of Assisi's admonition 6 above, does it say anything explicitly about the overarching theme I found in all twenty-eight admonitions, namely, the All Good God gives good gifts to all and requires a fitting response to those good gifts? Explicitly, no. Implicitly, yes. The Good Shepherd, as the model for the sheep, is God's good gift. The saintly "sheep" have willingly accepted God's good gifts, especially that of eternal life. And are we, in turn, to tell people of the good the good God has done to others but not respond courageously and generously to the good the good God gives us daily? Believe it or not, we are involved here in the larger question of the theory of interpretation or of hermeneutics. On its simplest level, I, along with Wall, Johnson, and Bauckham, am advocating a deeper reading of James that sees and makes connections between various sections. I am advocating turning around in our mind's eye the various words used in James 5:13-18. They are like a diamond whose facets can only be revealed from viewing it from different angles and with different intensities of light. Take the word "sick person" from James 5:14. What does it mean? Bauckham rightly says that sick people lack completeness of body and soul and are deprived of the strength that comes from attending the worship services of their community. Johnson maintains that the ways of those who love this world are to ignore the sick, to gloat over their misfortune, and to hatch greedy plots after their goods. And Wall sees sickness and sin as a spiritual test of the community's faith. Just as no one who sees a multifaceted diamond can claim to have a complete vision of its beauty, so too neither can Wall, Johnson, Bauckham or even Karris claim to have provided a full answer to the organizing principle of the paraenesis that is the Letter of James. But just as you can rent an audio program to guide your way through a special art exhibit for your greater appreciation, so too can you benefit from the guides I have introduced.

Having said so much about the literary form of the Letter of James as exhortation, I must complete this section with a few words about its format as a letter. Paul's letters have so captivated our view of what a first-century letter should be that we might be surprised to learn that letters could conclude without an ending such as "The grace of our Lord Jesus Christ be with your spirit" (Philippians 4:23). Scholars are indebted to Fred O. Francis (1970) for calling their attention to letters like that in 1 Maccabees 10:25-45, which has a double opening statement like the Letter of James and concludes without any "Sincerely yours in Christ." So the Letter of James is indeed a letter although it lacks the ending Paul's letters have accustomed us to expect. But there is more. Francis (1970, 125) rightly observes that "unquestionably prayer is an established element of the epistolary close in the NT epistles. Paul tends to recommend prayer as such, or ask for prayer 'for us,' or reaffirm that he is praying for the readers." So in its discussion of prayer in 5:13-18 the Letter of James has the functional equivalent of the ending of most New Testament epistles. If I might put the matter differently, I would say that the study of Fred Francis contributes to the impression we are gathering that the Letter of James is indeed well put together as exhortation in a letter format.

I conclude this section with the briefest of comments about the author of the paraenesis that is the Letter of James. All scholars agree that the James behind this letter is that outstanding figure of earliest Jewish Christianity referred to by Paul as a "pillar" in Galatians 2:9 and in Acts 12:17 and 15:13-21 and who was stoned to death in A.D. 62. Did this Jewish James write the good Greek of this letter? Or is this letter like some others in the New Testament written by someone else in the name of such an important figure of earliest Christianity? I follow Luke Johnson and others in taking James of Jerusalem to be the author of this letter, which stems from ca. A.D. 60

WHAT WERE THE SOURCES
FOR THE PARAENESIS OF JAMES?

This is a large question, whose complete answer lies outside the scope of this chapter and book. However, I must ask it because it pertains to our theme of prayer. I proceed on two levels. The first level deals with the influence that the sayings of Jesus had on the Letter of James. In the introduction of his commentary on the Letter of James, Franz Mussner (1975, 47–53) has a section "The Letter of James and Jesus' Ethic." The larger part of this section concerns the twenty-seven parallels that the Letter of James and the ethics of Jesus have in common. We will come back to two of these parallels, namely those between James 1:5 and Matthew 7:7/Luke 11:9 and James 1:6 and Mark 11:23-24 (Matthew 21:21), in a moment. Between James 5:17 and Luke 4:25 there is another parallel: they are the only two instances in the New Testament where Elijah and rain are mentioned. To this parallel we will return in our discussion of James 5:13-18. Mussner (1975, 51) comes to these four summary points. First, the material that the Letter of James and the teaching of Jesus have in common is almost exclusively in the area of ethics. Second, a majority of the common teaching belongs to the gospel tradition called Q. Third, the greater part of what has no parallel in Q comes from the tradition peculiar to Matthew; what is left comes from the tradition peculiar to Luke. Fourth, the majority of the common material is found in Matthew's Gospel within his Sermon on the Mount. And Mussner concludes this first part with the aphorism: What James teaches breathes the Spirit of Jesus! Later in his third edition Mussner (1975, 250–54) has much more to say about this question under the rubric of the Christology of the

Letter of James. In brief, he rightly argues that James has a strong but implicit Christology. Besides more explicit references to Jesus as Lord in 2:1 and 5:15 the fact that James takes over the teachings of Jesus shows in what high regard he held Jesus.

In his second part Mussner (1975, 52–53) raises the question: "Does the Letter of James 'Teach Christ'"? By raising the question in this form, Mussner explicitly addresses Martin Luther's negative evaluation of the Letter of James as "an epistle of straw." After pointing out that at least half of Jesus' preaching deals with ethics, that is, paraenesis, imperatives, concrete and practical instructions about life, Mussner (1975, 52–53; emphasis in original) concludes: "*To give heed to James is thus to give heed to Jesus!* Both are concerned with putting the word into practice! So the Letter of James does indeed belong to those writings of the New Testament that hand on and teach Christ in a completely special way." Mussner may be forgiven his sweeping generalization, but he is not alone in his attempt to rehabilitate the Letter of James from Luther's unsound evaluation and its influence on subsequent exegesis. The commentary by Luke T. Johnson (1995) is a major assault against Luther's influential but faulty reading. At the risk of being too schematic, I would say that the Pauline letters represent the early Christian preaching or kerygma and that the Letter of James represents baptismal catechesis on how to live the new life won by the death and resurrection of the Lord Jesus Messiah. And the baptismal catechesis of the Letter of James is greatly influenced by Jesus' ethics.

THE INFLUENCE OF JESUS' TEACHING ON PRAYER

From this large question of Jesus' influence on the Letter of James, I want to focus now on the two major parallels between James's paraenesis and Jesus' teaching that pertain to our topic of prayer. The first parallel focuses on James 1:5:

James 1:5	*Matthew 7:7, 11*	*Luke 11:9, 13*
If any of you is lacking in wisdom, ask God, who gives to all generously and without grudging. And it will be given to you.	Ask, and it will be given to you. . . . [H]ow much more will your Father in heaven give good things to those who ask him!	Ask, and it will be given to you. . . . [H]ow much more will the heavenly Father give the Holy Spirit to those who ask him!

The parallels to James 1:5 are from the materials that Matthew and Luke have in common (Q). James and Q seem to have at least two things in common: the words "Ask, and it will be given," and the assurance that God is good. James makes this point more straightforwardly, whereas Matthew and Luke use parabolic teaching. As each focuses on what God gives to those who ask, they differ according to their own theologies. Luke mentions "the Holy Spirit." Matthew has "good things." With his reference to "wisdom," James seems to tie the Jesus tradition to a wisdom tradition similar to that found in Proverbs 8:17, where Wisdom says: "I love those who love me. And those who seek me diligently, find me." Are we certain that James 1:5 is quoting Jesus' teaching on prayer? No, but the verbal allusions make it probable.

The second parallel focuses on James 1:6:

James 1:6	*Mark 11:22-24*	*Matthew 21:21-22*
But ask in faith, never doubting. For the one who doubts is like a wave of the sea, driven by the wind and tossed about.	Jesus answered them: "Have faith in God. Truly I tell you: If you say to this mountain: 'Be taken up and thrown into the sea,' and if you do not doubt in your heart, but believe that what you say will come to pass, it will be done for you. So I tell you: Whatever you ask for in prayer, believe that you have received it, and it will be yours."	Jesus answered them: "Truly I tell you: If you have faith and do not doubt, not only will you do what has been done to the fig tree, but even if you say to this mountain: 'Be lifted up and thrown into the sea,' it will be done. Whatever you ask for in prayer with faith, you will receive."

The main parallel is between the words: "Ask in faith, never doubting" of James 1:6 and "And if you do not doubt in your heart, but believe" of Mark 11:22-24. The imagery of "like a wave of the sea, driven by the wind and tossed about" probably stems from James who, as 3:4 indicates, relishes sea imagery. And as Sharyn Echols Dowd (1988, 69–94) has shown so well, the mountain-moving saying attests to God's omnipotence. It seems to be Mark's contribution to the saying. So what is common between James and the Jesus tradition in Mark are prayer, faith, and doubt. James seems to have tailored the Jesus tradition for his own purposes. In the conclusion of his study on the relationship between James 1:5-6 and Jesus' teaching in Matthew, Mark, and Luke, Richard Bauckham (1999, 86) is on target: "James' two verses together succeed in expressing very concisely the major elements of Jesus' teaching about prayer." That is quite an accomplishment for James, the brother of Jesus, writing about A.D. 60, and speaks eloquently about the role of Jesus' teaching in the life of the primitive Jewish Christian church.

JEWISH VIEWS OF PHYSICIANS' CARE OF THE SICK

On a second level I ask about the source or sources of James's teaching about "the sick" and put this material here rather than in my commentary on James 5:14 to prime the pump of interpretation. As far as I can tell, this topic is rarely broached in the commentaries, but it is very important for a sound discussion of James 5:14: " Someone is sick among you. Let him summon the elders of the church, and let them pray over him, anointing him with olive oil in the name of the Lord." I will deal with three passages, which I propose as interpretive parallels or sources.

In dealing with the story of the serpents that the Israelites encountered in the desert after their liberation from Egypt, the author of Wisdom says in 16:12: "For neither herb nor poultice cured them, but it was your word, O Lord, that heals all people." That is, the Lord, not a physician or physician's skill, healed the Lord's people. A second passage is found in Sirach 38:1-15 and contains praise of physicians, for example, 38:1: "Honor physicians for their services, for the Lord created them." But it also contains more traditional, cult-centered passages, for example, 38:9-12: "My child, when you are sick, do not delay. But pray to the Lord, and he will heal you. Give up your faults and direct your hands rightly and cleanse your heart from all sin. Offer a sweet-smelling sacrifice and a memorial portion of choice flour, and pour olive oil on your offering as much as you can afford. Then give the physician his place, for the Lord created him. Do not let him leave you, for you need him." It seems that the wisdom of Sirach is newfangled enough to sing the praises of physicians while at the same time acknowledging that God is the divine healer. But there is still distrust of physicians in some circles, for the Greek of Sirach 38:15 reads: "May the one who sins against his Maker fall into the hands of the physician!"

Our third and final passage stems from Philo of Alexandria who flourished in the first century A.D. In his writing *On the Sacrifices of Abel and Cain* 69–71, Philo is interpreting Exodus 8:9, where Moses says to pharaoh: "Appoint with me a time when I shall pray for you and your servants to take away the plague of the frogs." And although pharaoh should have said that Moses should pray at once, he puts his request off with the word "tomorrow." Then in paragraphs 70–71, which merit full quotation in a modified translation from F. H. Colson, Philo gives this tirade:

> This is the case with almost all the Facing-both-ways. . . . When anything befalls them which they would not, since they have never had any firm faith in God their Savior, they first flee to the help which things created give, to physicians, herbs, drug-mixtures, strict rules of diet, and all the other aids that mortals use. And if one say to them, "Flee, you fools, to the one and only physician of soul-sickness and cast away the help, miscalled as such, of the created and the mutable," they laugh and mock. And all their answer is "tomorrow for that," as though, whatever may befall, they would never supplicate God to save them from the ills that beset them. But when no human help avails, and all things, even healing remedies, prove to be but mischievous, then out of the depths of their helplessness, despairing of all other aid, still even in their misery reluctant, at this late hour they betake themselves to the only savior, God. He, for he knows that what is done under stress of necessity has no sure foundation, does not in all cases follow his law [of mercy], but only when it may be followed for good and with profit.

This passage from a contemporary of the Letter of James is remarkable. Although the adjective "facing-both-ways" is different than James's "double-mindedness" (1:8), the idea is the same. Just as the Letter of James 1:5-7 (no doubting) and 4:1-3 (no selfish pleasures) provide the conditions under which God will hear prayer, so too does Philo at the end of paragraph 71 (no prayer under duress). Finally, Philo shows how the sick might push God's curative powers aside, jettison prayer, and rush after human remedies.

In conclusion to this second level of the sources for the exhortations of the Letter of James I cannot prove that James consciously knew of what Wisdom 16:12, Sirach 38:1-15, and Philo *On the Sacrifices of Abel and Cain* 70–71 said about sickness and the differences between the saving power of human remedies and that of God, savior and physician. However, in a letter that has an abundance of wisdom themes, for example, the use of the tongue in 3:1-12, it would seem probable that in mentioning the sick in 5:14, James is alluding to yet another wisdom theme. Of course, he will take it his own way, as we will see in a few pages.

James 5:13-18

With the general background provided above on the literary form and sources of the Letter of James we are in position now to explore the teaching on prayer found in James 5:13-18. I will provide my own translation and put in bold type the many references to prayer.

13. Someone is suffering difficulties among you. Let him **pray**. Someone is feeling cheerful. Let him **sing a song of praise**.

14. Someone is sick among you. Let him summon the elders of the church, and let them **pray** over him, anointing him with olive oil in the name of the Lord.

15. And **the prayer** of faith will deliver the sick, and the Lord will restore him. And if he has committed sins, he will be forgiven.

16. Therefore, confess your sins to one another and **pray** for one another, so that you may be healed. The **prayer** of a righteous person is very strong and effectual.

17. Elijah was a human being with difficult experiences like ours, and he **prayed earnestly** that it not rain. And it did not rain on the earth for three years and six months.

18. And again he **prayed**, and the heaven gave rain, and the earth yielded its fruit.

After devoting so much space above to talking about paraenesis, we now have a paraenetic passage in our sights. Let's investigate it together, starting with some general observations and then proceeding verse by verse. As we look for catchwords, we note that verse 13 has a Greek verb, *kakopathein*, which I have translated as "suffering difficulties" and which functions as a double catchword. You see, it relates back to 5:10: "As an example of *suffering difficulties* and patience, beloved, take the prophets who spoke in the name of the Lord." (Could the prophet Elijah mentioned later in 5:17-18 be such an example?) And it relates forward to verse 17, where part of the Greek verb that commenced the entire section in 5:13 reappears in the author's description of Elijah, a human being *with experiences* like ours. And although different words are used for "prayer" throughout 5:13-18, the catchword "prayer" binds these verses together. Verse 15 introduces a new catchword, "sin," which flows through verses 16 and 19-20.

James 5:13

As we begin our detailed interpretation of James 5:13-18, let me tell my readers something that they may have intuited already. This passage really has no exact parallel in the New Testament, and therefore we have to find interpretive parallels as best we can. In this instance I remember a talk I heard during my graduate days. An expert in papyri documents was trying to recruit us New Testament types to reconstruct papyri with the promise of almost instantaneous publication of our research. His punch line was: "It isn't difficult work. Even if you just have a few words on a scrap of papyrus and know it's a receipt for goods, you can fill in the blanks of the missing words from the boilerplate all clerks used when they wrote out a receipt." Or to use a more contemporary example, just walk through a computer store and notice all the software programs that provide boilerplate materials, for example, for wills or resumes. With these boilerplates as your model you just have to fill in the blanks with your own particulars. Unfortunately, we have no boilerplate to help us interpret James 5:13-18. So my readers will have to be patient as we slowly move through these six verses of exhortation and find some passages from the Old Testament, the Gospels, and nonbiblical sources to assist our understanding. If you look at any other commentary on this passage, you will find the author doing the same thing.

The Letter of James opened in 1:5-7 with teaching about prayer. Presupposing what he said there about prayer without doubt and what he said in 4:1-3 about not praying for selfish pleasures, James begins his longest treatment of prayer in 5:13. He divides human experience into two categories: experiencing difficulties and feeling cheerful. For our purposes I want to accentuate the first category: "Someone is suffering difficulties among you. Let him pray." In mentioning "difficulties," James surely refers back to 1:2-18 of his overture and the test of faith that difficulties occasion and to the nature of God who gives good gifts and tempts no one. Peter H. Davids (1989, 122) captures well the meaning of James 5:13 as he interprets this verse from its larger and immediate context:

the misfortunes of life: persecutions, like those the prophets suffered (5:10; cf. 5:1-6); external misfortunes, like Job suffered (5:11); or being slandered by a community member (3:1-12; cf. 2:6-7). . . . The response to such evil is not counterattack (fighting violence with violence) or resignation (as the Stoics advised) but prayer. The psalmist appealed to God to deal with his persecutors (Pss. 30; 50:15; 91:15), and this is also the Christian response.

But at this juncture I raise a question that commentators infrequently ask: May the prayer of the person experiencing difficulties include the psalms of lament? That is, may James be not only encouraging his readers to pray that the Lord rescue them from their difficulties and strengthen their resolve in their difficulties, but also giving them leave to lament their plight? Could those experiencing difficulties, including sickness in the community of James, have had Psalm 38 on their lips? It contains verses like these:

¹O Lord, do not rebuke me in your anger or discipline me in your wrath.
³There is no health in my bones because of my sin.
⁵My wounds grow foul and fester because of my foolishness.
⁹O Lord, all my longing is known to you.
¹¹My friends and companions stand aloof from my affliction, and my neighbors stand far off.
¹⁷For I am ready to fall, and my pain is ever with me.
¹⁸I confess my iniquity. I am sorry for my sin.
²¹Do not forsake me, O Lord. O my God, do not be far from me.
²²Make haste to help me, O Lord, my salvation.

As Samuel E. Balentine (1993, 146–98) says so powerfully: Lament psalms with their explicit or implicit questions of "Why?" and "How long?" are real, but troublesome for the community of faith. Did the victim of suffering in the community of James dare to pray the psalms of lament? Just because we moderns in the Judaeo-Christian tradition have trouble with the lament psalms doesn't mean that our first-century Judaeo-Christians in the faith had similar problems. To me it seems that the first part of James 5:13 gives us permission to "complain" to God, the giver of good gifts, in the words of the prophet found in Jeremiah 11–20 or in the words of the psalms of individual lament such as Psalms 3, 6, and 7. In a word, it invites us to revisit on an experiential level and to appropriate in faith the meaning of James 1:2-4: "My brothers and sisters, whenever you face trials of any kind, consider it nothing but joy. For you know that the testing of your faith produces endurance. And let endurance have its full effect, so that you may be mature and complete, lacking in nothing."

James 5:14

Let me commence my discussion of this most important verse by making some general comments about the sick community member. First, I acknowledge that the Greek word I have translated as "sick" literally means "weak" and therefore could bear the meaning "spiritually weak." The immediate context of James 5:13-18, the parallels I cited above on how Wisdom 16:12, Sirach 38:1-15, and Philo *On the Sacrifices of Abel and Cain* 70–71 deal with sickness, and the mention of olive oil in this verse lead me to translate the Greek verb *asthenei* as "is sick." Second, as we have seen above, Robert Walls, Luke Johnson, and Richard Bauckham see the sick person as a person who needs to be made whole. Further, the community is not whole if its members do not attend to one who has become homebound, is out of sight, and set at the margins of the community. Moreover, the sick person occasions a test of the community's "friendship with the Lord" over against "friendship with the ways of the world." Will the members of the community gloat over another's sickness and lust after his property? With these general remarks under our belts, I turn to some specific issues.

Medical Care in Antiquity

The parallels I cited above about "sickness and physicians" prompted me to find out what type of medical care might have been available to the sick in antiquity. If we Americans bemoan our medical situation where more than forty million people in our country have no medical insurance, just think of a city like Rome or Alexandria or Antioch or even Jerusalem where no one had medical insurance. As a matter of fact life expectancy was between twenty and thirty years of age. And while Wendy Cotter (1999, 206) does provide some evidence "that towns hired certain physicians, *archiatroi*, to provide the indigent with free services in order to avert disease and epidemic," we must not think that health care was in any remote way similar to what first-world countries or even two-thirds-world countries have today. Remember that most of the wonder drugs we take for granted were just discovered in the last hundred years. Ralph Jackson in his book *Doctors and Diseases in the Roman Empire* (1988, 55) paints a somber and very realistic picture:

> In summary, it is difficult to over-estimate how important it was for the individual to maintain good health. In an age when both drugs and doctors were of uncertain quality, few illnesses were easily cured, and their prevention was therefore paramount. Leaving aside the rich, however, the preservation of health was hardly within the control of the individual. . . . The advice to their peers of medical writers like Celsus and Galen shows what was possible. However, it should not be allowed to obscure the evidence from other quarters, that ill health was a real and ever-present hazard of ordinary people, and one which the poor, above all, were least able to resist.

From Roy Porter's study of the medical history of humanity I gathered two more points about ancient health care. The first point deals with the policy of bedside visits adopted by the followers of the Greek physician Hippocrates (d. 370 B.C.). Porter (1997, 58) writes: "The Hippocratics specialized in medicine by the bedside, prizing trust-based clinical relations." As a matter of fact, a key line in the Hippocratic Oath runs: "Whenever I go into a house, I will go to help the sick and never with the intention of doing harm or injury." The Hippocratic therapeutic stance was expectant: "They waited and watched their patients, talking, winning trust and giving a helping hand to the 'healing power of nature . . .'" (Porter, 1997, 59). The second point I have garnered from Porter (1997, 69) deals with the Roman view of Greek physicians: "Romans enjoyed bad-mouthing Greek physicians: according to Pliny (A.D. c. 23–79), who deplored the recent influx of 'luxury' and worthless Greek physicians, an inscription, echoing Alexander, was now sprouting up on monuments in Rome: 'It was the crowd of physicians that killed me.' Romans liked to think healing should take place in the family, under the care of the paterfamilias, who would dispense herbs and charms." In a moment I will quote a cure for diarrhea that prescribes the use of olive oil and that Celsus (fl. A.D. c. 30) included in the eight books of his *De Medicina*. Celsus was not a physician but a wealthy estate owner who probably cared for the health of both family and workers from his store of accumulated "medical practices."

On the basis of the data mentioned above, I use my creative imagination to envision the situation of the sick person mentioned in James 5:14. The sick person is implicitly instructed not to call the physicians to his bedside. Nor is the sick person to call the *paterfamilias* to his bedside. He is to summon the elders (*paterfamilias*) of his new Christian community to his bedside. Is James anti-physician the same way that Philo *On the Sacrifices of Abel and Cain* 70–71 and Wisdom 16:12 are? Our next investigation on olive oil will give us additional materials upon which to construct an answer.

Anointing with Olive Oil

To my way of thinking the reference to olive oil in James 5:14 is very important. But alas, millions of Americans, perhaps even those reading this book, have little or no experience of olive oil and need some orientation to its qualities. In its basic reality olive oil is a food. Over the course of six years in administrative work in and out of Rome I left behind my bread-and-margarine fare and grew fond of bread-and-olive-oil. I also enjoyed pasta and other foods cooked in olive oil. And needless to say, I was overjoyed when I learned that health experts were proclaiming the good news that olive oil was friendly to the heart. With this briefest of backgrounds in mind let's take a look at what ancient authors said about olive oil. The references are multiple, and any attempt to classify them is already an interpretation. In his influential article on olive oil, H. Schlier (1964, 471–73) makes four points about its widespread significance and use in the ancient world: a form of agrarian produce; fuel for lamps; various kinds of anointing, for example, of the king; a means of healing the most diverse maladies. For our purposes I propose to reduce Schlier's four categories to three: food, anointing, and medicine.

Olive Oil as a Necessity of Life

Perhaps the most obvious meaning of olive oil is the one that's right in front of our noses. Olive oil is a food. As a matter of fact, the Jews considered it an essential food. Sirach 39:26 says: "The basic necessities of human life are water and fire and iron and salt and wheat-flour and milk and honey, the blood of the grape and *olive oil* and clothing." Deuteronomy 11:13-17, especially in its Greek version (Septuagint), is important for a number of reasons. It lists the necessities of life as "grain, wine, and olive oil." Just like James 5:7, it talks about the early and late rains. And it states explicitly what is implicit in James 5:17-

18: rebellion and sin against God can lead God to withhold rain, to cause drought, and thus cut off God's blessings of the necessities of life. Now I ask my readers to feast their eyes on what Deuteronomy 11:13-17 says and to see whether there are connections between its thoughts and those of James 5.

> If you shall only heed his every commandment that I am commanding you today—loving the Lord your God and serving him with all your heart and with all your soul—then he will give the rain for your land in its season, the early rain and the later rain. And you will gather in your grain, your wine, and your *olive oil*. And he will give grass in your fields for your livestock, and you shall eat your fill. Take care or you will be seduced into turning away, serving other gods and worshiping them. For then the anger of the Lord will be kindled against you, and he will shut up the heavens, so that there will be no rain and the land will yield no fruit. Then you will perish quickly off the good land that the Lord is giving you.

And as a basic component of life, olive oil became a symbol of life, indeed, a symbol for eschatological life. Bo Reicke (1964, 59), Franz Mussner (1975, 219–20), and John Christopher Thomas (1998, 26–28) have very valuable materials in this regard. *2 Enoch* dates from the time of the Letter of James. In the translation of F. I. Andersen, *2 Enoch* 22:8-10[A] reads as follows:

> The Lord said to Michael: "Take Enoch, and extract (him) from the earthly clothing. And anoint him with the delightful oil, and put (him) into the clothes of glory." And Michael extracted me from my clothes. He anointed me with the delightful oil. And the appearance of that oil is greater than the greatest light. Its ointment is like sweet dew, and its fragrance like myrrh. And its shining is like the sun. And I gazed at all of myself, and I had become like one of the glorious ones, and there was no observable difference.

In this passage biblical Enoch, who was snatched up to heaven and never died (Genesis 5:24), is transformed into one of the glorious ones through anointing with the olive oil that generates eternal delight and life.

From the use of olive oil as a food can I legitimately conclude that the use of olive oil in James 5:14 is symbolic and that one of the valences of this symbol is "life"? I would say that such a conclusion is legitimate. Can I also legitimately conclude from the use of olive oil as a food that the physically weak who are anointed with olive oil in the name of the Lord will experience life? I would again maintain that such a conclusion is valid.

Olive Oil as a Means to Heal the Most Diverse Maladies

Having treated some of the evidence for olive oil as food and as symbol for life, I now want to lay out pertinent passages about the healing qualities of olive oil. I state my conclusion in advance: Anointing with oil is generally one remedy among others and is generally for rich people who can afford using a necessity of life for massages. Nevertheless, it is an assured fact that the ancients maintained that olive oil had healing qualities.

I start with the sickness of diarrhea. In book IV, chapter 26, paragraphs 4–5 of his treatise on medicine (*De Medicina*) Celsus writes:

> It sometimes happens also that this disorder [diarrhea], having been neglected for several days, is more difficult to relieve. Such a patient should commence with something to induce vomiting. Then the following day at evening *be anointed with olive oil* in a warm room, take food in moderation, and the sourest wine undiluted. A wax-salve with rue should be applied to the abdomen. In this affection neither walking nor rubbing is of benefit (modified translation of W. G. Spencer).

Notice that anointing with olive oil is just one step in the treatment regimen.

Commentators are wont to refer to Josephus's description of the last illnesses of Herod the Great. I refer my readers to Josephus's *Jewish War* 1.656-58, and concentrate on what he says in his *Jewish Antiquities* 17.168-72: "But Herod's illness became more and more acute, for God was inflicting just punishment upon him for his lawless deeds" (168). Then Josephus lists Herod's medical problems, which include asthma, abdominal ailment, gangrene in his private parts, and "convulsions in every limb that took on unendurable severity." In his plight, Herod "made up his mind to use whatever remedies his physicians might suggest." For one of his remedies his physicians "decided to warm his body and had seated him in a tub of heated olive oil" (172). While Josephus goes on to say that this treatment knocked Herod unconscious, it was only one treatment among many.

Next I refer to the two biblical passages commentators invariably mention. Isaiah 1:6 reads: "From the sole of the foot even to the head, there is no soundness in it, but bruises and sores and bleeding wounds.

They have not been drained or bound up or softened with *olive oil*." And Luke 10:34 says: "The Samaritan went to him and bandaged his wounds, having poured *olive oil* and wine on them." By now my readers know my question: Is olive oil the only component in the treatment schemes of Isaiah 1:6 and Luke 10:34?

Finally, I cite a passage from a writing dated to the time of the Letter of James that tells the story of Adam's aches and pains and his desire to be anointed with the olive oil that flows from the tree in paradise. In the translation of M. D. Johnson, *The Apocalypse of Moses* 13:1-2 reads:

> And Seth went with his mother Eve near to Paradise. And they wept there, praying God that he would send his angel to give them the oil of mercy. And God sent Michael the archangel, and he said to them: "Seth, man of God, do not labor, praying with this supplication about the tree from which the oil flows, to anoint your father Adam. It shall not come to be yours now but at the end of times."

In this passage the sin of Adam and Eve has brought about pain and woe which will not be relieved in this life. The healing olive oil will come at the end of time.

In conclusion I would venture that the healing aspects of olive oil may help explain its use in James 5:14. And incidentally, they may also help explain a mysterious verse in Mark. Mark 6:13 describes the activity of the Twelve sent on mission by Jesus: "The Twelve cast out many demons. And they anointed with olive oil many who were sick and cured them."

Olive Oil Used for Various Kinds of Anointing

Kings like David were set aside for their responsibility through anointing with oil. But more important to me seems Isaiah 61:3, a passage to which Franz Mussner (1975, 220) alludes. The one upon whom the spirit of the Lord God rests and whom the Lord has anointed is "to give the oil of gladness instead of mourning." In Luke 4:18-19 Jesus quotes the first two verses of Isaiah 61:1-3 to describe his mission of eschatological reversal when, for example, freedom is proclaimed to captives. Although the Greek behind "oil" in Isaiah 61:3 is the generic *aleimma*, it includes olive oil. And thus the reference to anointing with "oil" for gladness' sake in Isaiah 61:3 is another sign of the arrival of God's end time.

Is the allusion to olive oil in James 5:14 an indication of the arrival of the eschatological time of glad reversal predicted by Isaiah 61:3 when the mourning of those physically weak and weary will be turned into joy?

Conclusions on Olive Oil

I must confess that I came to this study of the meaning of olive oil with the preconception that it was a medicament and symbolized restoration to health. Upon reflection I have come to realize that I had limited the symbol of olive oil to one meaning. After my investigation I favor the valence of olive oil as a symbol of life, but have to remind myself that symbols by nature are polyvalent, that is, capable of multiple meanings. I cannot imprison the symbol of olive oil into one cell of meaning. And if olive oil has at least a threefold symbolic meaning, then it might be functioning in a number of ways. In the light of the materials I have collected on ancient health care I would venture to say that James 5:14 is anti-physician. In effect, James is saying that the sick person has life, restoration to health, and eschatological gladness not from the bedside visits of the observant Hippocratic physicians or from the lord of the manor (*paterfamilias*) who may prescribe a health treatment that involves anointing with olive oil, but from the power of prayer and from the name of the Lord.

In the Name of the Lord

Commentators are unanimous in proclaiming that the anointing of the sick person with olive oil is not magic. Prayer is made to the Father of lights, from whom every generous act of giving comes (1:17). Healing will come from that source. Further, the anointing is done "in the name of the Lord." While there is some ambiguity whether "Lord" refers to God or Jesus, the expression "our glorious Lord Jesus Christ" in James 2:1 and similar expressions in Acts, for example, 19:5, tip the scales in favor of Jesus the Lord. It is not participation in the Jewish sacrificial system (see Sirach 38:11) or even in the cult of the healing god Asclepius that invokes God's healing, but the Lord Jesus.

It goes without saying that James 5:14 has had a long and often tumultuous history in the churches. As a Roman Catholic, I am led to look at this passage in the light of the renewal at the Second Vatican

Council of the sacrament of the sick, and particularly in light of the rite of communal anointing of the sick. As a Chicagoan, I am reminded of the late Joseph Cardinal Bernardin, archbishop of Chicago, who died in 1996 of pancreatic cancer. In his *The Gift of Peace* (1997, 131) Bernardin, a terminally ill "elder," who called himself the "chaplain to cancer patients" wrote: "I told my Cabinet what a moving experience it was as the sick, the elderly, and the dying came forward for the laying on of hands and anointing with the oil of the sick. As a cancer patient, I, too, had been anointed. Receiving this sacrament in the company of so many members of this local church was a moving experience for me and for them." During his last days Cardinal Bernardin would attend as many as four services of communal anointing daily. His was a ministry of compassionate solidarity with the sick. Pheme Perkins (1995, 137) mentions another dimension of the communal anointing of the sick in the Roman Catholic Church: "One of the most important effects of healing services that involve the whole community, not just the sick, is breaking the barriers of silence and isolation that illness often imposes on the sick and their families." What a wonderful and powerful legacy James has left us in 5:14.

James 5:15

As with the previous verse, commentators have sought to find parallels to interpret this passage: "And the prayer of faith will deliver the sick, and the Lord will restore him. And if he has committed sins, he will be forgiven." Take, for example, the word "to save." In James 1:21; 2:14; 4:12; and 5:20, "to save" means final salvation. Yet if James 5:15 is to be connected to 5:14, "to save" here should be interpreted to mean "to deliver" from sickness to health. And that is the meaning "to save" has in the gospel tradition. And as a matter of fact, in the gospel tradition "to save" is linked with faith. Yet there is a twist here, too, for it is not the faith of those who pray, but the faith of the one restored to health and wholeness. See Mark 5:34: "Jesus said to the woman who had had the hemorrhage: 'Daughter, your faith has saved you [restored you to health].'" Or look at Luke 17:19: "Then Jesus said to the Samaritan leper who had returned to give Jesus thanks, 'Get up and go on your way. Your faith has saved you [restored you to health].'"

And scholars also interpret the meaning of the verb "to raise up" from the gospel tradition. For example, in Mark 1:31 Jesus cures Simon Peter's mother-in-law who was sick in bed with a fever: "Jesus came and took her by the hand and raised her up. Then the fever left her, and she began to serve them." From a parallel such as this in Mark 1:31 scholars take "to raise up" to mean "to cure" and not "to raise up on the last day in the resurrection."

And because scholars have interpreted "to save" and "to raise up" from the gospel tradition and linked these interpretations to the sick person of 5:14, they are led to interpret another word in 5:15 along the same lines. That is, the Greek word *kamnein*, which can mean "weary," "sick," or "dead," is taken to mean "sick."

Thus far I have presented the common way of understanding this first part of James 5:15, but I think that Philo's *On the Sacrifices of Abel and Cain* 70–71 provides a more apt parallel. If you recall, Philo taught that it is God, not the physicians, who save from various ills. I italicize the key phrases in my quotation from Philo:

> When anything befalls them which they would not, since they have never had *any firm faith in God their Savior,* they first flee to the help which things created give, to physicians, herbs, drug-mixtures, strict rules of diet, and all the other aids that mortals use. And if one say to them, "Flee, you fools, to the one and only physician of soul-sickness and cast away the help, miscalled as such, of the created and the mutable," they laugh and mock. And all their answer is "tomorrow for that," as though, whatever may befall, *they would never supplicate God to save them from the ills that beset them.*

Much of what Philo says is expressed negatively. His positive teaching is this: When an illness descends upon you, pray to God, your savior, who will save you from this ill and all others.

In summary and on the basis of the interpretive parallels from the gospel tradition and Philo's *On the Sacrifices of Abel and Cain,* I maintain that in the first part of James 5:15 the author continues his anti-physician stance. It is the prayer of faith, made by the sick person, the elders, and the rest of the community—and not physicians' remedies—that call upon the savior Lord to restore the sick to health.

The last part of James 5:15 introduces the notion of "forgiveness of sins" and provides the link with 5:16 and 5:19-20. Two parallels help us interpret the connection between sickness and forgiveness of sin. In Sirach 38:1-15, a passage to which I alluded earlier, we read: "My child, when you are sick, do not delay. But pray to the Lord, and he will heal you. Give up your faults and direct your hands rightly. And cleanse your heart from all sin" (38:9-10). The thought behind these verses seems to be at least twofold. First, God is the healer and the one who restores the sick to wholeness. Second, God more readily hears those who try to get right with God through confession of sin and righteous activity toward their neighbors. A second parallel comes from the gospel tradition and is John 5:14. After Jesus had cured the man who had been sick for thirty-eight years, he told him: "See, you have been made well. Do not sin any more, so that nothing worse happens to you." It seems implied in John 5:14 that Jesus' healing also included the forgiveness of the man's sins. At least a connection is obvious between sickness and sin. In brief, the prayer of faith prompts the Lord to forgive sins, which like physical sickness is an obstacle to the wholeness of the individual and of the community.

James 5:16

This verse continues the theme of prayer but with a decided emphasis on sin: "Therefore, confess your sins to one another and pray for one another, so that you may be healed. The prayer of a righteous person is very strong and effectual." The elders of the church and the sick person mentioned in 5:14 fade from the scene as James addresses the entire church. And now the healing envisioned is restoration to spiritual and communal health and wholeness rather than physical healing. While these twists of meaning may strain our normal ways of logical thinking, they are bread and olive oil for exhortatory writers. Let's find some parallels to help us interpret this new dimension of the thought process leading from "sickness/physical cure" and "sin/forgiveness of sin" and "confession of sins to and prayer for one another/healing in the community."

I take the list of parallels found in Peter Davids (1989, 135) as representative of what the commentators provide and select some key passages. Three passages speak powerfully of individual confession of sin to God. Psalm 32:5 reads: "Then I acknowledged my sin to you, and I did not hide my iniquity. I said: 'I will confess my transgressions to the Lord.' And you forgave the guilt of my sin." And at the beginning of a long prayer of confession, Daniel 9:4-5 has: "I prayed to the Lord my God and made confession, saying: 'Ah, Lord, great and awesome God, keeping covenant and steadfast love with those who love you and keep your commandments, we have sinned and done wrong, acted wickedly and rebelled, turning aside from your commandments and ordinances.'" And in response to the preaching of John the Baptist, people "were baptized by him in the river Jordan, confessing their sins" (Matthew 3:6).

The three parallels I have just mentioned are very helpful in showing how sin destroys one's relationship with God and that it must be acknowledged before a gracious and forgiving God. Two other parallels give us a better indication of confession of sin to one another. Both come from the conclusion of the exhortatory or paraenetic section of writings dating at the end of the first Christian century. *Didache* 4.13-14 reads: "¹³Do not abandon the commandments of the Lord, but keep what you have received, without adding or subtracting. ¹⁴You shall confess your offences in church, and shall not come forward to your prayer with a bad conscience. This is the way of life." The *Letter of Barnabas* 19.11-12 has: "¹¹Keep the teachings which you have received, adding nothing and subtracting nothing. Hate the Evil One thoroughly. Pass righteous judgment. ¹²Do not cause quarrels, but bring together and reconcile those who quarrel. Confess your sins. Do not go to prayer with an evil conscience. This is the way of Light." I offer a few comments. The fact that *Didache* and *Barnabas* mention the topic of confession of sin at the end of their writings on the way of life/light may help explain why James ends his letter with a similar exhortation. Moreover, *Barnabas* 19.12 and especially *Didache* 14.14 show that confession of sin could take place in the assembly of one's brothers and sisters. We have been left no rubrics on how confession of sins to one another took place. But it did take place. Finally, *Didache* 14.14 and *Barnabas* 19.12 agree that believers should not go to public prayer with a bad/evil conscience. Left open is the question of whether the believer's conscience is troubled because of sins against God or neighbor. In any case, steps must be taken to remove what is causing the bad/evil conscience.

At this point I cannot help but think of those worship services in many religious traditions that commence with a confession of sins to one another such as "I confess to Almighty God and to you, my brothers and sisters, that I have sinned. . . ." Before we worship together, we seek mutual forgiveness and forgiveness from the gracious God we approach in worship. And the revised rite of the sacrament of reconciliation in the Roman Catholic Church allows for a communal penance service. I have participated in congregations of a thousand or more as we penitents confessed our sins of social injustice, bigotry, racism, and hybris against God, our fellow human beings, and the environment and sought mutual forgiveness and wholeness. What a moving and integrating experience! And for many centuries monastic communities and those influenced by monastic traditions held a weekly penance service called "the Chapter of Faults," during which the members would confess their faults in the presence of their brothers. A confession might take this form: "Through my negligence I broke a serving bowl. I ask the community's pardon for squandering our resources." In these three ways and in many others the community of faith has sought over the centuries to actualize the teaching of James 5:16.

As I went through seminary and religious formation, I learned to sign letters to confreres with the Latin exhortation *Oremus pro invicem*, "Let's pray for one another." Today I find that I am still led to sign letters with similar sentiments and do so in English. And these days, too, I have learned that James 5:16 is the only passage we have in Scripture that gives voice to that sentiment in so many words. Sure, in his letters Paul talks about his prayer for his converts, for example, "We always give thanks to God for all of you and mention you in our prayers" (1 Thessalonians 1:2). And Paul ends his earliest letter with "Beloved, pray for us" (1 Thessalonians 5:25). 1 John 5:16 and Galatians 6:1-3 imply that Christians pray for one another. But it is only in James 5:16 that believers are explicitly exhorted to pray for one another.

And the goal of mutual prayer is healing. The community that confesses its sins to one another is healed. The community that prays for one another is healed. And the community that experiences healing is a complete and whole community.

The last part of 5:16 rounds off the thought of its verse and leads into the next two verses: "The prayer of a righteous person is very strong and effectual." A very helpful parallel is found in Psalm 34:15: "The eyes of the Lord are on the righteous. And his ears are open to their cry." See also Proverbs 15:29: "The Lord is far from the wicked. But he hears the prayer of the righteous." Taken within the context of James 5:13-18, "righteous" does not mean someone who is a canonized saint. Rather the righteous are those who have acknowledged their sinfulness and asked for forgiveness from God and neighbor. They have been made right by God, who, in turn, is open to hear their pleas.

What have we learned about prayer in James 5:16? The sickness of one of its members is not the only malady that can afflict the Christian community. There is also the devastating power of the spiritual malady, sin. Mutual confession of sin and mutual forgiveness lead to deep healing in the community of faith. Then, too, Christians stand together and need the support of mutual prayer.

James 5:17-18

James 5:17-18 reads: "Elijah was a human being with difficult experiences like ours, and he prayed earnestly that it not rain. And it did not rain on the earth for three years and six months. And again he prayed, and the heaven gave rain, and the earth yielded its fruit." What Bo Reicke (1964, 61) says of Elijah in James 5:17-18 is very important and can be applied to much of the Letter of James: "Thus by taking into account the various thought patterns that may be associated with the story of Elijah's prayer, we can more easily understand why the author used this episode to illuminate the present passage."

One such thought pattern is found in *The Lives of the Prophets* 21. In the translation of D. R. A. Hare, 21.4-5 says this about Elijah: "The signs which he did are these. Elijah prayed, and it did not rain for three years, and after three years he prayed again and abundant rain came." While James 5:17-18, as well as Luke 4:25-26, mention "three years and six months," this passage from a contemporary document shows how people quantified the power of Elijah's prayer.

Another thought pattern is to see Elijah as a person "who had difficult experiences like us." James 5:17-18 does not directly allude to Elijah's troubles with the prophets of Baal, the recalcitrant King Ahab, and the murderous Jezebel. Nor does 5:17-18 explicitly refer to Elijah's despondent dejection, which prompted him to take a day's journey into the wilderness and pray to the Lord: "It is enough. Now, O Lord, take away my life, for I am no better than my ancestors" (1 Kings 19:4). But is not the total picture of Elijah in the author's view? Is not the entire story of God's dealings with Elijah part of what James said earlier in 5:10: "As an example of suffering and patience, beloved, take the prophets who spoke in the name of the Lord"?

And Giovanni C. Bottini (1981) in his monograph on the prayer of Elijah has illumined yet another thought pattern in James 5:17-18. I summarize his work very briefly. Besides investigating the background of Elijah's prayer in 1 Kings 17–19, Bottini has found parallels between James 5:13-20, 1 Kings 8:35-36, and Jeremiah 14:1–15:4 primarily by studying the Septuagint translations of these Old Testament passages. These last two passages are similar to the one from Deuteronomy 11:13-17 I quoted earlier and have this message: If the people sin, God will withhold the rain. And then the grain, the wine, and the olive oil will cease. Bottini (1981, 172) writes: "One could say that the mention of the shutting of heaven and the theme of drought-rain carried with them an entire series of other themes such as sin, prayer, calling upon the name of God, conversion, pardon for sins, the correct way of life, etc." I think that Bottini's analysis helps us to see the deeper connections between 5:17-18 and the references to sin in 5:15-16. Indeed, it is because of sin that God withheld the rain.

Another pattern of thought is mentioned by Luke Johnson (1995, 337). He interprets the phrase "the earth produced its fruit" found in James 5:18 thus: "The literary connection with James 5:7 seems patent: there also we have the farmer awaiting the precious fruit of the earth . . . which is given after a first and second rain. The vivification of the earth expressed by fruit also establishes a parallel between sickness/dry land and health/fruit-bearing land. . . ."

I began my consideration of James 5:17-18 with a reference to Bo Reicke. In typical Jacobean fashion let me end with an inclusion. Reicke (1964, 61) has an insightful interpretation of Elijah's effective intercession for rain. Surely, James is not encouraging his readers to imitate Elijah and pray for rain! "Rather his main interest is to show that a righteous man praying effectively can delay or hasten the saving grace of God which is symbolized by rain, as also in vs. 7."

CONCLUSION

Through various interpretive means I have tried to evoke meaning from the imperatives of James 5:13-18. If I am correct in using ancient health care practices to analyze James 5:14-15, then we find that James is insisting on bringing the God and Christ quotient into health care. James is saying: Don't run off to the physicians and abandon the Lord, who is savior and healer. Just maybe, in our U.S. health care system, which is dominated by physicians and managers, we need to hear James's message of who is actually in control of our lives. Besides lessons about prayer and physical sickness James 5:13-18 has taught lessons about a healthy and whole community that asks for forgiveness from one another and prays for one another.

Since I invited them into our earlier discussions about overarching themes in the Letter of James, I invite Johnson, Bauckham, and Wall back for final comments and give the podium to Johnson. Luke Johnson (1995, 343) has grasped in a profound way some of the dimensions of having "the sick" in the Christian community. He ties this reality into his overarching thematic of the opposition between "friendship with God and friendship with the world" and writes:

> The logic of the world, therefore, is to isolate the sick from the healthy. . . . This "natural reflex" of survival, however, also becomes the opportunity for sin, when it becomes the deliberate exclusion of the sick person from care and support, when the physical alienation imposed by sickness is embraced as a spiritual alienation from the sick. It is not by accident, I think, that James here (5:14) for the first time uses the term *ekklesia,* for it is the identity of the community *as* community that sickness threatens.

And in the very formulation of his insights Johnson touches on the overarching themes championed by Richard Bauckham, namely, "wholeness and inclusion, not exclusion," and by Robert Wall, namely, "the community of the wise," which is home for all.

At the end of this chapter and of this book I'm glad I spent time on James 5:13-18 and didn't succumb to the temptation to keep my book tidy by excluding its exhortations on sickness and prayer from my book on prayer. It has influenced the churches in so many positive ways and has so much to teach us today. Praise the Lord for James!

For Further Reading

Balentine, Samuel E. 1993. *Prayer in the Hebrew Bible: The Drama of Divine-Human Dialogue.* Overtures to Biblical Theology. Minneapolis: Fortress.

Bauckham, Richard. 1999. *James: Wisdom of James, Disciple of Jesus the Sage.* London and New York: Routledge.

Davids, Peter H. 1989. *James.* New International Biblical Commentary. Peabody, Mass.: Hendrickson.

Elliott, John H. 1993. "The Epistle of James in Rhetorical and Social Scientific Perspective Holiness-Wholeness and Patterns of Replication." *Biblical Theology Bulletin* 23: 71–81.

Johnson, Luke Timothy. 1995. *The Letter of James: A New Translation with Introduction and Commentary.* Anchor Bible 37A. New York: Doubleday.

Martin, Ralph P. 1988. *James*. Word Biblical Commentary 48. Waco, Tex.: Word Books.

Peterson, David G. 1990. "Prayer in the General Epistles." In *Teach Us to Pray: Prayer in the Bible and the World*, 107–12, 330–31. Ed. D. A. Carson. London: Paternoster; Grand Rapids: Baker Book House.

Wall, R. W. 1997a. "James, Letter of." *Dictionary of the Later New Testament & Its Development*, 545–61. Ed. Ralph P. Martin and Peter H. Davids. Downers Grove, Ill.: InterVarsity.

———. 1997b. *Community of the Wise: The Letter of James*. New Testament in Context. Valley Forge, Pa.: Trinity Press International.

Bibliography

Allison, Dale C. 1998. *Jesus of Nazareth: Millenarian Prophet.* Minneapolis: Fortress.

Ayo, Nicholas. 1992. *The Lord's Prayer: A Survey Theological and Literary.* Notre Dame, Ind.: University of Notre Dame Press.

Barr, James. 1988. "'Abba' Isn't 'Daddy.'" *Journal of Theological Studies* 39: 28–47.

Barrett, Charles Kingsley. 1978. *The Gospel According to St. John: An Introduction with Commentary and Notes on the Greek Text.* 2nd ed. Philadelphia: Westminster.

———. 1979. "Theologia Crucis — in Acts?" In *Theologia Crucis—Signum Crucis: Festschrift für Erich Dinkler zum 70. Geburtstag,* 73–84. Ed. Carl Andressen and Günter Klein. Tübingen: J. C. B. Mohr (Paul Siebeck).

———. 1982. "Christocentric or Theocentric? Observations on the Theological Method of the Fourth Gospel." In *Essays on John,* 1–18. Philadelphia: Westminster.

Bassler, Jouette M. 1989. "Mixed Signals: Nicodemus in the Fourth Gospel." *Journal of Biblical Literature* 108: 635–46.

Bauckham, Richard. 1993b. *The Climax of Prophecy: Studies on the Book of Revelation.* Edinburgh: T&T Clark.

Beck, Brian E. 1989. *Christian Character in the Gospel of Luke.* London: Epworth Press.

Bernardin, Joseph Cardinal. 1997. *The Gift of Peace: Personal Reflections.* Chicago: Loyola Press.

Bloomfield, Morton W. et al. 1979. *Incipits of Latin Works on the Virtues and Vices, 1100–1500 A.D. Including a Section of Incipits of Works on the Pater Noster.* Cambridge, Mass.: Mediaeval Academy of America.

Boff, Leonardo. 1983. *The Lord's Prayer: The Prayer of Integral Liberation.* Maryknoll, N.Y.: Orbis.

Boismard, M.-É. 1993. *Moses or Jesus: An Essay in Johannine Christology.* Minneapolis: Fortress; Leuven: Peeters.

Bonaventure, Saint. 1895. *S. Bonaventurae Commentarius in Evangelium S. Lucae.* Volume VII. Quaracchi: Collegium S. Bonaventurae, 1895.

———. Forthcoming. *Commentary on Luke's Gospel.* Translated and annotated by Robert J. Karris. St. Bonaventure, N.Y.: The Franciscan Institute.

Borg, Marcus J. 1994. *Meeting Jesus Again for the First Time: The Historical Jesus & The Heart of Contemporary Faith.* New York: HarperSanFrancisco.

———, and N. T. Wright. 1999. *The Meaning of Jesus: Two Visions.* New York: HarperSanFrancisco.

Bottini, Giovanni C. 1981. *La preghiera di Elia in Giacomo 5,17-18: Studio della tradizione biblica et giudaica.* Studium Biblicum Franciscanum Analecta 16. Jerusalem: Franciscan Printing Press.

Brown, Raymond E. 1965. "The Pater Noster as an Eschatological Prayer." In *New Testament Essays,* 275–320. Garden City, N.Y.: Doubleday.

———. 1966. *The Gospel According to John (I–XII): Introduction, Translation, and Notes.* Anchor Bible 29. Garden City, N.Y.: Doubleday.

———. 1994. *The Death of the Messiah: From Gethsemane to the Grave, A Commentary on the Passion Narratives in the Four Gospels.* Volume Two. Anchor Bible Reference Library; New York: Doubleday.

Brucker, Ralph. 1997. *"Christushymnen" oder "epideiktische Passagen? Studien zum Stilwechsel im Neuen Testament und seiner Umwelt.* Forschungen zur Religion und Literatur des Alten und Neuen Testaments 176. Göttingen: Vandenhoeck & Ruprecht.

Brueggemann, Walter. 1997. *Theology of the Old Testament: Testimony, Dispute, Advocacy.* Minneapolis: Fortress.

Bultmann, Rudolf. 1971. *The Gospel of John: A Commentary*. Oxford: Blackwell.

Cargal, Timothy B. 1993. *Restoring the Diaspora: Discursive Structure and Purpose in the Epistle of James*. Society of Biblical Literature Dissertation Series 144. Atlanta: Scholars Press.

Charlesworth, James H., ed. 1983, 1985. *The Old Testament Pseudepigrapha*. Vols. 1–2. New York: Doubleday.

———. 1986. "Jewish Hymns, Odes, and Prayers (ca. 167 B.C.E.—135 C.E.)" In *Early Judaism and Its Modern Interpreters*, 411–36. Ed. Robert A. Kraft and George W. E. Nickelsburg. Society of Biblical Literature The Bible and its Modern Interpreters 2. Philadelphia: Fortress; Atlanta: Scholars.

Chester, Andrew. 1994. "The Theology of James." In Andrew Chester and Ralph P. Martin, *The Theology of the Letters of James, Peter, and Jude*, 1–62. New Testament Theology. New York: Cambridge University Press.

Clements, R. E. 1986. *The Prayers of the Bible*, 205–59. London: SCM.

Collins, Raymond F. 1976. "The Representative Figures of the Fourth Gospel." *The Downside Review* 94: 26–46; 118–32.

Cosgrove, Charles H. 1984. "The Divine Dei in Luke-Acts: Investigations into the Lukan Understanding of God's Providence." *Novum Testamentum* 26: 168–90.

Cothenet, Edouard. 1981. "Earthly Liturgy and Heavenly Liturgy according to the Book of Revelation." In *Roles in the Liturgical Assembly, the Twenty-Third Liturgical Conference Saint Serge*, 115–35, 313–15. New York: Pueblo Publishing Company.

Cotter, Wendy. 1999. *Miracles in Greco-Roman Antiquity: A Sourcebook*. London/New York: Routledge.

Crossan, John Dominic. 1991. *The Historical Jesus: The Life of a Mediterranean Peasant*. New York: HarperSanFrancisco.

———. 1994. *Jesus: A Revolutionary Biography*. New York: HarperSanFrancisco.

———. 1998. *The Birth of Christianity: Discovering What Happened In the Years immediately after the Execution of Jesus*. New York: HarperSanFrancisco.

———. 1999. "What Victory? What God? A Review Debate with N. T. Wright on *Jesus and the Victory of God*." *Scottish Journal of Theology* 50: 345–58.

Crump, David M. 1992. *Jesus the Intercessor: Prayer and Christology in Luke-Acts.* Wissenschaftliche Untersuchungen zum Neuen Testament 2.49; Tübingen: J. C. B. Mohr (Siebeck). Reissued in 1999 by Baker Books of Grand Rapids, Michigan as part of its Biblical Studies Library.

D'Angelo, Mary Rose. 1992a. *"Abba* and 'Father': Imperial Theology and the Jesus Traditions." *Journal of Biblical Literature* 111: 611–30.

———. 1992b. "Theology in Mark and Q: *Abba* and 'Father' in Context." *Harvard Theological Review* 85: 149–74.

Davids, Peter H. 1988. "The Epistle of James in Modern Discussion." In *Aufstieg und Niedergang der römischen Welt.* Part II: Principat Volume 25.5. 3621–45. Ed. Wolfgang Haase and Hildegard Temporini. Berlin/New York: Walter de Gruyter.

Day, Dorothy. 1938. *From Union Square to Rome.* Silver Spring, Md.: Preservation of the Faith Press.

Deichgräber, Reinhard. 1967. *Gotteshymnus und Christushymnus in der frühen Christenheit: Untersuchungen zu Form, Sprache und Stil der frühchristlichen Hymnen,* 44–59. Studien zur Umwelt des Neuen Testaments 5; Göttingen: Vandenhoeck & Ruprecht.

Dibelius, Martin. 1976. *James: A Commentary on the Epistle of James.* Hermeneia. Philadelphia: Fortress.

Doble, Peter. 1996. *The Paradox of Salvation: Luke's Theology of the Cross.* Society for New Testament Studies Monograph Series 87. New York: Cambridge University Press.

Doohan, Helen, and Leonard Doohan. 1992. *Prayer in the New Testament: Make Your Requests Known to God.* Collegeville, Minn.: Liturgical Press.

Dowd, Sharyn Echols. 1988. *Prayer, Power, and the Problem of Suffering: Mark 11:22-25 in the Context of Markan Theology.* Society of Biblical Literature Dissertation Series 105. Atlanta: Scholars Press.

Duke, Paul D. 1985. *Irony in the Fourth Gospel.* Atlanta: John Knox.

Dunn, James D. G. 1993, *The Theology of Paul's Letter to the Galatians.* New Testament Theology; New York: Cambridge University Press.

Evans, Craig A. 1993. *Word and Glory: On the Exegetical and Theological Background of John's Prologue.* Journal for the Study of the New Testament Supplement Series 89. Sheffield: JSOT Press.

Farris, Stephen. 1985. *The Hymns of Luke's Infancy Narratives: Their Origin, Meaning and Significance.* Journal for the Study of the New Testament Supplement Series 9; Sheffield: JSOT Press.

Feldkämper, Ludger. 1978. *Der betende Jesus als Heilsmittler nach Lukas.* Veröffentlichungen des Missionspriesterseminars St. Augustin bei Bonn 29. St. Augustin: Steyler.

Fitzmyer, Joseph A. 1985. *The Gospel According to Luke (X–XXIV): Introduction, Translation, and Notes,* 896–907. Anchor Bible 28A. Garden City, N.Y.: Doubleday.

———. 1998. *The Acts of the Apostles: A New Translation with Introduction and Commentary.* Anchor Bible 31. New York: Doubleday.

Francis, Fred O. 1970. "The Form and Function of the Opening and Closing Paragraphs of James and I John." *Zeitschrift für die neutestamentliche Wissenschaft* 61: 110–26.

Freyne, Seán. 1992. "Hellenistic/Roman Galilee." *Anchor Bible Dictionary,* 2:895–99. New York: Doubleday.

Funk, Robert W. 1996. *Honest to Jesus: Jesus for a New Millennium.* New York: HarperSanFrancisco.

———, Roy W. Hoover, and The Jesus Seminar. 1993, 1997. *The Five Gospels: The Search for the Authentic Words of Jesus.* New York: HarperSanFrancisco.

García Martínez, Florentino. 1994. *The Dead Sea Scrolls Translated: The Qumran Texts in English.* 2d ed. Leiden: Brill; Grand Rapids: Eerdmans.

Garrett, Susan R. 1989. *The Demise of the Devil: Magic and the Demonic in Luke's Writings.* Minneapolis: Fortress.

Grant, Colin. 1999. "The Greying of Jesus." *Expository Times* 110/8: 246–48.

Green, Joel B. 1997. *The Gospel of Luke.* The New International Commentary on the New Testament. Grand Rapids: Eerdmans.

Guthrie, Donald. 1992. "Aspects of Worship in the Book of Revelation." In *Worship, Theology and Ministry in the Early Church: Essays in Honor of Ralph P. Martin,* 70–83. Ed. Michael J. Wilkins and Terence Paige. Journal for the Study of the New Testament Supplement Series 87. Sheffield: JSOT Press.

Harding, Mark. 1994. "The Lord's Prayer and Other Prayer Texts of the Greco-Roman Era: A Bibliography." In *The Lord's Prayer and Other Prayer Texts from the Greco-Roman Era,* 101–257. Ed.

James H. Charlesworth. Valley Forge, Pa.: Trinity Press International.

Harris, Oscar G. 1966. "Prayer in Luke-Acts: A Study in the Theology of Luke." Nashville, Tenn.: Vanderbilt University Doctoral Dissertation.

Hayden, Daniel R. 1981. "Calling the Elders to Pray." *Bibliotheca Sacra* 138: 258–66.

Hays, Richard B. 1996. *The Moral Vision of the New Testament: A Contemporary Introduction to New Testament Ethics.* New York: HarperSanFrancisco.

Heinemann, Joseph, and Jakob J. Petuchowski, eds. 1975. *Literature of the Synagogue.* New York: Behrman House.

———. 1977. *Prayer in the Talmud: Forms and Patterns.* Studia Judaica 9. Berlin/New York: Walter de Gruyter.

Hoffman, Lawrence A., ed. 1997. *My People's Prayer Book: Traditional Prayers, Modern Commentaries.* Volume 1: *The Sh'ma and Its Blessings.* Woodstock, Vt.: Jewish Lights Publishing.

———, ed. 1998. *My People's Prayer Book: Traditional Prayers, Modern Commentaries.* Volume 2: *The Amidah.* Woodstock, Vt.: Jewish Lights Publishing.

Hooker, Morna. 1969/70. "John the Baptist and the Johannine Prologue." *New Testament Studies* 16: 358–64.

Jackson, Ralph. 1988. *Doctors and Diseases in the Roman Empire.* Norman/London: University of Oklahoma Press.

Johnson, Elizabeth A. 1992. *She Who Is: The Mystery of God in Feminist Theological Discourse.* New York: Crossroad.

Johnson, Luke Timothy. 1996. *The Real Jesus: the Misguided Quest for the Historical Jesus and Truth of the Traditional Gospels.* New York: HarperSan Francisco.

———. 1999. *Living Jesus: Learning the Heart of the Gospel.* New York: HarperSanFrancisco.

Jörns, Klaus-Peter. 1971. *Das hymnische Evangelium: Untersuchungen zu Aufbau, Funktion und Herkunft der hymnischen Stücke in der Johannesoffenbarung.* Studien zum Neuen Testament 5. Gütersloh: Gütersloher Verlagshaus, 1971.

Karris, Robert J. 1985. *Luke: Artist and Theologian: Luke's Passion Account as Literature.* Theological Inquiries. New York: Paulist Press.

———. 1999. *The Admonitions of St. Francis: Sources and Meanings.*

Text Series 21. St. Bonaventure, New York: The Franciscan Institute.

Käsemann, Ernst. 1968. *The Testament of Jesus: A Study of the Gospel of John in the Light of Chapter 17.* Philadelphia: Fortress.

Kirk, Alan Kenneth. 1999. "Peasant Wisdom, the 'Our Father' and the Origins of Christianity." *Toronto Journal of Theology* 15: 31–50.

Koenig, John. 1998. *Rediscovering New Testament Prayer: Boldness and Blessing in the Name of Jesus.* Harrisburg, Pa.: Morehouse.

Krentz, Edgar. 1995. "Epideiktik and Hymnody: The New Testament and Its World." *Biblical Research* 40: 50–97.

LaVerdiere, Eugene. 1994. *Dining in the Kingdom of God: The Origins of the Eucharist according to Luke.* Chicago: Liturgy Training Publications.

Laws, Sophie. 1980. *The Epistle of James.* Black's New Testament Commentary. Peabody, Mass.: Hendrickson.

LeFevre, Perry. 1995. *Modern Theologies of Prayer.* Chicago: Exploration Press.

Lindström, Fredrik. 1994. *Suffering and Sin: Interpretation of Illness in the Individual Complaint Psalms.* Coniectanea Biblica, OT Series 37. Stockholm: Almquist & Wiksell International.

Longfellow, Henry Wadsworth. 1902. *The Complete Poetical Works of Henry Wadsworth Longfellow.* Boston: Houghton, Muffin and Company.

Magrassi, Mariano. 1998. *Praying the Bible: An Introduction to Lectio Divina.* Collegeville, Minn.: Liturgical Press.

Malina, Bruce J. 1980. "What Is Prayer?" *The Bible Today* 18: 214–20.

Manns, Frédéric. 1994. *Jewish Prayer in the Time of Jesus.* Studium Biblicum Franciscanum Analecta 22. Jerusalem: Franciscan Printing Press.

Meeks, Wayne A. 1993. *The Origins of Christian Morality: The First Two Centuries.* New Haven, Conn.: Yale University Press.

Meier, John P. 1991. *A Marginal Jew: Rethinking the Historical Jesus.* Vol. 1: *The Roots of the Problem and the Person.* New York: Doubleday.

———. 1994. *A Marginal Jew: Rethinking the Historical Jesus.* Vol. 2: *Mentor, Message, and Miracles.* New York: Doubleday.

Miller, Patrick D. 1994. *They Cried to the Lord: The Form and Theology of Biblical Prayer.* Minneapolis: Fortress.

Moloney, Francis J. 1978. "From Cana to Cana (John 2:1–4:54) and the

Fourth Evangelist's Concept of Correct (and Incorrect) Faith."
In *Studia Biblica 1978*, II, 185–213. Ed. E. A. Livingstone. Jour-
nal for the Study of the New Testament, Supplement Series 2;
Sheffield: JSOT Press, 1978.

————. 1997. *A Body Broken for a Broken People: Eucharist in the New
Testament.* Rev. ed. Peabody, Mass.: Hendrickson.

Monloubou, Louis. 1976. *La prière selon Saint Luc recherche d'une
structure.* Lectio divina 89. Paris: Cerf.

Montanari, Massimo. 1994. *The Culture of Food.* Cambridge: Blackwell.

Mussner, Franz. 1975. *Der Jakobusbrief.* 3d ed. Herders Theologischer
Kommentar zum Neuen Testament XIII.1; Freiburg: Herder.

O'Brien, P. T. 1973. "Prayer in Luke-Acts." *Tyndale Bulletin* 24: 111–
27.

Omanson, Roger L. 1986. "The Certainty of Judgment and the Power
of Prayer: James 5." *Review and Expositor* 83: 427–38.

Ott, Wilhelm. 1965. *Gebet und Heil: Die Bedeutung der Gebets-
paränese in der lukanischen Theologie.* Studien zum Alten und
Neuen Testament 12. Munich: Kösel.

Painter, John. 1993. *The Quest for the Messiah: The History, Literature and Theology of the Johannine Community.* 2d ed.
Nashville: Abingdon.

Patterson, Stephen J. 1998. *The God of Jesus: The Historical Jesus and
the Search for Meaning.* Harrisburg, Pa.: Trinity Press International.

Perkins, Pheme. 1995. *First and Second Peter, James, and Jude,*
83–140. Interpretation. Louisville: John Knox, 1995.

Pervo, Richard I. 1987. *Profit with Delight: The Literary Genre of the
Acts of the Apostles.* Philadelphia: Fortress.

Petersen, Norman R. 1993. *The Gospel of John and the Sociology of
Light: Language and Characterization in the Fourth Gospel.*
Valley Forge, Pa.: Trinity Press International.

Plymale, Steven F. 1989. "The Lucan Lord's Prayer." *The Bible Today*
27: 176–82.

————. 1990. "Luke's Theology of Prayer." *Society of Biblical
Literature 1990 Seminar Papers,* 529–51. Ed. David J. Lull.
Society of Biblical Literature Seminar Papers Series 29.
Atlanta: Scholars Press.

————. 1991. *The Prayer Texts of Luke-Acts.* American University
Studies Series VII, Volume 118. New York: Peter Lang.

Porter, Roy. 1997. *The Greatest Benefit to Mankind: A Medical History of Humanity.* New York: Norton.

Powell, Mark Allan. 1998. *Jesus as a Figure in History: How Modern Historians View the Man from Galilee.* Louisville: Westminster John Knox.

Reicke, Bo. 1964. *The Epistles of James, Peter, and Jude: Introduction, Translation and Notes.* Anchor Bible 37. Garden City, N.Y.: Doubleday.

Reid, Barbara E. 1996. *Choosing the Better Part? Women in the Gospel of Luke.* Collegeville, Minn.: Liturgical Press.

Ruiz, Jean-Pierre. 1994. "The Apocalypse of John and Contemporary Roman Catholic Liturgy." *Worship* 68: 482–504.

Sanders, E. P. 1985. *Jesus and Judaism.* Philadelphia: Fortress.

———. 1992. *Judaism: Practice and Belief 63 BCE–66 CE.* Philadelphia: Trinity Press International.

———. 1993. *The Historical Figure of Jesus.* London: Penguin.

Schillebeeckx, Edward. 1979. "Jesus' Original *Abba* Experience, Source and Secret of His Being, Message, and Manner of Life." In *Jesus: An Experiment in Christology,* 256–71. New York: Seabury.

Schlier, H. 1964. "*Elaion.*" *Theological Dictionary of the New Testament,* 2:470–73. Grand Rapids: Eerdmans.

Schnackenburg, Rudolf. 1980. *The Gospel According to John.* Vol. 1. New York: Seabury.

Schnelle, Udo. 1992. *Antidocetic Christology in the Gospel of John: An Investigation of the Place of the Fourth Gospel in the Johannine School.* Minneapolis: Fortress.

Scholer, David M. 1975. "Sins Within and Sins Without: An Interpretation of I John 5:16-17." In *Current Issues in Biblical and Patristic Interpretation: Studies in Honor of Merrill C. Tenney Presented by his Former Students,* 230–46. Ed. Gerald F. Hawthorne. Grand Rapids: Eerdmans.

———. 1986. "The Magnificat (Luke 1:46-55): Reflections on Its Hermeneutical History." In *Conflict and Context: Hermeneutics in the Americas,* 210–19. Ed. Mark L. Branson and C. Rene Padilla. Grand Rapids: Eerdmans.

Smalley, Stephen J. 1973. "Spirit, Kingdom and Prayer in Luke-Acts." *Novum Testamentum* 15: 59-71.

Squires, John T. 1993. *The Plan of God in Luke-Acts.* Society for New

Testament Studies Monograph Series 76. New York: Cambridge University Press.

————. 1998. "The Plan of God in the Acts of the Apostles." In *Witness to the Gospel: The Theology of Acts,* 19–39. Ed. I. Howard Marshall and David Peterson. Grand Rapids: Eerdmans.

Thackeray, H. St. J. 1957. *Josephus, Jewish Antiquities,* Books I–IV. Loeb Classical Library. Cambridge, Mass.: Harvard University Press.

Theissen, Gerd, and Annette Merz. 1998. *The Historical Jesus: A Comprehensive Guide.* Minneapolis: Fortress.

Thomas, John C. 1998. *The Devil, Disease and Deliverance: Origins of Illness in New Testament Thought,* 17–37. Journal of Pentecostal Theology Supplement Series 13. Sheffield: Sheffield Academic Press.

Trites, Allison A. 1978. "The Prayer Motif in Luke-Acts." In *Perspectives on Luke-Acts,* 168–86. Ed. Charles H. Talbert. Perspectives in Religious Studies Special Studies Series 5. Macon, Ga.: Mercer University Press.

Turner, M. M. B. 1990. "Prayer in the Gospels and Acts." In *Teach us to Pray: Prayer in the Bible and the World,* 58–83, 319–25. Ed. D. A. Carson. London: Paternoster; Grand Rapids: Baker Book House.

Vanni, Ugo. 1991. "Liturgical Dialogue as a Literary Form in the Book of Revelation." *New Testament Studies* 37: 348–72.

Vassiliadis, Petros. 1997. "Apocalypse and Liturgy." *St. Vladimir's Theological Quarterly* 41: 95–112.

Verseput, Donald J. 1997. "James 1:17 and the Jewish Morning Prayers." *Novum Testamentum* 39: 177–91.

Vögtle, Anton. 1978. "The Lord's Prayer: A Prayer for Jews and Christians?" In *The Lord's Prayer and Jewish Liturgy,* 93–117. Ed. Jakob J. Petuchowski and Michael Brocke. New York: Seabury.

Waetjen, Herman C. 1999. *Praying the Lord's Prayer: An Ageless Prayer for Today.* Harrisburg, Pa.: Trinity Press International.

Wells, C. Richard. 1986. "The Theology of Prayer in James." *Criswell Theological Review* 1: 85–112.

Wilkinson, John. 1998. *The Bible and Healing: A Medical and Theological Commentary,* 236–60, 318–21. Edinburgh: Handsel; Grand Rapids: Eerdmans.

Witherington, Ben, III. 1998. *The Paul Quest: The Renewed Quest for the Jew of Tarsus.* Downers Grove, Ill.: InterVarsity Press.

Wright, N. T. 1992. *The New Testament and the People of God.* Christian Origins and the Question of God 1. Minneapolis: Fortress.

——. 1996. *Jesus and the Victory of God.* Christian Origins and the Question of God 2. Minneapolis: Fortress.

——. 1999. "Doing Justice to Jesus.: A Response to J. D. Crossan: 'What Victory? What God?'" *Scottish Journal of Theology* 50: 359–79.

Yarbro Collins, Adela. 1977. "The History-of-Religions Approach to Apocalypticism and the 'Angel of the Waters' (Rev 16:4-7)." *Catholic Biblical Quarterly* 39: 367–81.

——. 1980. "Revelation 18: Taunt-Song or Dirge?" In *L'Apocalypse Johannique et l'Apocalyptique dans le Nouveau Testament,* 185–204. Ed. J. Lambrecht; Bibliotheca ephemeridum Theologicarum Lovaniensium 53. Leuven: University Press; Gembloux: Duculot.

Yoder, John Howard. 1994. *The Politics of Jesus: Vicit Agnus Noster.* 2d ed. Grand Rapids: Eerdmans.

Index of Authors

205

Index of Ancient Sources